The DOUBLE GODDESS

Women Sharing Power

VICKI NOBLE

Illustrated by

KIMBERLEY EVE

Bear & Company

Rochester, Vermont

Bear & Company
One Park Street
Rochester, Vermont 05767
www.InnerTraditions.com

Bear & Company is a division of Inner Traditions International

Library of Congress Cataloging-in-Publication Data

Noble, Vicki.
  The double goddess : women sharing power / Vicki Noble ; illustrated
by Kimberley Eve.
        p. cm.
Includes bibliographical references and index.
  ISBN 1-59143-011-9
  1. Goddesses. 2. Goddess religion. 3. Women—Religious life. 4.
Lesbianism—Religious aspects. 5. Shamanism. I. Title.

  BL473.5.N63 2003
  291.2'114—dc21

                                2003004479

Printed and bound in the United States at Lake Book Manufacturing, Inc.

10 9 8 7 6 5 4 3 2 1

Text design and layout by Priscilla Baker
This book was typeset in Bembo with Village and Avenir as display typefacse

Contents

Acknowledgments

This book has taken ages to write, partly because of my travel and teaching obligations and the special needs of my adolescent son, but also because of the obscure nature of the material itself. Although there is bountiful evidence—which I have done my best to gather—in support of my Double Goddess thesis, it is widely scattered among many different kinds of texts, museums, libraries, and archives, with many of the sources old, remote, out of print, hard to acquire, and patently expensive. I am grateful to have been living, until recently, in Berkeley, California, where independent bookstores (both new and used) still flourish: I have been especially helped by Shambhala and Black Oak Books, as well as the University Press Bookstore. And the University of California Library system—although floundering somewhat—is still a fabulous resource.

Along this eight-year journey I have been mainly helped financially by private "sponsors" who took me under their wing by making pledges to support my independent research so that I could take the time to do it. For their substantial support during the early stages I would especially like to thank Susun Weed, Angie Thieriot, Beatrice Bowles, Samantha Lyons, B. J. Miller, Minerva Gow, Kyle King, Jaye Martin, Brenda Nicholson, Cristina Biaggi, Rita Pasotti, Katherine Neville, Tollie Miller, Carole Barlas, and the Vaughan Family Foundation. Thanks also to Jonathan Tenney, Sally Craig, Alev Croutier, Nancy Baer, Clare Luce Abbey, Caroline Drivers, and Elizabeth Comstock. Recently I am grateful as well to Gisken Crawford, Joan Poor, Sumedha Khanna, Donna Read, Starhawk, Stasi Martin Truyts, Jennifer Berezan, Faith Freewoman, Mary Ann Mierzwa, JoAnn Gunnarson, Hope Rhode, Susan McLaughlin, Shannon Morris, and Cindy Zamzow. My Webmistress Shawn Hancock even donated her time putting an excerpt of the book up on our site (www.motherpeace.com).

I thank the Bogliasco Foundation for a fabulous month-long writing retreat in northern Italy in the fall of 1997, during which time I was able to explore the ancient Grimaldi caves, museums, and other sacred sites in the area, as well as acquire important texts published in Italy. I deeply appreciate Rita Pasotti's support and affirmation of my work, for providing me with a wonderful trip around Tuscany in the spring of 1998 to visit Etruscan museums, and for taking hundreds of photographs along the way.

I am forever indebted to Jeannine Davis-Kimball for her work with Amazon excavations and her generous invitation for me to go on an investigatory trip to Russia in 1997 to visit museums and archival collections and meet with Russian archaeologists; the trip and her mentoring have been absolutely invaluable, right up to the publishing deadline when she critically read several pertinent chapters. Likewise I want to thank my friend Miriam Robbins Dexter for her excellent in-depth, rigorous, and supportive reading of the text before I sent it to the publisher for final viewing. And thanks to Will Roscoe, who offered valuable suggestions for the section on Two-Spirit people.

With regard to Tibetan Buddhist material, in addition to my passionate eclectic studies over the years, I am indebted to Tsultrim Allione for introducing (transmitting) several dakini practices to me beginning in 1995, and Tulku Thubten Rinpoche for his insightful and profound support for my work in general. Thanks also to my fabulous guide in Crete, George Spiridakis, who has deepened my research by believing in my theories, sharing his own in-depth knowledge of the ancient women-centered culture there, and escorting my tour groups off the beaten track for homecooked food and inspiring interactions with wonderful local people. With George leading the way, we have climbed to several sacred mountain shrines and explored most of the important ancient caves that honeycomb the island. Hiking almost to the top of Mt. Ida to enter the Kamares Cave, where a Bronze Age High Priestess left her stone offering table four thousand years ago, I count as one of the accomplishments of my life.

I am grateful to several other friends who were willing to read and comment on various drafts of the book: Barbara Higbie, Elinor Gadon, Ubaka Hill, Cristina Biaggi, Krissy Keefer, Mary B. Kelly, and especially Jennifer Berezan—who, after all, shared with me the initial "aha" in regard to the many Double Goddess figures we saw in museums around the world as we traveled together from 1991 through 1994.

From Australia, Chris Sitka generously shared much more documentation than I was able to use in this book. Her well-developed theories and inspired, scholarly understandings of the Double Goddess as images of prehistoric and original lesbianism deserve publication in their own right. And I'm grateful to the German author Gabriele Meixner for generously sending me a copy of her *Frauenpaare* (Womenpairs). I only wish my German were better; in that regard, thanks to my friend Hanna Soule for translating sections of Meixner's book, so that I could see how our two approaches intersected.

But for some vigilant friends and colleagues, I would have never found some of the images in the first place, since they are rarely indexed under "Double Goddess." Thanks to Constance (Nieburg) Tippett for calling my attention to a 1967 copy of *Horizon Magazine* featuring on the cover a Double Goddess ceramic pot from Hacilar, and then when she saw how interested I was, just mailing me her copy of the valuable out-of-print magazine. Thanks also to Willow La Monte for the slide of a Double Goddess I hadn't seen from Marija Gimbutas's collection from Achilleion in Greece; to Karen Vogel for bringing me a copy of *Sculpture Magazine* with the first published images of the plaster Double Goddesses from Ain Ghazal; to Layne Redmond for sending me an image from the Metropolitan Museum; to Max Dashu for the image from Lithuania, and to Mary Lou Miller for a variety of Amazons and Maenads from Greek vase images.

Thanks again to Susun Weed for finding my inspired illustrator, Kimberley Eve, whose fresh drawings have given a lively expression to the ideas I'm sharing in this complex book. Kimberley's responsiveness and positively agreeable presence in relation to the text and my challenging timetable have been a blessing to me. At a midpoint in the process, my friend Sandy Boucher worked as a clear-headed and compassionate freelance editor on the book, contributing her astute sense of the written word along with her personal commitment to feminist spirituality. Our extended back-and-forth editorial encounter was a truly successful exercise in women sharing power. And at a crucial transitional moment, Willow La Monte made a momentous intervention in the way of a generous unsolicited donation that allowed the book to be completed. Since the fall of 2001, the good people of Inner Traditions • Bear & Company have wholeheartedly contributed their knowledge and creativity to the final birthing of my book, and I've enjoyed our collaboration very much.

I take full responsibility for whatever errors are present in these pages. Eight years seems a long time for me to work on a book, and if I have neglected to mention anyone's name, it may be because your contribution to this effort occurred years ago. I apologize for my inadequate memory and hereby thank you for your help. Likewise, it is difficult for any scholar to stay on top of the archaeological material, since every excavation changes the known "facts" by adding data that must be integrated. I rely a lot on older books, because they don't have the antifeminist agenda that has appeared in archaeology as a backlash to the 1970s women's spirituality Goddess vision. More recent scholarly works benefit from the discoveries of carbon-14 and tree-ring dating methods, which have made dating and chronologies more technically reliable at the same time that many of their doctrinal antifeminist interpretations seem skewed and even patently wrong. I have attempted to keep the best of the older nondefensive assessments of the pervasiveness of the ancient Great Mother while utilizing the most up-to-date research in my dates and places.

In that vein I am still and always manifestly grateful to my mentor and scholarly role model, the iconoclastic archaeologist, folklore expert, and linguist Marija Gimbutas, whose active intelligent physical presence in the world I miss very much. I offered a little incense to her picture most days before I began, and I feel quite certain that her ancestral spirit has been guiding my work. Part of what I hope this book will accomplish is helping to keep alive her marvelous and coherent inspiration, even in a time when she is deliberately being forgotten by mainstream archaeology (while being proven, in retrospect, to have been uncannily accurate).

MAPS OF ARCHAEOLOGICAL SITES OF ANCIENT GODDESS CULTURES

The maps on these pages show the locations of the worldwide archaeological sites where the artifacts referenced in this book were found. The first map shows the Western Hemisphere; the second shows Africa, Europe, and Asia; the third is a closer detail map of Eurasia; and the fourth a detail map featuring the Cycladic Islands and the Aegean.

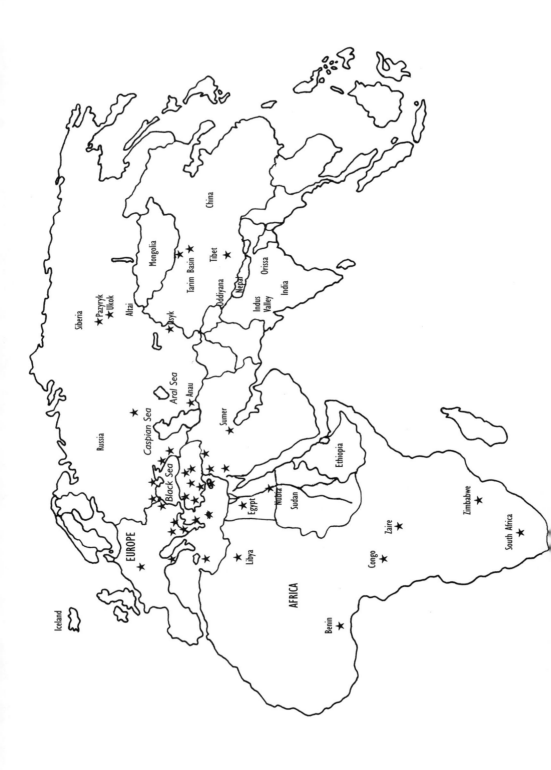

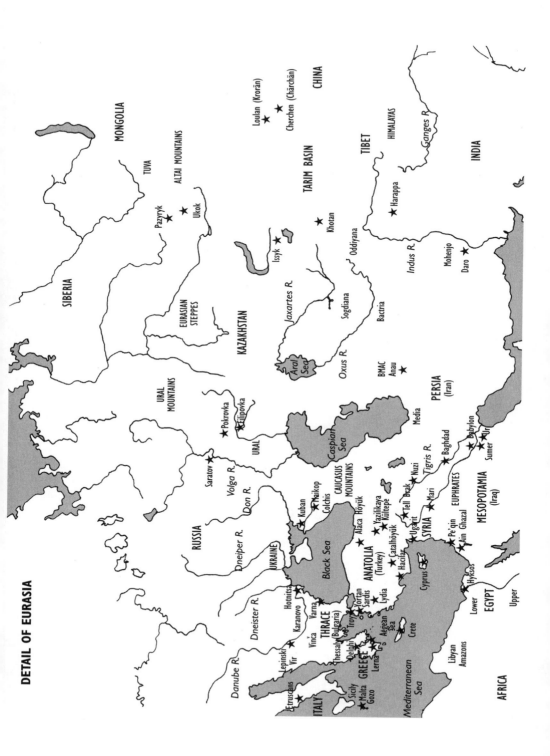

DETAIL OF EURASIA

SIBERIA

MONGOLIA

TUVA

ALTAI MOUNTAINS

Pazyryk ★

Ulok

★ Loulan (Kroian)

Cherchen (Chärchän) ★

CHINA

EURASIAN STEPPES

KAZAKHSTAN

TARIM BASIN

HIMALAYAS

Ganges R.

TIBET

★ Issyk

★ Khotan

★ Harappa

INDIA

Jaxartes R.

Oddiyana

Indus R.

Mohenjo Daro ★

URAL MOUNTAINS

Aral Sea

Sogdiana

Bactria

★ Pokrovka
★ Filipovka

URAL

Oxus R.

BMAC
Anau ★

PERSIA
(Iran)

Saratov ★

Volga R.

Don R.

Caspian Sea

Media

★ Babylon
Ur ★

Baghdad ★

Sumer ★

RUSSIA

Dneiper R.

CAUCASUS MOUNTAINS

Tigris R.

Nuzi ★
★ Tell Brak

EUPHRATES

UKRAINE

Kuban ★

★ Maikop
Colchis

Alaca Höyük ★

Yazilikaya ★
Kültepe

Mari ★

Ugarit ★

MESOPOTAMIA
(Iraq)

Dneister R.

Black Sea

ANATOLIA
(Turkey)

Çatalhöyük ★

SYRIA

Pe qin ★
Ain Ghazal ★

Hotnitsa ★

Hacilar ★

Danube R.

Karanovo ★

THRACE

Varna ★

Troy
Sardis ★

Lydia

Cyprus

HYKSOS

Vinča ★

Thessaly (Bulgaria)

Aegean Sea

EGYPT

Lower

Upper

Lepinski Vir ★

Delphi ★

GREECE

Lerna ★

Crete

Libyan
Amazons

AFRICA

ITALY

Etruscans ★

Sicily ★
Malta ★
Gozo

Mediterranean Sea

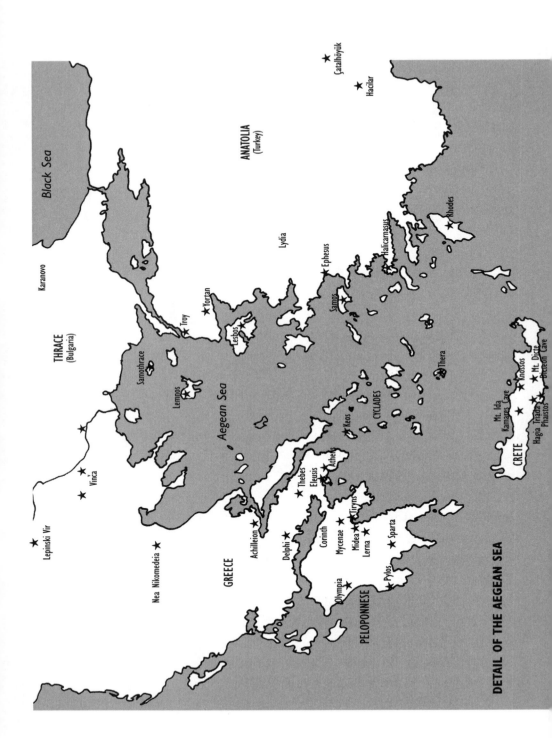

Black Sea

THRACE
(Bulgaria)

Karanovo

Samothrace

Troy

Lemnos

Lesbos

Aegean Sea

ANATOLIA
(Turkey)

Çatalhöyük

Hacılar

Lydia

Ephesus

Samos

Halicarnassus

Rhodes

Lepinski Vir

Vinča

Nea Nikomedeia

Achilleion

Delphi

Thebes
Eleusis
Athens

Corinth
Mycenae
Midea
Lerna
Tiryns

Olympia

Sparta

Pylos

GREECE

PELOPONNESE

Keos

CYCLADES

Thera

CRETE

Mt. Ida
Kamares Cave

Knossos

Mt. Dicte
Psichron Cave

Hagia Triada
Phaistos

DETAIL OF THE AEGEAN SEA

INTRODUCTION

What Is the Double Goddess?

The Double Goddess is an ancient icon with luminous meaning for contemporary women, expanding on the single images that have prevailed in prior considerations of the Goddess. Among the numerous female figures important in the ancient world appear many twin figures of two women as well as symbolic dual female representations such as the Double Axe, birds, lions, leopards, and snakes. Found in cultures from different times in many places around the world, some are sculpted from stone, bone, or clay; others are painted on walls or crafted as vessels. As I discuss throughout the book, I see these Double Goddess figures as profoundly representational of the whole yin-yang female biological cycle and its shamanistic relationship to life on this planet, human evolution, and the development of civilization.

The long and rich heritage of Double Goddess figurines and painted images described in this book reflect the organic cycles of nature that informed the ancient Goddess religion, archetypally

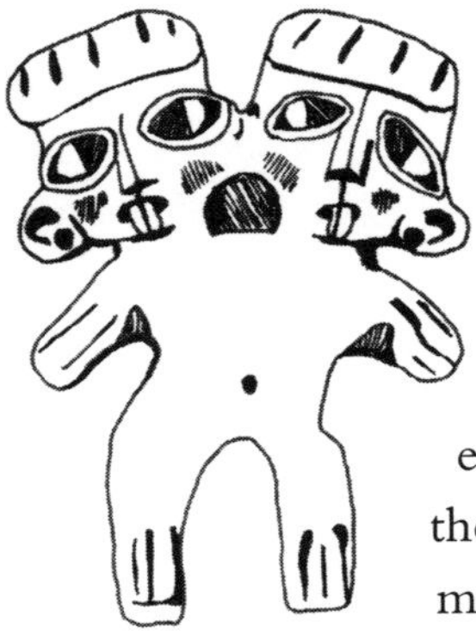

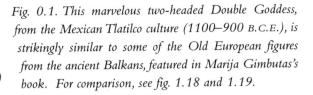

Fig. 0.1. This marvelous two-headed Double Goddess, from the Mexican Tlatilco culture (1100–900 B.C.E.), is strikingly similar to some of the Old European figures from the ancient Balkans, featured in Marija Gimbutas's book. For comparison, see fig. 1.18 and 1.19.

expressed through the body of every woman as the repeating alternation between ovulation and menstruation. These two aspects of the feminine are iconographically depicted in the multivalent and widespread image of two divine women, expressing the dual poles of nature: death and life, dark and light. Many of the twin figures literally share a body, several depicting one woman with two heads, such as one from Mexico. Many others—like Siamese twins—show two women emerging out of one shared lower body, their two torsos having four clearly delineated breasts but their hips being joined.

The image of the Double Goddess is a vital missing piece for modern women, as it graphically portrays our exquisite and unique bipolar existence in a positive, healthy way. Coming from a time before the exclusion of the woman as "subject"—rather than object—the Double Goddess reflects *female autonomy*, offering very important icons for modern women trying to find again (re-member) our ancient, integral sense of self and wholeness.

In male-dominated societies, women are perceived as "other," and our differences from men

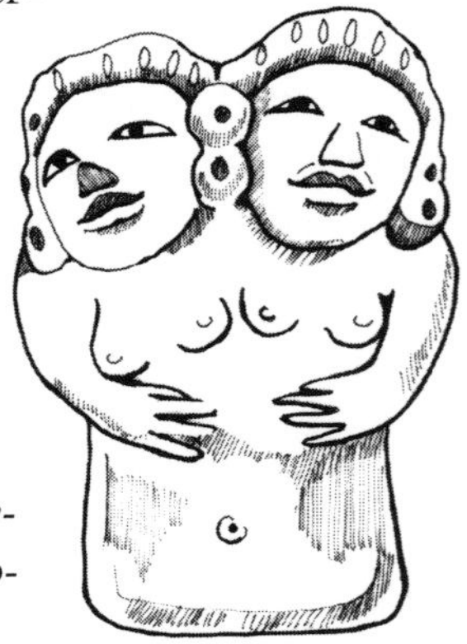

Fig. 0.2. This Double Goddess from the north Gulf Coast of Mexico, Huaxtec culture, dates to approximately 200 C.E. Her loving expression(s) and the way that she embraces herself is a model of the "Two-in-Oneness" of the Double Goddess archetype in the New World, as well as the Old. Goddess cultures everywhere sanctified both sides (light and dark, active and receptive) of every woman as a representation of natural law.

are typically ignored, pathologized, or even demonized. A few people have been disturbed by what seems like my casual use of the word *bipolar* to describe women's supposedly "natural" state, fearing that it somehow plays into the Western medical negative psychological diagnosis by that name that so heavily targets women. What I am describing as our innate "bipolarity" signifies a lot more than disruptive mood swings. My use of the word *bipolar* has been carefully chosen to discuss, and consciously reframe, the innate back-and-forth mystery of ovulation and menstruation, unique to our species and magically (magnetically) synchronized with the cycles of the Great Goddess Herself in Her dual planetary aspects as Earth and Moon, and the mythic forces of life and death.

The human female link to the lunar cycle through menstruation and ovulation represents a key evolutionary step in the process of becoming human. Menstruation is a fundamental characteristic of our evolutionary leap from the primate ancestor, being central to what differentiates us from our closest relations—the chimpanzees and bonobos—who share 98 percent of our DNA. Our separation from both of these primate cousins can mainly be seen in our lack of *estrus*. During estrus the female is sexually receptive and her "bleeding" signals the male for coitus; in the female human, bleeding happens entirely apart from fertility every month, and only ovulation (without bleeding) signals to the male for reproduction. In other words, human sexuality detached itself from reproduction through the aegis of the vacillating female hormonal cycle, in which the female human is "continuously sexually receptive," to quote the male-based anthropological view.[1]

I first became interested in this idea in 1975 when I met Dr. Judith Shirek, a physical anthropologist from U.C. Berkeley. Sadly, Shirek died the same year, but her pioneering work on the human female's lack of estrus—and the implications of that evolutionary development—sparked my lifelong inquiry. The opening chapter of my 1991 book, *Shakti Woman: Feeling Our Fire, Healing Our World,* asserts that female shamanism is based in the lunar blood cycle, and female authority depends on being in touch with this primal power. More recently, Judy

Grahn, in her book *Blood, Bread and Roses,* developed what she calls a "metaformic theory" of human evolution, documenting the pervasive presence of menstrual rituals found around the world and throughout time.[2] Now Grahn, in collaboration with Dianne Jenett, directs the Women's Spirituality program at New College in San Francisco where I also teach as an adjunct professor, and where the evolutionary blood mystery is part of the core master's degree curriculum.

What is frequently overlooked in mainstream scholarship, but illuminated by Goddess scholars, is the unique and powerfully synchronized connection with the monthly cycle of the Moon in the sky. The focus here is a powerful female agency in human women who—because of the innate ritual base present in their own biological existence—emerged as the original magicians, shamans, and inventors of culture. The word *mensis* (month) links *menstruous* (monthly), *measure, and mental,* and Mensa is the name of an organization designed to honor the brainiest people alive. The Double Goddess is a code for this ancient and potent evolutionary blood mystery.

When archaeologist Marija Gimbutas looked at Double Goddess figures or temples shaped as two women, such as Gigantija in Malta (see fig. 2.5 in chapter two) she described them as mother and daughter, and referred to Demeter and Persephone of the Greek Eleusinian Mysteries. But she also focused more broadly on the *matrilineal descent* that characterized ancient Goddess-worshipping cultures, that is, the transmission of property and knowledge through the female line from mother to daughter. A living example of female descent can be seen in contemporary Navaho women in the southwestern United States, who still own and control their own flocks of sheep. When a Diné (Navaho) woman wants to divorce her husband, she simply puts his belongings outside the door of the hogan.

The Double Goddess represents the idea of *female sovereignty* in a context of ancient female yogic and shamanistic practices and principles that formed the organizing structure of most ancient cultures in the

Fig. 0.3. Two crowned heraldic sphinxes carved of ivory wear typical Mycenaean priestess hats with a fez-style base and something flowing out the top (hair?), as depicted in Aegean murals throughout the second millennium B.C.E. This one comes from Mycenae, during the late Bronze Age, when women still actively facilitated religious ceremonies.

world before patriarchy. These double images—as well as the varied mythologies of Double Queens found in different parts of the ancient world—suggest that the icons represent a female lineage (matrilinearity) in the form of a continuous "storied tradition"* of female sovereignty.

The heraldic sphinxes on the ivory carving illustrated here are one of many such Double Goddesses from Mycenaean Greece in the late Bronze Age. In some depictions, the two women are sitting in chairs or thrones side by side like queens, such as one found in Malta near the ruins of Gigantija (see fig. 2.4 in chapter two) and others from Homer's Greece (see fig. 2.17 in chapter two). In the broadest sense, they portray *women sharing power* and thereby provide us with an egalitarian model. This widespread dual image of the Double Goddess (later identified in writing as the "Mothers," the "Two Ladies," or the "Two Queens") represents quintessential female rule. Implicit in the archetype is the mirrorlike wisdom present in the profound intimacy of female bonding, whether it is between mother and daughter, blood sisters, female friends, respected colleagues, or lesbian lovers.

---

*This is the phrase used by Alexander Marshack to discuss the original matrix figure (ancestress) and the great body of oral tradition built around her that he inferred from the works of human cave-painters during the Paleolithic era (50,000 to 14,000 years ago).

Fig. 0.4. This double female carving from India, taken from a temple, perhaps depicts the Dual Mothers, or Sakhiyani ("woman-to-woman bonding"), or an age-old Indian concept of "jami" (twins), describing two women who "share a yoni." According to Giti Thadani, these concepts point to a kind of prepatriarchal "women's friendship" that potentially includes erotic relationship.

Apropos of this idea is Giti Thadani's fascinating book on prepatriarchal India, in which she discusses the ancient motif of *jami*: "the dual sisters inhabiting the same yoni space which is representative of an entire social and kinship formation."[3] Thadani relates that "one of the earliest cosmogonies recorded in the Rig Ved is that of the dual feminine deities—Dyava . . . referred to often as twins (*jami*) . . . dual mothers . . . in a feminine kinship genealogy with *prithvi* (earth), and as a generative chain of dual mothers."[4] She reiterates my central point regarding the Double Goddess when she speaks of "the notion of birth (as) a cyclic transformation of the dual, diverse jami-sisters generating and renewing each other. Light and dark are not opposing forces but transforming and revolving halves of the same wheel."[5] And she quotes an Indic hymn, "twin sisters of various alternating forms, of the two, one glowing, the other dark," which seems to express the female biological cycle of menstruation and ovulation to perfection.[6]

During the eight years it has taken me to compile and write (and rewrite) this book, I have noticed that certain key questions (perhaps "issues" is a better word) consistently emerge from the audiences who view my slide lectures, or the readers who have looked over various drafts of the book along the way. Like a psychological ink blot test, the

Double Goddess figures seem to bring up our personal (and often hidden) stuff!

The whole question of whether or not the figures I am describing are *actually* Goddesses, as opposed to *simply* women, or priestesses, or female figurines, has upset a number of people who would prefer the descriptive categories to be more clear-cut. Although traditional academic references to some of the figures do seem indicative of embarrassed or dismayed scholars, still it was traditional academic scholars who originally named the pairs Double Goddess. Many of the figures were found in "cult" settings, such as temples or shrines, strongly supporting the assumption that they represent deities, whereas others found in burials or refuse piles have elicited more disagreement over their titles. The Double Goddesses fit into a larger debate ("culture war" is more like it), in which the whole category of "Goddess" is being called into question by archaeologists who would prefer that all the thousands of female figures and images found all over the ancient world be viewed as less than divine. Why is this?

A brief glance at recent history might refresh our understanding of the hidden issues in this highly charged encounter between the academy and the so-called Goddess movement. Before the 1960s, archaeologists and prehistorians more or less unanimously agreed that ancient cultures were religious "cults" of the Great Mother and that the ubiquitous female figures were images created as representations of this female deity. These scholars were mostly detached, mostly not "feminist," and many of them perceived the Great Goddess as an early (primitive) feature of evolving human societies, later improved upon by the inevitable invention of God-the-father. Nonetheless, there was—in the first hundred years of archaeology—no real disagreement about Her identity.

Then something revolutionary happened. In 1970s America (and now internationally), a movement developed among feminist women called the women's spirituality movement, in which we discovered, reclaimed, and seriously reappropriated the ancient icon of the Goddess as our own. In the subsequent thirty years, we have created oracles, liturgies, rituals, songs, and chants in celebration of Her; we have developed a pedagogy and programs of graduate study within accredited university settings, such as California Institute for Integral Studies (CIIS) and New College in San Francisco, providing modern women students with masters and Ph.D. degrees on the subject; and we have collectively written enough published books and articles to comprise an impressive body of literature defining and further refining this new and unorthodox "women's religion." In fact, we have dug in our heels and grounded ourselves for the duration, taking a patient and long-term view of the transformation happening at this root level of (female) society.

At exactly the same time, the media has professed (over and over again in a tiresome effort to convince us) that feminism is dead and that the Goddess is no longer fashionable for the hip, postmodern women of today. The fact that Western women had not only shown scholarly interest in the ancient widespread religion of the Great Mother, but also recognized it as meaningful in our own everyday lives, has precipitated a frenzy of reactivity in the academic world, leading to an active effort to deny that there was any Goddess religion at all, ever, anywhere. Former Goddess sites (such as Çatalhöyük in Turkey) are "debunked," female figurines are described as "dolls," "toys," or even reframed as men in skirts, and buildings long believed to be temples or shrines are now called into question by the self-styled "New Archaeology."

The double female figures discussed in this book have never before been collected together and viewed coherently in terms of their sheer numbers, geographic distribution, and historical written references.* Since many of them were originally referred to as Double Goddess figures in the scholarly literature, I have kept that title, believing that it dignifies and acknowledges their sacred authority. But I am also linking earlier Double Goddess figures with much later references to Amazons

*A German woman, Gabrielle Meixner, wrote the only other book surveying the figures.

ruling in Dual Queenship, and seeing their division of labor (priestess and warrior) as the functions of twin priestesses who served as religious and temporal leaders of ancient societies. I have used the words *Goddesses, priestesses,* and *queens* more or less interchangeably in this book in order to call attention to their stature and to overcome the consistent archaeological bias that regards every high-ranking female burial as housing a noblewoman or the wife of a chieftain or king.

A number of women have wondered whether I am too timid to come right out and call *all* the figures lesbians, whereas others think it foolhardy and extreme of me to suggest that *any* of them might be lovers. Although I immediately saw the Double Goddess images as woman-identified women, I don't believe the figures are *only* lesbian (in the contemporary way that we conceptualize it). Along with my identification as a lesbian feminist, I am also a healer and have spent the last twenty-five years researching, practicing, and teaching the ancient arts of female shamanism. I am using *shaman* as a generic word here, as in this general definition from the *American Heritage Dictionary*: "A member of certain tribal societies who acts as a medium between the visible world and an invisible spirit world and who practices magic or sorcery for the purposes of healing, divination, and control over natural events." I hope to demonstrate that these female functions of priestess or shaman were original to and fundamentally alike in northern Africa, the Mediterranean and Aegean areas, Central Asia, the Middle East, India, Tibet, and Old Europe; that far-reaching trade, commerce, war, and migrations made for constant cross-cultural contact and meaningful connection between them; and that their shared traits can be seen in the artifacts and images left to us from their settlements, cult sites, and burials. African Artemis figures painted on rock walls of the Sahara before it was a desert exemplify these shared traits. Women depicted with bows and arrows, such as the ones depicted in Fig. 0.5 on page 10 from southwestern Africa, were perhaps huntresses, as is generally assumed, but are known more esoterically for rain-making and weather-working activities as well.

Fig. 0.5. This exquisite rock-art image, discovered in southwest Africa, at Leopard's Ravine (north of Windhoek), could be an African version of Artemis and her nymphs. The running women might be rain-making shamans in a tradition that has resonance with the ancient Chinese women, called "wu," who were documented as the official shamans there until the end of the Tang dynasty. In Egypt, the annual rains, bringing the crucial flooding of the Nile, were connected with the central religious rites of the culture for thousands of years.

My research shows provocative connections between the Amazons that Herodotus wrote about and the roots of Tibetan Buddhism, found in the pre-Buddhist Bön and earlier "folk" religions of Central Asia. I'm also interested in the Etruscans, gorgons, winged Nikes, and the Valkyries and Völvas (warriors and priestesses) of Norse mythologies, as well as the so-called *dakini* witches and *yogini* queens mentioned by scholars of Buddhism in Tibet. (*Dakini* is a Tibetan word meaning "sky-goer" or "sky-walking female," and a *yogini* is a practitioner of supernatural yogic powers.) I am convinced that buried in the past, and unnoticed in recent history, is a coherent female lineage of shamanistic practices and ecstatic rituals that cuts across the boundaries and nationalisms that take up so much space in our modern history books. I have always felt called to rekindle this forgotten lineage of female-to-female transmission, so deftly expressed through the icon of the Double Goddess.

When women governed society (which I will demonstrate throughout this book), the sacred and the sexual were joined. "Make love, not war"—surely the most famous slogan from the 1960s—shows a deeply intuitive grasp of prehistory when the Goddess ruled and women's ecstatic religion was central to every predynastic civilization. As I have asserted in earlier works (*Motherpeace: A Way to the Goddess*, the imagery of the *Motherpeace Tarot Cards*, and *Shakti Woman: Feeling Our Fire, Healing Our World*), thousands of female figurines, murals, painted vases, and burial artifacts from Neolithic, Bronze, and Iron Age cultures demonstrate that one essential role of the female priestess in matristic societies was the performance of the sacred sexual rites. No matter what religions have replaced the ancient religion of the Mother Goddess, and no matter how harshly women have been treated, the underground stream of Goddess images and ancient rituals in most places has never been completely suppressed.

There may not be a lot of women these days calling themselves feminists, but women at the beginning of this third millennium are nothing if not agents of our own reality. A whole generation of women are having babies without husbands, choosing alternative medicine instead of going to the doctor, and sleeping with whomever they choose without regard to that person's gender. Modern women no longer find it contradictory to be

Fig. 0.6. A Canaanite goblet showing the Goddess as a great yonic triangle flanked by ibexes or mountain goats comes from Palestine, dating to the late Bronze Age. The vulva is the earliest sign expressed by humans. Pervasive from the Paleolithic era in Europe, and everywhere amongst tribal people, it is a shorthand way to say "Goddess."

female and accomplish important work in the world, and often the most important work of changing the world is part of our vision. Peace demonstrations by Mothers for Peace and Code Pink, and collaborative performances of Women Against War show that there is a huge and growing global leadership movement fueled by female solidarity and unification demanding peace rather than war. Rather than trying to become just like men, proving that our perceived differences (like the menstrual cycle, and the fact that we are capable of giving birth) are irrelevant and merely "constructed," what I aim for as a feminist is no less than a reinstatement of our original biological right to rule this planet. What could be more timely in this hour of threatened planetary destruction at the hands of horrific male technologies of war?

Although the deconstruction of gender begun by feminists in the midtwentieth century has gone to absurd lengths in the postmodern age, positing that there is no essential difference at all between male and female, a recent study of men's and women's responses to stress added yet another layer of proof to the fact that there is a significant biological basis for such differences.[7] The results of this landmark study, conducted at UCLA by Doctors Laura Cousin Klein and Shelley Taylor, provide evidence that the "fight or flight" mechanism describes only how *men* respond to stress. When under stress, males produce testosterone, whereas in women this response is buffered by the release of oxytocin, which ultimately produces a calming effect. Though the researchers describe women's response to stress in a slightly trivializing way as "tend and befriend" (gather the children and collaborate with other women), their research documents a significantly different response to stress in women than the fight-or-flight response long held as the generic human standard of what happens to *all* people under stress. Because 90 percent of the scientific research over the last four decades has been done on men, no one noticed that women had an entirely different response to stress until these women scientists decided to check it out.

These researchers have combined their findings with other studies, which show that having friendships keeps people healthy, to point to the biological necessity of a network of female friendships for women. The doctors stopped there in their published interpretations. However, it does not take much to recognize that this special biological capacity in women to become calm under stress and act from wisdom and concern for others points far beyond the need for female friendship to strongly suggest that the world would be in a far better state if it were women who governed society.

As I visited one museum after another in my travels over the last decade, especially in Europe and the Mediterranean area, I kept unexpectedly coming upon more of the Double Female figures—large ones, small ones, Neolithic, Bronze Age, classical period—even though you may not see them in most books written about the places, they are actually found almost everywhere! My imagination was captured repeatedly by figures of the Double Goddess. I came across several in a powerful exhibit in Istanbul in 1994. I saw a miniature Egyptian Double Ankh in a case at the Hermitage in St. Petersburg in 1997, which bears a striking resemblance to the double-Venus symbol used to represent lesbianism in modern times, and is also the glyph for an asteroid named Sappho placed in modern astrology charts.

Double Goddesses go all the way back to the beginnings of human culture—one appearing on a cave wall at Laussel in France from thirty thousand years ago (see fig. 1.7 in chapter one)—and throughout later Neolithic, Bronze, and Iron Age cultures. (See Time Line at end of book.) They continue even into the modern age through the underground streams of "folk" and textile art all across Eurasia. Some unique pairs from Ain Ghazal, Jordan, seventh millennium B.C.E., are life size (see

Fig. 0.7. This tiny Egyptian Double Ankh is on display in a case at the Hermitage Museum in St. Petersburg, Russia. It is made of faience, like the Cretan Snake Goddesses, date unknown. The Ankh is basically a women's symbol, like the sign of Venus, and two of them add up to a Double Goddess, providing quite an effective glyph of symbiotic union or lesbianism (similar to the astrological symbol for Sappho, which is also formed of two attached women's symbols).

Fig. 0.8. These two female figures side by side, dark and light, with two flanking animals (leopards?), Double Eagles, and a Double Axe above them are from a contemporary Cretan embroidery. Marija Gimbutas points out that the Goddess tradition, although underground, was continuous for many millennia, with motifs remaining essentially the same all over Europe and the Mediterranean area for thousands of years.

fig. 1.14 in chapter one), and there are dozens of smaller ones from Old Europe and Anatolia (ancient Turkey). A small figurine from Çatalhöyük ("Cattle Hill"), an ancient city in Turkey, also dates from the seventh millennium B.C.E. The figure shows two women embracing in what could be a template of the easy intimacy found in so many of the Double Goddess figures around the world. In addition to powerful female imagery, archaeological evidence from Çatalhöyük suggests a peaceful civilization where people domesticated animals, cultivated enough food to have abundance, and lived lives filled with art, ritual, and ceremonial activity.

All my work is a celebration of such cultures and of female sovereignty, and this book is offered in the same spirit.

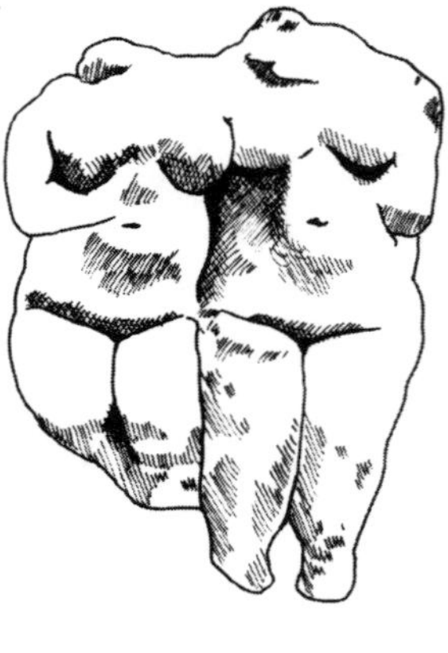

Fig. 0.9. This tiny Double Goddess comes from Çatalhöyük, in ancient Anatolia (modern Turkey), and dates to the seventh millennium B.C.E. Çatalhöyük may be the most important ancient Goddess site, which (somewhat ironically) is the current target of an active effort to erase the whole idea of a Great Goddess who was worshipped all over the ancient world.

ONE

Power of Two: The Legacy of the Double Goddess

BIOLOGY IS DESTINY: ALL WOMEN ARE TWINS

All women are twins. All women are fundamentally two in one, our most essential structural feature being our bipolar nature entrained with the ceaseless rhythms of the "inconstant Moon," to quote Shakespeare's Juliet. Each one of us, for much of her adult life, moves monthly between the light and dark poles of hormonal and emotional fluctuation—from ovulation to menstruation. At one point expanded, then introverted; reaching out and going within; we descend to depths of unfathomable complexity and return to the world empowered and ready to begin again. Unlike the linear, one-pointed man, women (and thus the ancient religions of the Goddess) flow with the cyclic rhythms of the waxing and waning Moon, with its birth, death, and rebirth.

In health classes in the 1950s, they showed us a graph with curvy lines representing the opposite poles of experience we women go through every month of our adult lives, until "the pause." What they didn't tell us in health class, but what the image of the Double Goddess expresses to a T, is the way we sometimes feel split into two very different personalities—our twin selves—at those different times of the month. This undulating rhythm matches the lunar phases and oceanic tides of our planet. Unfortunately, it is only in a natural world that this cyclic fluctuation is respected, and where we don't have to rush off to the office at "that time" of the month while trying to keep our period to ourselves. The mass epidemic of PMS in America today (more than 80 percent of adult women) has to be at least partly blamed on the fact that we no longer celebrate our menstruation, but instead designate it as a medical disorder and relate to it as an unwanted "curse." There is a clear correlation between the end of Goddess worship and the demonization, erasure, and denial of women's blood mysteries.

Fig. 1.1. Double Duck Goddess from the Hittite capital of Hattusas, central Turkey, at the end of the Bronze Age. Double figures like this represent a continuing tradition of the Amazon Queens who ruled in Dual Queenship all across Anatolia during the third and into the second millennium B.C.E.

Fig. 1.2. This Double Bird Goddess from Nazca, Peru, dated to the first millennium B.C.E., suggests a powerful connection between the Old World and the New, either through the force of the collective unconscious, which would generate such similar motifs, or even by some form of migration that remains to be proven. It is interesting that legends of South American Amazon warrior women prevail even to this day and that the state of California was supposedly named for an Amazon, Califia.

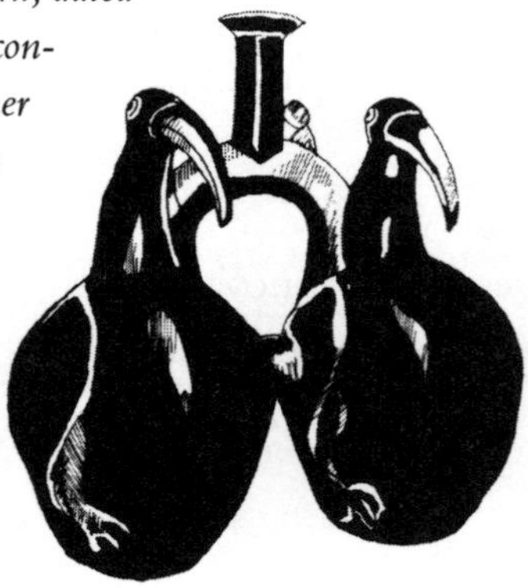

It makes sense that this bipolar quality would have first been deified, since on a primordial level it is a metaphor of creation itself as well as of the inflow and outbreath of the *pneuma*—or breath—that sustains us. Andrew Weil describes this universal reality in *Spontaneous Healing*. Speaking of the rhythmic pattern of expansion and contraction in the breath, he says, "Oscillation between two phases exists at every level of reality, even up to the scale of the observable universe itself, which is presently in expansion but will surely at some point contract back to the original, unimaginable point that is everything and nothing, completing one cosmic breath."[1] The Double Bird Goddesses pictured here come from different continents and suggest a common recognition of the two-in-one theme of female cyclic reality, as well as showing the female affinity with flight and with the egg of generation (and regeneration).

THE DIVINE TWO-IN-ONE

The icon of the Double Goddess has the capacity to reinvigorate the autonomy of women and reenliven (in a positive, nonpathological way) the innate bipolar state of consciousness that women have every right to proudly call our own. Although ancient matristic cultures (with their multifaceted female icons of birth, death, and regeneration) have been reductively labeled "fertility cults," the pioneering work of archaeologist Marija Gimbutas has gone a long way toward rectifying this oversimplification. Gimbutas—a Lithuanian woman who fled the Germans and then Stalin—arrived in the United States with a baby under one arm and her Ph.D. dissertation under the other. She was given a temporary office at Harvard where she could do her research, and then headed an innovative new interdisciplinary department at UCLA until her retirement. Renowned for having written twenty-eight books on the Bronze Age Indo-Europeans with their "weapons, weapons, weapons" (as she put it in an interview with me in 1988), she turned her attention to the deeper level of artifactual evidence she was seeing in her excavations in Greece and Macedonia. There she discovered the civilization of the Goddess, which occupied her intellectual investigations until she died in 1994 on Candlemas, one of the most important Goddess holidays marking the yearly seasonal cycle. Feminist scholars are forever grateful to her for grounding our work in strong scientific documentation that clearly supports our intuitions.

Most modern people who imagine the Goddess at all tend to see Her only as the nurturing fertile Great Mother. Or, if they see Her other side, they demonize it as a vile ogress, bent upon human sacrifice, castration, and other practices that came into being during a late transitional time when patriarchal male domination was beginning and things were becoming confused. Her ancient and integral complexity—the original dual nature of the Great Mother—often seems to overwhelm contemporary scholars, causing male scholars particularly to perceive Her as ambivalent, whimsical, fundamentally frightening, and untrustworthy. It seems to them contrary or unfair that She who gives life can also take it away.

Yet it is this dual rhythm, this two-sided nature that most essentially characterizes the Great Goddess: life and death are two parts of the same whole picture, with little more than a revolving door in between. She *is* the Tao (pronounced "dao"), symbolized by a circle with two fishlike images swimming around and meeting eye to eye, one black and one white, each with the opposite color as its eye. This is a stylized representation of the Two-In-One, the pregnant Great Mother with Her

Fig. 1.3. The Tao symbol from China represents the Two-in-One as the pregnant Great Mother and her fluctuating twins, the yin and yang, each containing a dot of color from the opposite other. Ancient shamans in China were women, known as "wu," who danced to make it rain, practiced sacred sexual rites, and facilitated other magical religious practices and ceremonies until well into the modern epoch.

Fig. 1.4. Double Goddess of wood from Lithuania, Marija Gimbutas's homeland, depicting Laima (Fate) and her sister, Giltine (Death). Laima decreed a child's fate at birth, and birth rituals honored her with offerings made in the sauna, where bathing preceded the birth event and a feast took place after. Giltine announced fateful decrees regarding death by standing at the foot of the person's bed.

capacity of giving birth to twins, both male and female, dark and light, which contain within themselves the seed of the other. These two aspects exist eternally in perpetual motion, one turning into the other in the ceaseless eternal return that expresses life on earth. In the absolute sense, it doesn't matter which side we're on at any given time; they're equal. We need not fear. The Goddess holds us in *and is* the whole, and we go back and forth between the two states. It is the function of Her double priestesses to facilitate these transitions.

It is this back-and-forth process that the Goddess-centered religions acknowledge and celebrate in the icon of the "Regeneratrix," as Gimbutas repeatedly referred to her. The Mother Goddess as the great Two-in-One reminds us of summer and winter, day and night, even alternating right- and left-brain functions, as well as the reincarnational coming and going. More specifically, the twin aspect of the Double Goddess points to the unique lunar cycle of ovulation and menstruation in every adult woman, which ranks as a quintessential differentiating characteristic of the human primate family. The snake—with its innate transformative ability to shed old skin—is totemically related to human women, who menstruate (shed the lining of the uterus) every month, as metaphorically represented on the Double Snake vase from Rhodes shown in fig. 1.5 on page 20.

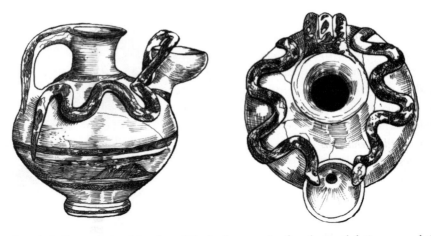

Fig. 1.5. Spouted ritual jug from Rhodes has a pair of snakes undulating around the top, preparing to drink from the spout; it dates to the late Bronze Age. Rhodes is an island, like Cyprus, off the coast of Turkey (ancient Anatolia), where the Goddess tradition has a long history.

MIRRORING HER, MIRRORING TIME

A mural painted at Çatalhöyük in the seventh millennium B.C.E. contains an iconic image that reflects the bipolar nature of the female human and of all existence, along with summing up the whole cosmology and chronology of the Goddess religion. According to James Mellaart—the archaeologist who originally excavated at Çatalhöyük in the 1960s—the scene depicts Artemis as the Goddess on the Mountain, an ancient shamanistic icon of power and creativity. In a complementary tradition that can still be affirmed today, many important mountains carry their original female names, such as Nanda Devi (a form of Parvati, called "Goddess of Bliss") in the Indian Himalayas, or the Goddess Annapurna ("She Who Is Filled with Food"). The Goddess of Mount Everest, the highest mountain in the world, is known by Tibetans as Lady Langma (Miyolangsangma).[2]

Predating written language, the Mountain Goddess in the mural at Çatalhöyük within her tree-covered mountain shrine wears a headdress

Fig. 1.6. Found in Çatalhöyük, this Double Goddess image from the seventh millennium B.C.E. could serve as a prototype for all the others that follow. The Mountain Mother Goddess wearing headdress and necklace provides the fertile ground for the dual expression of her Priestess-Queens and several pairs of animal guardians (boars or bears, lions, leopards, and vultures) that flank her. The earliest known Double Axes bear witness to this female-centered society governed by women.

and necklace that can be taken as power insignia. Gimbutas focused a great deal of attention on the importance of the pervasive headdresses and necklaces shown on Goddess figurines from hundreds of sites in Old Europe, many of which she excavated herself.[3] These classic ornaments are the identifying characteristics of the Goddess, the necklace (with breasts) symbolizing her "presence and her regenerative potential"[4] and the crown in particular "a symbol of her omnipotence and omniscience."[5] The enclosed shrine or "cave niche" is cleverly created by the "negative" space that is actually, when you look closer, two boars (or perhaps bears) whose faces meet above her head. Inside the space of the two boars are portrayed two leopards whose faces also meet at her face. Below the leopards and boars are her two priestesses or queens—the sacred sisters, jami, the Double Goddess in human form—with arms holding or emphasizing their bare breasts and wearing characteristic scalloped or fluted skirts that reappear in Malta and Crete thousands of years later. Flanking the two priestesses and facing outward are two more leopards or lionesses who seem to be guarding the women and could be their alter egos; and in the space of their bodies, created by dark on light space, are images of vultures. In the center of the two priestesses, creating their shared girdle, is the head of an aurochs (one of the first domesticated animals, similar to an ox), with its horns stretching out and linking the women together. Beyond the cats are the earliest known Double Axes, the original emblem of the Double Goddess and the sovereignty of the female, creating a powerful symbolic border for the whole scene.

The ancient symbols and images of Çatalhöyük have sustained themselves for nine thousand years, continuing to be stylized and reproduced in the tribal rugs (kilims) still woven today by the women of Turkey, Afghanistan, and other nearby regions.[6] Even though the populations are now Islamic, the kilims are still woven in the same artistic style as this ancient mural, in which the negative spaces create images that give a complexity to the artwork and cause your eyes to have to continually refocus and rediscover new images in what looked like blank or contrasting space. In a way, the form of the expression and the content are exactly the same: The Double Goddess (in art or women) represents the way in which the twinning motif is a mirror reflection, back to back, of something that isn't really its own opposite (as in different), but more like a mirror reflection of it (sameness); yet the dual poles dance. The dark pole of the lunar, menstrual cycle can't actually be separated out from the ovulation end of the month, and this truth is the nugget of ancient Goddess wisdom that later became codified into other traditions such as Taoism. This quintessentially female divine duality is understood to be a verb, a process of being and becoming, rather than a fixed entity.

Kilims often have borders of Double Goddesses as well as more central female images in mirror reflection and otherwise. A Double Goddess motif found in many murals at Çatalhöyük and stylized in contemporary kilims—the one that seems to have the most longevity— is a generic mirror image in which one figure sits above the other in "playing-card" style with their two heads pointed in opposite directions. The probable precursor of these images is one that appears in the

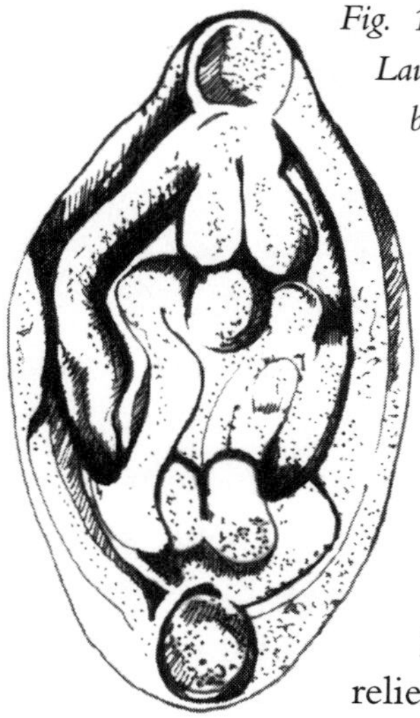

Fig. 1.7. This image from inside the cave sanctuary of Laussel, France, Paleolithic period (ca. 30,000 B.C.E.), has been variously identified as a male-female copulation scene, a birthing scene, or (most recently) a Double Goddess in mirror reflection. Perhaps as a "playing card" image of two women, it represents the changing of the seasons from winter to summer, and the resulting dark and light cycle that occurs.

Paleolithic cavern at Laussel, France (30,000 B.C.E.). At the door of the cave-sanctuary, one passes under the famous "Venus of Laussel"—a relief sculpture about two-and-a-half feet high carved some thirty thousand years ago on an overhang at the entrance—to enter into the cave-womb where a double human figure is incised. Some have seen it as a heterosexual image of reproduction or even tantric (supernatural or magical) sex, as I suggested in *Shakti Woman.*[7] The two anthropomorphic figures could be engaged in an act of copulation as seen from above in the style of male-female images found in historical Indian temples. Others have thought it to be a depiction of active birth.[8] But more recently—and perhaps more accurately—the image has been interpreted by James Harrod as two Goddesses, "facing and entwined, to symbolize the mystery and creative energy flowing between mother and daughter or between two women."[9] It is quite likely that this Paleolithic image of the Double Goddess also represented the seasonal cycle of the solar year, functioning as a symbolic calendar. It is certainly no accident that tribal people around the world—as well as pagans of European descent—keep a traditional circular calendar of the seasonal cycle marking eight major power points that we call the winter and summer Solstices, spring and fall Equinoxes, and four cross-quarter days that fall in between. Just as the monthly lunar cycle begins with the invisible dark Moon, the yearly cycle of the Sun begins in a similar way when that light is almost invisible, at the dark of winter. Long celebrated by people around the world as the birth moment in the solar year, this holiday was adapted by Christianity and designated as the "birth of Christ" only two thousand years ago. The sacred calendar has been reclaimed by modern feminist women and pagans around the world who celebrate the Solstices, Equinoxes, and the potent cross-quarter holidays in between: Candlemas, Beltane, Lammas, and Hallowe'en.[10]

If we look at the icon of the Double Goddess in mirror reflection as a sacred calendar, we see one head as a representation of the New Moon/Winter Solstice (hibernation, when the light is born from within the potent darkness) and the other as the Full Moon/Summer Solstice (when the light is at its strongest, days are longest, energy at its furthest extension, and the Sun begins to turn back again toward the dark as the long days begin to shorten). These two opposing points in the yearly cycles mark the yang and yin of the year as experienced alternately in the northern and southern hemispheres. Ancient agricultural societies would have been especially likely to pay attention to this seasonal calendar, which marked the times for ploughing, planting, and harvesting, with all the attendant festivities to celebrate each phase.

But the sacred calendar is as old as humanity and predates agriculture by many thousands of years. Lunar menstrual calendars were incised on bones by our Paleolithic hunter-gatherer ancestors, a fact documented by Alexander Marshack's microscopic analysis of bones found at ancient Cro-Magnon sites. Marshack believes that rather than primitive or random notations, the "time-factored" menstrual calendar bones and the Venus figures in the caves represented a simple everyday shamanistic component of a much larger and more elaborate system of mathematics and science that our ancient ancestors understood and developed over thousands of years. In this context, the Laussel Double Goddess figure can be perceived as containing the whole cosmological system of understanding in one glyph that functions similarly to the Chinese image of the Tao. The tenacity of the mirror image Double Goddess is more easily understood when seen in this light.

The story of Demeter and Persephone—the most famous Greek

Double Goddess—is a remnant of this ancient seasonal calendar. Worshipped together as "the Two Goddesses,"[11] their mysteries celebrated at Eleusis (near Athens) every year were known all over the classical world into the Christian Era, from the time that the first buildings were placed there in the fifteenth century B.C.E. Demeter's barrenness represents the withdrawal of life force in the frozen winter, bereft of fertility, when the seed is underground and the night is long; Persephone's return in the spring is the powerful quickening of life as the solar power grows toward its apogee at Summer Solstice when the light is great. When I created the Motherpeace Empress tarot card in the late 1970s, it was Demeter I had in mind; the long history of female and agricultural

Fig. 1.8. Motherpeace Empress card—this image of the Empress from the Motherpeace tarot cards was created by the author. It embodies a continuous span of sacred women's history, from the paleolithic "Venus of Laussel" (ca. 25,000 B.C.E.), to the enthroned Queen Mother and her leopards (Çatalhöyük, seventh millennium B.C.E.), to the Roman Ceres with her snakes and sheaves of grain. The Great Mother Goddess in her fertile aspect was classically represented by the Greek Demeter, whose Eleusynian Mysteries were famous all over the ancient world.

Fig. 1.9. Motherpeace Daughter of Wands card—this image of the Daughter of Wands from the Motherpeace tarot cards was created by the author to express the return of Persephone to her mother in the spring, and the resurrection of life on earth after the cold, barren winter. The young enthusiastic daughter rushes headlong into life, carrying the Wheel of Nemesis and a sprig of witch hazel for healing.

fertility is depicted behind the reclining figure of the Goddess herself. When I made the Daughter of Wands, I was thinking of Persephone's return; she is shown running exuberantly, with a cave in the background, and carrying a budding branch of the healing tree, witch hazel.

A similar mother-daughter pair was worshipped on the island of Samothrace and in the Anatolian region of Phrygia, according to Monaghan. Like Demeter and Persephone, Anieros and Axiocersa were "doubles of each other: the young earth of springtime and the mature earth of autumn; the young woman of promise and the fulfilled matron." Their religion was "the ancient one of Asia Minor, based on the divinity of the female body," which was seen as a "microcosm of the forces of life, growth, death and rebirth."[12]

Dark and light, these two Goddesses of female duality could be a late version of what was poetically represented in ancient Sumer as the Goddess Inanna making her descent into the underworld at the beck and call of her dark sister, Ereshkigal, who ruled there.[13] The story of Inanna's descent and return—as much a monthly menstrual mythology as a seasonal description—is part of the earliest piece of epic writing in the world, and this most ancient pair of Divine Sisters functions as a likely prototype for the later seasonal story of Demeter and Persephone. The late patriarchal intrusion of the daughter's abduction by Pluto or Hades (male god of the underworld) into the story and Persephone's forced presence in the underworld for half of each year robs the female characters of the personal agency that each of them possessed in the earlier version. Inanna descended to the underworld because she wanted to, or instinctually *needed* to, having heard the call of the Dark Goddess of menstruation and birth (death and rebirth). When she returned to the upper world, she was empowered by the descent and rebirth experience, which functioned like a primal initiation process.

In the same sense Demeter, the Goddess of life and fertility, has to withdraw her energies within herself for the cyclical renewal that is symbolized by her daughter's return in the spring and the budding of new life that always happens then. My early introduction to the basic qualities of Demeter and Persephone came through Erich Neumann's wonderful text, *The Great Mother,* which I discovered in the 1970s. Earth Mother Demeter represents Neumann's "elementary" feminine axis: the physical, fertile planet Earth and the lush, abundant growth that

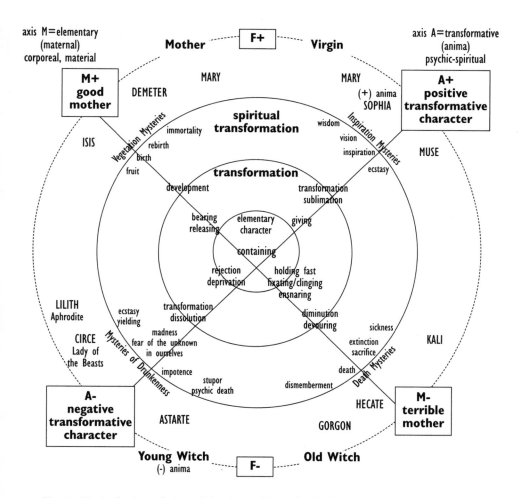

Fig. 1.10. Author's rendering of the Axis of Double Goddess from Erich Neumann's The Great Mother—*this image was significant in catalyzing the original research done by the author before co-creating the* Motherpeace *cards and before writing her book,* Motherpeace: A Way to the Goddess through Myth, Art and Tarot *(Harper & Row, 1983). The idea of the "elementary" feminine (Earth Goddess) and the "transformative" feminine (Moon Goddess) overlapping and interconnecting in the female psyche and in the universe felt deeply logical to her, even though it would be more than a decade before she saw her first Double Goddess figurine.*

feeds all life.[14] Her daughter Persephone belongs to the transformative feminine axis and has to descend to the underworld in order to partake of the unconscious, invisible, and other-worldly aspects of the primal feminine cycle. The Goddesses of Earth and Moon (upper and under-world, physical and psychic) represent the polar fluctuations of the monthly cycle, and it's interesting that modern women still say we are "having our Moon" when referring to the menstrual period.

Tellingly, Demeter is described (like Inanna) as *ruler* of the upper world, and Persephone is similarly crowned queen of the underworld, which she *rules* for half the year. Yet Demeter and Persephone both ended up as victims of male violence. They are perceived as making the best of a bad situation, but even so, were known as the "Demetres, a name that stresses the oneness of their divinity . . . one goddess in two guises."[15] The Eleusinian Mysteries depicting the Demeter-Persephone story were so popular that people came by the thousands to gather in the amphitheater at Eleusis and experience the divine event, a secret epiphany, which participants were sworn never to reveal.

DARK-LIGHT GODDESS SPIRITUALITY

We women with our lunar, bipolar biology are like the Double Goddess, partaking equally of life and death. At one time of the month we might be friendly and self-sacrificing, receptive, open to relation-ship and the accommodation it implies; at the other end of the cycle, look out—we can be bitchy and out of sorts, difficult, easily upset. Like the tides, we ebb and flow. In our modern culture, the ovulation point of the cycle is recognized as "good" and the menstruation side of it per-ceived as "dark," if not generally "bad" (the "curse"). But in ancient primal cultures, both sides were acknowledged and sanctified, and human culture itself was organized around this rhythmic duality, as suggested in this gold pectoral (a necklace that rests on the chest like a breastplate) unearthed at Knossos in Bronze Age Crete. Women invented the arts of pottery and basketry, often fashioning containers

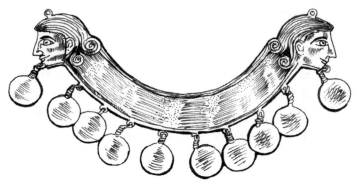

Fig. 1.11. This Greek gold pectoral from the so-called Aegina Treasure of Cretan artifacts, once housed in the British Museum, has now been returned to Athens where it is on display in the National Archaeological Museum. The pectoral shows two female figures in profile facing away from each other; from Knossos, late Bronze Age.

in their own image reflected in the image of the Divine Female, like this Double Goddess vessel from the Nazca culture of Peru.

The ovulation point in the female blood cycle corresponds to the light and all that goes with it. At that (symbolic) Full Moon time of the month, many women feel genuinely receptive and nurturing, creative, expressive, and open to bonding. At that other, dark end of the cycle, most of us don't particularly want to relate and can't gracefully give up ourselves for an "other," no matter how important or intimate a relationship might be to us; instead, we respond to another call. Like the Sumerian Inanna who heard the call of her dark sister, Ereshkigal, and responded, we women must listen within.

Fig. 1.12. This Double Goddess vessel representing two women from Nazca, Peru, 400 B.C.E., is not unlike those found in Anatolia and other places. With lightheartedness, it makes the visual assertion that the female body is a sacred container and that two women are better than one. Note the hands holding the breasts and the markings around the eyes that might indicate tattooing, an intricate part of the priestess tradition around the world.

The descent motif so beautifully depicted in this earliest of epic stories belongs particularly to the realm of the female initiate. The death and rebirth graphically depicted in the Inanna story (she dies and hangs on a meat hook for three days) is classically shamanistic. In shamanistic terms, women die every month, constantly rehearsing that break in consciousness that allows us regularly to travel to the invisible terrain of the dreamtime and safely return. Like a snake shedding its skin, we die and get reborn through our descent to the underworld of blood and loss of ordinary consciousness. This periodic psychic disintegration (what we now label PMS) belongs at the far end of the transformative axis in Neumann's structure, along with sickness and death.

At ovulation, there is the potential of new life—an awesome biological capacity inherent in the female organism and celebrated from the earliest times. Life calls, and reproduction is possible. But there is an equal luminosity in the sacred darkness of the menstruation time, as evidenced in ancient Indian tantric texts that regarded a menstruating Shakti (female priestess) as the most powerful guru (teacher who transmits knowledge) to initiate a male adept into the yogic mysteries. Indian *Devadasis* (temple dancers) were still performing their ancient rituals of initiation and celebration in worship of the Divine until the middle of the twentieth century—when the British outlawed their "lewd" activities and brought an end to their long lineage. In those rituals their sexual and menstrual fluids were venerated as sacred substances.[16] Kirlian photography tells us something similar: that when a woman bleeds, she emanates white light. Miranda Shaw's definitive investigation of the female roots of north Indian Buddhist tantric principles and practices provides a context for the re-membering of modern women's active and grounded dark-light Goddess spirituality.[17]

In the West, yang and yin—the Taoist expression of the bipolar nature of the whole—have been diminished, reduced exclusively to mean "male" and "female." It is as if the two biological sexes, clearly gendered, have been hammered into a hallowed institution. Yet this bipolarity so strongly felt by individual women is part of our biological heritage; although certainly felt as yang and yin, it is not necessarily experienced as male and female. Contemporary Jungian thought has strongly emphasized the idea of a woman's "inner male" that she is supposed to "get in touch with," but I find it at least as useful (therapeutically) to deal with the actuality of the lived female experience as "feminine yang" and "feminine yin," to use terms coined by Sylvia Perera in her commentary on the Inanna myth.[18] Other polar images that come to mind are Kwan Yin and Kali or Medusa and the Virgin Mary. To reclaim the buried, demonized, dark feminine self is a profound act of actualization and integration for any contemporary woman, and to imagine being female as including the usual male prerogatives of aggression, power, and physical intensity is potentially liberating.

Gimbutas informed us of this dual female nature by focusing on the ubiquitous representations of the Bird and Snake Goddess found all over Old Europe. Bird and snake figures exist elsewhere in the ancient world as well, such as the winged figure from the Valley of Mexico (1200–900 B.C.E.). The bird-woman hybrid represents for Gimbutas a quality of bisexualism, but rather than male and female, it is that of the bird (sky and mind) and snake (earth and body).[19] Just as in the female cycle, "their functions are so intimately related that their separate treatment is impossible."[20] The motif is one of integration of opposites within the self and again points to the female biological

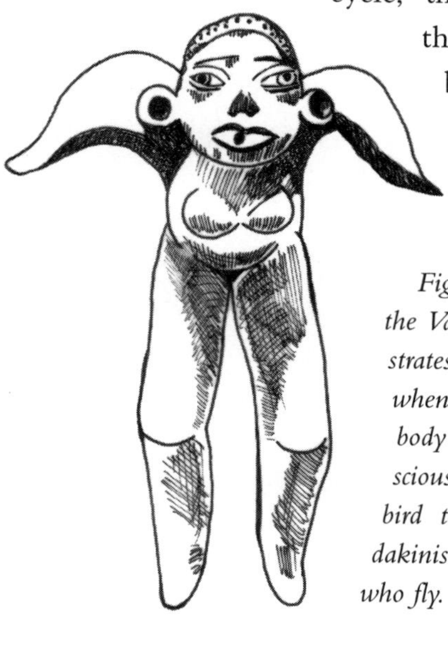

Fig. 1.13. This lovely winged female figure from the Valley of Mexico (1200–900 B.C.E.) demonstrates the shamanistic power of "kundalini rising," when the awakened serpent power in a woman's body rises up and culminates in enlightened consciousness and the ability of her spirit to fly like a bird to other realms. Similarly, Tibetan Buddhist dakinis are referred to as "sky goers," that is, females who fly.

reality. When a woman experiences her monthly flow, she bleeds "without a wound," as pagans like to say. Contained within this extremely physical state of being (the snake) is a spacious, open psychic reality in which our spirits detach and fly (the bird); we are generally understood to be more psychic during our periods.

Sometimes the snake (physical being) spontaneously arises and becomes the bird (consciousness) in flight. In Eastern yoga teachings, the kundalini energy is depicted as a snake coiled three times at the base of the spine, lying dormant, awaiting any event that would catalyze it to awaken and arise through the seven chakras or energy centers in the body. When this high-voltage spiritual energy reaches the top of the head (crown chakra), it spills out and the initiate achieves bliss. What men have to meditate for twenty years to achieve through discipline and hard work, many women experience through the physiological processes of menstruation, natural birthing, and sacred sexuality. My own kundalini awakened in my adolescence as I explored my sexuality for the first time, and it developed with each intense sexual encounter I had after that. By the time I was practicing yoga consciously in my late twenties, it was clear to me that all the things I read in esoteric yoga texts referred to experiences I was having consistently by then. In my yoga teachings with women over the years, I have encouraged my students to practice yoga for the purpose of opening and clearing channels so that the natural process of kundalini arousal might take place spontaneously through their biological life activities.

It is equally important for women that we allow natural healing processes to take place in our lives, rather than relying on Western medical interventions to interrupt our menstruation, birthing, and menopausal experiences. Otherwise we sacrifice the opportunities presented by nature for our personal enlightenment and evolutionary development. Surely the Double Goddess images that appeared so early in the history of civilization reflect this understanding of the organic female nature, with its two integrated aspects of body and spirit, which are naturally activated by participating in the cycles of nature: birth, death, and regeneration. "Virgin and mother stand to one another as flower and fruit, and essentially belong together in their transformation from one to the other."[21]

SIAMESE TWINS: MERGED DOUBLE GODDESS IMAGES

Some of the most beautiful and enigmatic Double Goddesses are the merged ones resembling Siamese twins whose two heads share one body, or others whose two bodies are linked together as if attached. Still others share a girdle that holds their two bodies together in an intimate merging. Some early Neolithic figurines fall into this category, such as an exquisite alabaster figurine from Çatalhöyük (see fig. 1.25) and several from the Vinča (Balkan) culture of the late sixth to early fifth millennium B.C.E. (see figs. 1.18–1.20).

The largest Double Goddesses ever discovered were found in two separate caches at Ain Ghazal in Jordan, an ancient site not far from Jericho in Amman north of the Dead Sea where plaster appeared for the first time in the eighth millennium B.C.E. It is probably here that agriculture was first practiced extensively and here that some of the most intriguing Double Goddesses were discovered from a Neolithic site active several thousand years before the Old Testament was written. After a decade of patient retrieval by archaeologists, some of the figures from the later of the two caches were installed at the

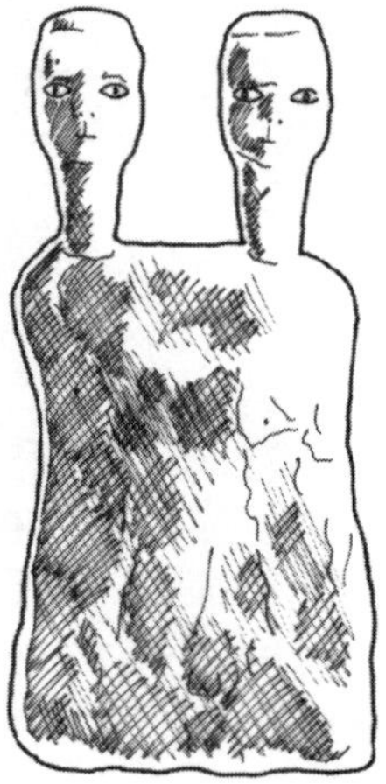

Fig. 1.14. This unique Double Goddess is one of five life-size plaster busts (about 3 1/2 feet tall) found in a cache buried at Ain Ghazal in Jordan around 6700 B.C.E. Archaeologists believe the two separate caches of plaster figures were buried when they were no longer used for religious purposes at the site. The plaster technique developed at Ain Ghazal is used in the wall paintings at Çatalhöyük in ancient Turkey from about the same time period. Green eyeliner could be something like the malachite used later by Egyptian priestesses during the dynastic period.

Fig. 1.15. Museum photo from the Smithsonian of the Double Goddess plaster bust from Ain Ghazal, Jordan. This amazing life-size plaster bust of two women, recently unearthed along with four others from a cache at Ain Ghazal in Jordan, dates from the early seventh millennium B.C.E., representing the earliest and largest neolithic expressions of a Double Goddess. Imagine the power of this icon when dressed in woven (linen or flax) robes, animal skins, wigs, headdresses, or crowns for overseeing communal festivities. The penetrating trance-like stare of this double-headed female deity is enhanced by the use of a green substance like malachite around the eyes, typical of other figurines and living priestesses in the later neolithic period.

Smithsonian in an exhibit focused on restoration techniques. The odd figures are flat and sculpted without arms, and five of them have the two heads of a Double Goddess. Archaeologists think they must have been dressed in elaborate costumes that would have given clues to their identities.[22]

The archaeologists insist on describing the statues as ungendered, because the figures (which were meant to be clothed) lack any obvious breasts or a marked pubic triangle to prove them female. The author of a book in the popular *Eyewitness Guide* series, in association with the British Museum, used the totally inappropriate caption, "*man* of straw" (my italics), referring to the straw structure used as a base under the plaster, and thereby designating male gender absolutely without justification.[23] The figures, to the contrary, have the large staring eyes of divinely inspired trance so often seen in Goddess figurines in all areas around the Mediterranean and the Near and Middle Eastern areas over a period of several millennia, outlined in the pervasive eye ointments used regularly by women from Egypt to India. (And if anything, the straw "doll" underneath the plaster resembles much smaller Irish "corn dollies" more than any "straw man.")

The excavating team has found shrines at this site that to them represent the beginnings of organized religion. Because the figures are so large and from such an early date—from temples that are the oldest known religious structures in the southern Levant—they carry a lot of significance. The current politics of Western archaeology would very much prefer that they *not* be Goddesses, yet they fall within a context and time period that simply precludes male images. The large plaster figures found at Ain Ghazal—the oldest Double Goddess figurines—are not by far the only ones found in the Levant where the concept clearly held power from the early Neolithic through the late Bronze Age. (See Time Line at end of book.)

The figures have ridges on their heads that would have held some form of hair, headdresses, headbands, diadems, or veils, and their bodies would have been clothed in whatever sacred fabrics the women of the area were weaving at that time (from flax, hemp, wool, or cotton, for example). From the archaeological record, we learn that women of this region in 6500 B.C.E. were making linen from the nettle plant and creating intricate beaded "hair nets" or high ceremonial hats found by archaeologists in caves near the Dead Sea. We might imagine that the people of Ain Ghazal dressed their Double Goddess (and corresponding priestesses?) in linen robes or tunics and fine linen beaded hair nets. The tunics or gowns could have been white, as in Egypt, or perhaps they were dyed with natural materials found in that area and processed by the women into color. After that, beads or cowrie shells might have been sewn onto the garments for added talismanic power, or—as in the case of the nettle hair nets—a stone button could have been added at the top, creating a peaked effect that would be replicated down through the ages and across vast geographical spaces.

Recent exciting discoveries in a cave in Israel at Peqi'in in the north produced another early Double Goddess whose image was published in 1999 in *Archaeological Odyssey*, a popular American archaeological magazine. The site is considered important mainly because the cave burial housed artifacts from a diversity of peoples living all around the large area of what is now Palestine-Israel, proving that they were in contact with one another in the fifth millennium B.C.E., much earlier than was believed before this discovery. The cave held ossuaries, or ceramic boxes filled with bones of the deceased, pointing to rites of excarnation or secondary burial. Gimbutas reminds us that the "exhumation of the body is

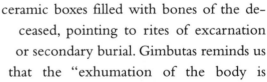
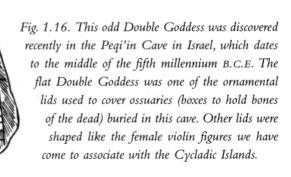

Fig. 1.16. This odd Double Goddess was discovered recently in the Peqi'in Cave in Israel, which dates to the middle of the fifth millennium B.C.E. The flat Double Goddess was one of the ornamental lids used to cover ossuaries (boxes to hold bones of the dead) buried in this cave. Other lids were shaped like the female violin figures we have come to associate with the Cycladic Islands.

women's work." The ossuaries had decorated lids that included violin-shaped female figures typical of hundreds of similar shapes found later in the Cycladic Islands. The Double Goddess found there was painted in crisscross to look like a weaving or mat, a motif that can clearly be seen on the much later "Myrtos Goddess" unearthed at a site by that name in Crete (second millennium B.C.E.). The flatness and the abstract quality of the image corresponds to much later "plank" Goddesses found in Cyprus during the late third millennium B.C.E.

Several two-headed Double Goddess figures appear over a period of almost a thousand years of Vinča culture (mid–sixth to mid–fifth millennium) in the central Balkans, where war was recently raging in Kosovo. Archaeologists have uncovered Vinča temples where ox skulls covered with clay and painted blue with a red triangle on their foreheads were attached to clay columns or painted walls; these "bucrania" suggest rituals such as those later depicted on classical Greek vases showing Maenads ("mad women") dancing in ecstasy in front of pillars hung with a mask of Dionysus. Along with offering tables and portable hearths, more than *two thousand* Goddess figurines and anthropomorphic vases were found at Vinča sites.

Fig. 1.17. These flat Double Goddesses from Cyprus, dating to the third millennium B.C.E., are unique. Lovingly inscribed with shared necklaces and the markings familiar to the "language of the Goddess," they clearly represent an ongoing tradition of shared rulership and matrilineal descent. Their large noses are reminiscent of the Double Goddess from Peqi'in Cave in Neolithic Israel.

The double-headed figures are all more or less the same type—two Goddesses sharing one body—and they all seem to be variations on what Gimbutas defined as the Bird Goddess. A whopping forty percent of all the figures found at Vinča sites have bird features.[24] The figurines are marked with an early abstract sacred script, designated "the language of the Goddess" by Gimbutas. From the earliest times, the Bird Goddess has been most simply and universally represented by "the designating mark" of the V or chevron, which stands in for vulva or pubic triangle.[25] "The association of the V or chevron, interconnected Vs, juxtaposed Vs, or a V joined to a meander, with images of the ornithomorphic Goddess and objects used in her cult remains constant for millennia." So frequent was its use that Gimbutas believes the "chevron family of symbols" was used to mark objects "as belonging to the Deity."[26]

In her earliest Goddess research, Gimbutas connects the Bird Goddess to rainmaking, an ancient women's shamanistic art practiced all over the world.[27] She further connects rain with milk, mentioning "an old and widespread belief which induced people to see women's breasts or cow udders in the clouds."[28] Any stylized Bird Goddess can be recognized by her V-shaped necklace and her nourishing breasts.

At the Parta temple in western Romania (a Vinča site), in the main (eastern) hall of the upper temple near the entrance, on a podium of clay and sand more than one meter wide, "towered a life-sized statue that had one torso but two heads."[29] Of the "abundance of Vinča double-headed goddess figurines recovered from other sites," an early fragmented one shows only the bust of a woman with two arms that look like wings and two breasts, but with two heads, and the heads look like they

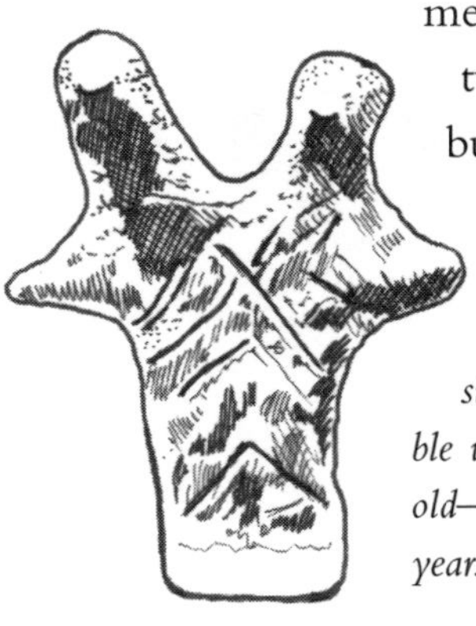

Fig. 1.18. A two-headed Double Goddess with both heads singing, from Vinča culture, western Romania, sixth millennium B.C.E. Clearly, the tradition of incredible vocal expression, so characteristic of the Balkans, is age old—obvious in this image from more than eight thousand years ago.

are singing. Given the world-renowned voices of today's Bulgarian Women's Choir, or their California counterpart, the women's choral group Kitka, this indicates a special kind of sacred singing that women in Eastern Europe have been doing for millennia. A slightly later, more complete figure shows two winged Bird Goddesses arising out of one lower body, marked with chevrons and signs associated with the Bird Goddess all over Old Europe.[30] The third image, a later version from northern Yugoslavia, shows two Bird Goddesses (they look like ducks) with their two arms and hands on their shared hips, heads attached, bodies inscribed with meanders and perforations where someone would have attached perishable materials like feathers to add to their costuming.[31] All of these images that have survived from the Vinča culture are quite abstract and probably served cultic functions, represented shamanistic rites, and referred to deities embodying the concepts of the sacred quality of female twin-being and female sovereignty.

The unique Vinča complex, partially influenced by the Karanovo culture nearer to the Black Sea in Bulgaria, was a highly evolved culture that sustained itself beautifully for a thousand years of habitation (5300–4300 B.C.E.) until the first wave of invaders from the steppes came in and obliterated their civilization. These early people, who spent their days making art, celebrating what look to be some of the earliest Dionysian rituals ever performed and apparently

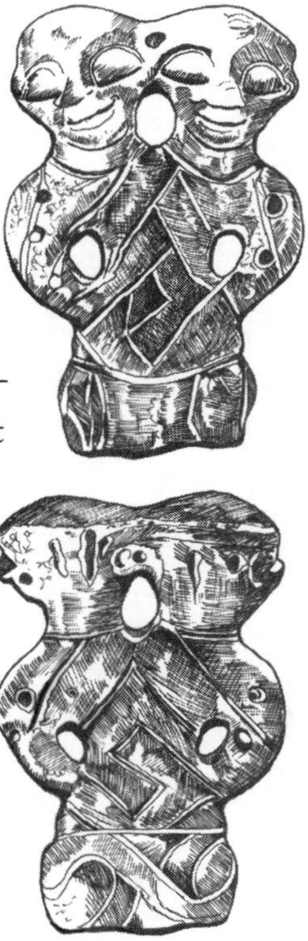

Fig. 1.19. The Double Goddess in this figure comes from northern Yugoslavia, with two heads and hands on her (their) hips, from the highly evolved Old European Vinča culture, dated to around the fifth millennium B.C.E. A Double Bird Goddess, they would have had feathers and other perishable materials attached through the perforations made for that purpose.

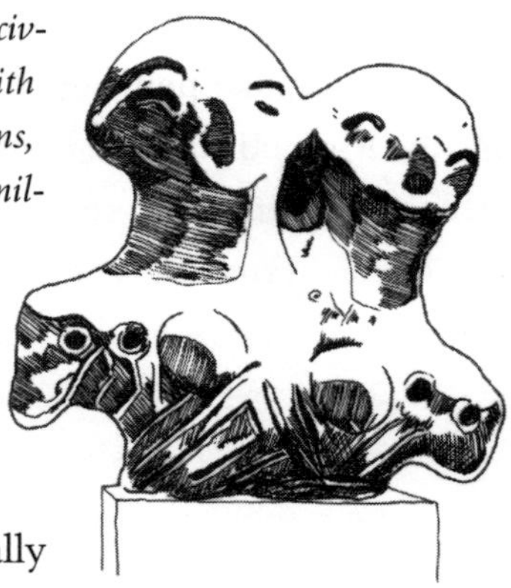

Fig. 1.20. Like most of the figurines from the Vinča civilization, this Double Bird Goddess is incised with the "language of the Goddess," including chevrons, meanders, and other early script signs. Vinča, fifth millennium B.C.E.

creating the world's first writing (the "language of the Goddess"), were wiped from the archaeological record practically without a trace, although flasks from Vinča have been found at the Greek mainland site of Lerna.[32] Some probable Vinča refugees found their way there, as well as to "regions where no human community had settled since Paleolithic times" such as "hilly terrain . . . settlements in the highest places, surrounded by cliffs or girded by rivers" suggesting "an extreme concern for defense" and also occupying caves.[33] Perhaps on account of the isolation of these meager communities of refugees, something of the original culture remained and has continued to reappear in the folk art and women's religion, as shown by Mary Kelly's work, up into the current century in Greece, the Balkan countries, and Eastern Europe.

Some of the strangest, most mysterious Double Goddesses are the so-called Disc Goddesses found in central Anatolia dating from the late-third and early-second millennia. Round alabaster discs from Kültepe (an Assyrian site not far from Alaca Höyük) have long necks poking

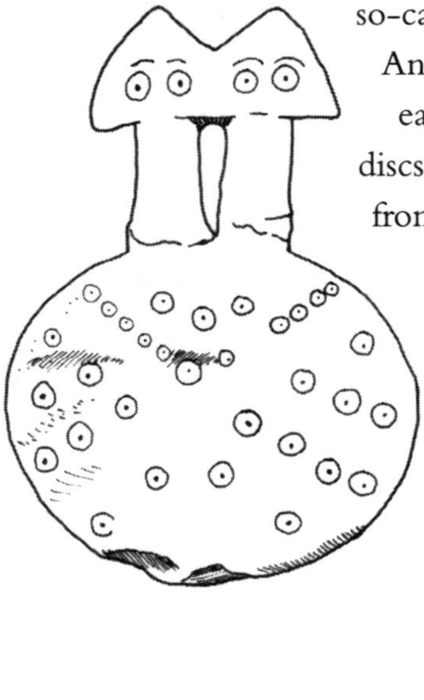

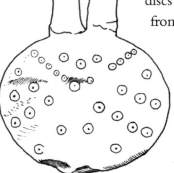

Fig. 1.21. This Double Disc Goddess, made of alabaster, comes from Kültepe in Cappadoccia (Anatolia), late third millennium B.C.E. *These weird Goddesses match the surrounding landscape of magical, surreal fairy chimneys naturally fashioned from volcanic rock.*

up from them with various multiple heads that look a little like arrows or, some say, like penis heads. I found these figures enigmatic at first, to say the least, but then I saw photos of the area in which they are located, which is called Cappadoccia. The whole landscape there is surreal, having been created by volcanic lava that cooled down and became fairy

Fig. 1.22 (a & b). Fairy chimneys in Cappadoccia, Turkey. Author photos.
a. These enigmatic forms are found all over the region of Cappadoccia in central Turkey. They were created by volcanic lava that cooled down leaving conical towers topped by boulders and creating what the locals call "fairy chimneys," a surreal landscape that must have been implicated in the inspiration for the so-called Disc Goddesses found all over central Turkey in the third millennium B.C.E. *(especially the ones that look like fig. 1.21). The hollow towers have been cultivated as cave-houses by monks, hermits, and hippies.*
b. This particular "fairy chimney" has a large central figure and two smaller ones in front, reminiscent of the Çatalhöyük Mountain Goddess and her Double Priestesses (fig. 1.6) from the same general area several thousand years earlier. Perhaps this is not too far-fetched, considering the Cimmerians (from whom Amazons may have been descended) lived in subterranean dwellings, practicing mining, smithcraft, and perhaps divination.[34]

chimneys, strange conical towers topped by boulders of a different color. These weird shapes are echoed in the local Goddess figures.

The classic Double Disc Goddesses are round with two heads, their disc bodies incised with the same figure that creates their eerie eyes, a round circle with a dot in the center. One of them has strongly incised eyebrows linking the two pointy heads together (are the pointed heads supposed to represent witches' hats?). Another one has two lovely neck-laces and a band or belt that crosses at the level of both of their breasts and could be said to link them together in the same way that a girdle or, more likely, a shawl might. One such Disc Goddess harkens back to the mural at Çatalhöyük of the Mountain Goddess and her Double Priestesses sharing the same girdle. This Disc Goddess has one elabo-rately refined head and face (unlike the others who are faceless except for large trancelike eyes), with a well-marked incised braid down her back and a headband. Inside her body is a replica of a Double Disc Goddess like the others, with triangle pointy heads arising out of one disc body incised with circle-and-dot decorations.

I also saw a triple-headed and one four-headed disc-shaped idol in

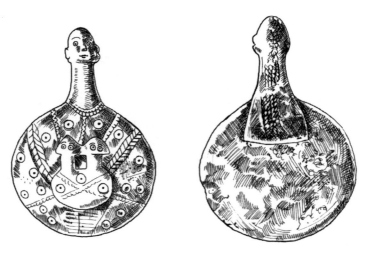

Fig. 1.23. This Double Disc Goddess of alabaster with twins inside takes after the mural at Çatalhöyük (see fig. 1.6) of a "Mother Goddess and her two daughters," according to the exhibition called "Nine Thousand Years of the Anatolian Woman," held in Turkey in 1994. The image comes from central Anatolia, third millennium B.C.E.

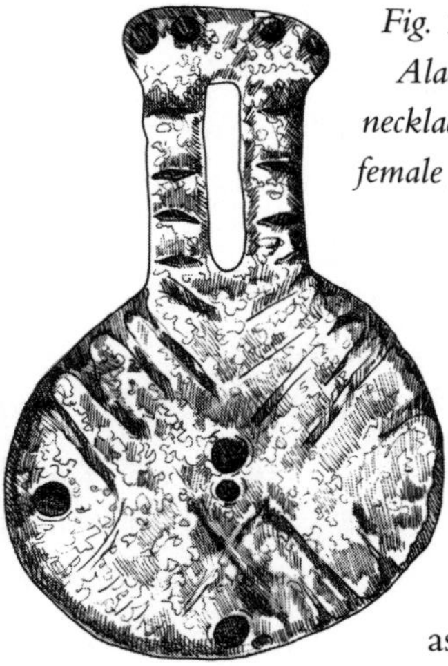

Fig. 1.24. This Double Disc Goddess, made of lead, from Alaca Höyük, dated to about 2300 B.C.E., wears two necklaces, and (if the curator of an exhibit is correct) has both female genitalia and a stylized male organ as well.

an exhibit in Istanbul, as well as a Double Goddess made in the disc shape but cast from lead rather than carved from alabaster, its two heads joined together and the body marked in a similar way to the others. A single navel is marked, as well as the pubic triangle, by raised dots, as are the two sets of eyes and even, according to the curator, breasts (although they are not anatomically correct). The curator also thinks that the raised dot in the center of the pubic triangle is a "male organ"[35] but there is no particular reason to think so. The Double Goddess wears two necklaces.

A particularly beautiful sculpture of a Double Goddess comes from Çatalhöyük and shows two women in a loving embrace, their torsos emerging out of one pelvis and bound together by one shared girdle of power. The girdle looks like a woven flat belt, similar to the kilims (flat-woven rugs) depicted in murals at that site, and to belts woven and worn by women, such as the Guatemalan Mayans, in other places all over the world. The relationship portrayed in this image is loving and tender, mutually nurturing. Closer than sisters, the pair could represent mother and daughter, and by extension the

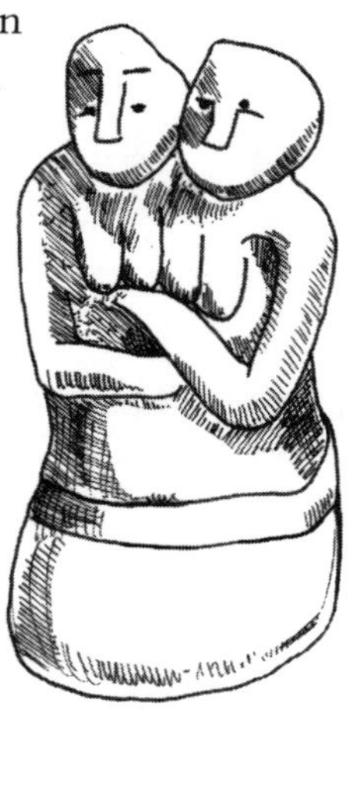

Fig. 1.25. This Double Goddess comes from Çatalhöyük, dated to the seventh millennium B.C.E. The two women portrayed in an intimate embrace, their bodies emerging out of one shared girdle or woven belt, suggest the concept of "jami," or twins sharing one womb, as discussed by Giti Thadani in her book Sakhiyani.

matrilineal chain of a female lineage. At the same time, if it weren't for the distinctly demarcated breasts on the two figures, I am certain this figure would have been described as depicting a *hieros gamos* ("sacred marriage" of the male and female, through which the female's sacred power confers kingship on the male partner) because of the intimacy, emotion, and apparent eroticism expressed in the piece.

The girdle is an interesting vehicle for expressing the closeness of the twin or merged relationship, the "jami" or "dual sisters inhabiting the same womb space."[36] In the Bronze Age it is Ishtar's girdle that refers to her royal power and the loosening of Aphrodite's girdle that gets so much attention in the Greek classical period. Hera's girdle represented her ancient power, and it was the girdle of the Amazon queens that every hero in the Homeric epics apparently wanted to steal. In Elizabeth Barber's fine study of women's relationship to textiles, *Women's Work: The First 20,000 Years*, the girdle refers back to the earliest string belts shown on Paleolithic Goddesses from some 20,000 years ago and was perhaps "associated with childbearing."[37] Barber notes that female figurines wear skirts and belts like this for the next twenty thousand years or so, until they emerge in Hera's famous girdle in the *Iliad*, "fashioned with a hundred tassels." Homer, she tells us, stated that into all girdles "have been crafted all the bewitchments," and when Hera borrows Aphrodite's girdle, Aphrodite tells her "what you wish for in your mind will not go unaccomplished!"[38] Clearly it represented both her sexual power and a woman's magical will.

The most common symbol in flat-weave Anatolian kilims is also interpreted as a birth symbol. Called the *elibelinde* (literally "hands on hips"), it refers to a "head-like form with two incurving hooked arms, (which) represents the fertility-mother-goddesses of Near Eastern prehistory, whose cults, with variations and under different names, continued up to the Christian era."[39] The funny arrow-shaped heads sticking out from the bodies of the Anatolian Disc Goddesses mentioned above (see fig. 1.21) could be the precursors of (or inspired by) the double hooked heads: a beautiful kilim with large central medallions features,

Fig. 1.26. Contemporary Turkish kilims (flat-weave tribal rugs) containing stylized images of the Mother Goddess from a lineage that dates back to ancient Çatalhöyük wall paintings. Here a rug-dealer holds out a kilim to show a customer the variety of "fertility symbols" or Elibelinde figures still woven into the rugs by village women today.

in mirror reflection, two-headed figures "reminiscent of the flat, double-headed goddess figures from the Bronze Age of Anatolia and Mesopotamia."[40]

Elibelinde figures come in many variations: One fine kilim in a contemporary collection of earlier pieces shows elibelinde figures with the triangular skirt topped by *two* hooked heads that look almost like bird heads facing each other. These two-headed images are interpreted by scholars as female fertility symbols of the "double-headed Goddess" type, "the origins of which go back to the neolithic cult of the Mother Goddess."[41] But perhaps an underlying, somewhat hidden layer of meaning in the two-headed images is more along the lines of the Indian "jami" or twinship of profound female bonding.

THE DOUBLE AXE: SHORTHAND FOR WOMEN

The Double Axe or *Labyris* (or *Labrys*) is the preeminent symbolic representation of the Double Goddess, portraying the "supernatural potency, expressed by the doubling device, 'the power of two.'"[42] Clearly the two crescent-shaped blades of the axe refer to the Moon in its waxing and waning, birthing and dying, and the monthly rhythm of our periodic bleeding that is aligned with this ever-renewing lunar cycle. It

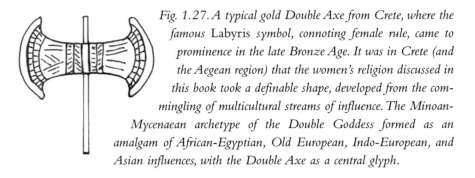

Fig. 1.27. A typical gold Double Axe from Crete, where the famous Labyris *symbol, connoting female rule, came to prominence in the late Bronze Age. It was in Crete (and the Aegean region) that the women's religion discussed in this book took a definable shape, developed from the commingling of multicultural streams of influence. The Minoan-Mycenaean archetype of the Double Goddess formed as an amalgam of African-Egyptian, Old European, Indo-European, and Asian influences, with the Double Axe as a central glyph.*

is these horned crescents, placed back to back, that formed the Double Axe of the ancient Goddess cultures, creating one of the earliest and most long-lasting glyphs of the Double Goddess. A tremendously powerful hourglass figure with bird's claws or wings is painted on a pot from Hungary (5000 B.C.E.), and a similar image found on the interior of a dish from the Sesklo culture in northern Greece (6000 B.C.E.) shows a Double Hourglass figure in mirror reflection with bird's wings (or feet) and crested (crowned) heads. A beaked jug from mid-second millennium B.C.E. Mycenae shows the persistence of the image.

According to Gimbutas, "The double axe of the Bronze Age was originally an hourglass shaped Goddess of Death and Regeneration."[43] And—although linguists tend to think not—surely the word *Labyris* has some relationship to "labia," which in turn relates so graphically to the Double Axe. Esoterically, the concept of the Double Goddess as expressed in the Double Axe could point to the clitoris and labia of every female as the sacred seat of regenerative power, housing the multiorgasmic female sexuality that marks the woman as sacred center of all tantric devotional rituals. In her book on the female role in Tibetan Buddhist tantric rites, June Campbell reminds us that OM MANI PADME HUM ("hail to the jewel in the lotus") is the "most commonly recited mantra" in Tibet.[44] Noting that the mantra is addressed to a female deity (Manipadma), Campbell linguistically reconstructs the mantra as an invocation to "the deity of the clitoris-vagina."[45] Long before the

Fig. 1.28. This beaked jug from Mycenae, Greece, comes from a long tradition of such vessels connected with Goddess cultures, especially the earlier cultures of mainland Turkey and mainland Greece. This one, from the mid-second millennium B.C.E., shows an hourglass Goddess figure in the naturalistic style generally used by Minoan artists. The hourglass or figure-of-8 is a form of the Double Axe, and as such continues a long tradition of honoring female power.

invention of the "hieros gamos" (sacred marriage of the male and female), the Double Axe served as a widespread reminder of the intact two-in-oneness of every female.

The best evidence for the pervasive and continuous importance of the Double Axe as a female symbol can be found in the nine-thousand-year history of the patterns in tribal rugs and folk embroideries from Turkey, Greece, and the Balkans. Double Axes were woven into the earliest kilims, if scholars are correct in thinking that the wall paintings of Çatalhöyük replicated existing tapestries of the time, the inhabitants of that place being "far more advanced and civilized than we had thought possible."[46] Double Axe motifs are still prevalent today in the handmade flat-woven rugs crafted by the women of Turkey and the surrounding areas. Given the variety of female representation found at Çatalhöyük—in wall paintings, pots, and sculptural figures—it seems likely that the Double Axes represented the simplest female form, the hourglass created from two triangles that meet at a center (the waist), shorthand for woman.

In her earliest work on the Goddess, Marija Gimbutas stressed the butterfly shape of the axe, insisting that "the emblem of the Great Goddess in its origin has nothing to do with the axe; it antedates the appearance of metal axes by several thousand years." Bronze Age people made their axes in the shape of a butterfly (double-bladed), and when the "butterfly became a double-axe, the image of the goddess as a butterfly continued to be engraved on double-axes."[47] The transformation of butterfly into axe is attributed to the newly arrived Indo-Europeans and the importance they placed on the axe of their Thunder-god, Zeus, to whom it was sacred and believed to be imbued with potency.[48] But the butterfly as a central symbol of the regenerative Goddess goes back at least to the sixth millennium B.C.E., where She embodies the principle of transformation. Geometric Double Axes ("butterflies") are incised on a pottery dish from Bohemia (5000 B.C.E.), and the Double Axe on the Mycenaean vase in this sketch makes it look like a Butterfly Goddess. Schematic butterflies continue to appear in more stylized forms throughout early Greek history, remaining one of the most frequent design motifs. A Serbian proverb from our time sums up seven thousand years of this unbroken connection: "If you kill a butterfly, you kill a witch."[49]

The special conflation of woman, witch, butterfly, and Double Axe goes back several thousand years in Old Europe, where it is part of what Gimbutas called "the language of the Goddess." Vases from the fifth millennium civilizations of Vinča, Cucuteni, and Karanovo in the Balkans depict stylized women made of two triangles (a Double Axe) performing ritual dances similar to later Sardinian scenes. Old European dancers depicted on the walls of a cave in northwestern Bulgaria—surely ancestors of the Thracian "wild women" or "witches" recorded so much later—look like Double Axes wearing fringe skirts, and some even wear

Fig. 1.29. The Double Axe was found everywhere in Crete, as protection in front of ritual storage supply areas, as ceremonial weapons found in hoards, and as votive offerings to the Goddess in sacred cave sanctuaries. The Double Axe on this Mycenaean vase has been stylized as a Butterfly Goddess, dated to the late Bronze Age.

ritual belts that stick out from the dresses in the shape of Double Axes. Gimbutas suggests that "the shape of the axes corresponds with that of actual copper axes of the Vinča and Karanovo cultures dated to 4500–4000 B.C."[50]

Most astonishing of all, the Double Axe hourglass women are not limited to Old Europe, but clearly traveled across the steppes along what would come to be known as the Silk Road. An article by Jeannine Davis-Kimball in the *Indo-European Studies Bulletin* shows rock art at a site in western China. The nine-foot-tall images were created by a Europoid people from the Balkans sometime during the late Bronze Age or early Iron Age, when documented migrations took place from West to East.[51] The scene—not far from sites where Europoid mummies have been excavated—shows hourglass figures dancing, including phallic men and women wearing conical horned hats. A Double Goddess figure in red leads the dance, and double pairs of animals flank the dancers. Scholars describe the montage as a "fertility scene." My

Fig. 1.30. Rock art in western China's Xinjiang region shows figures nine feet tall wearing conical horned hats, including a central red Double Goddess figure, in what scholars call a "fertility scene" from the late Bronze Age. The site is near where Europoid mummies in tall conical black witches' hats were discovered in the Tarim Basin north of Tibet. Archaeologist Jeannine Davis-Kimball has hypothetically identified the creators of the petroglyphs as "peoples from Eastern Europe" who made the mind-boggling cross-continental journey to the Tarim Basin.[52]

own research suggests that there were actual cultural and trade connections between Crete and the Tarim Basin in the second millennium B.C.E.[53] Beginning even earlier, from 3000 B.C.E. to the end of the second millennium B.C.E., Goddess populations were on the move as they were displaced from their ancient sites by violent invaders who sought to dominate them. (See chapter four for more details on this.)

THE DOUBLE AXE AND FEMALE RULE

It is in the Greek island of Crete that we are most familiar with the Double Axe, since it is there that it came into its full power as a symbol of female rule. Double Axes are ubiquitous in sites in Crete dating to the second millennium B.C.E. In Crete and the Aegean Islands, "a completely theacentric, gynocentric civilization and religion endured through the first half of the second millennium B.C."[54] However, as we have already seen, the Double Axe didn't spring full blown in Crete. More likely the prominence of the Labyris in Crete, along with other convincing artifactual evidence of presiding queen-priestesses (which we will take up in chapter four), represents the final glory of the ancient Goddess cultures in the Mediterranean region. As Gimbutas remarks, "The Minoan culture of Crete, as a result of its geographical location, preserved matrilineal customs much later than its counterparts on the mainland."[55]

Although wildly misnamed "Minoan" after an entirely legendary

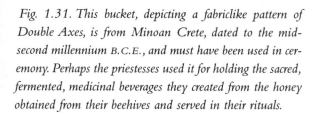

King Minos, the culture that actually developed in Crete and the other Aegean Islands during the third and especially the second millennium B.C.E. was female centered, peaceful, artistic,

Fig. 1.31. This bucket, depicting a fabriclike pattern of Double Axes, is from Minoan Crete, dated to the mid-second millennium B.C.E., and must have been used in ceremony. Perhaps the priestesses used it for holding the sacred, fermented, medicinal beverages they created from the honey obtained from their beehives and served in their rituals.

affluent, and highly religious, leading some scholars to posit that the so-called "palaces" of the time (such as Knossos and Phaistos) were really ceremonial centers or even monasteries. Like Christian monasteries in medieval Europe, they acquired "great wealth," supported a "large hierarchy," and acted as a "redistribution center" where, according to Rodney Castledon, "priestesses may have presided over the complex, with any king acting only in subordination to them."[56] In her final work, *The Living Goddesses*, Gimbutas summarizes, "Now we know that those 'palaces' were in reality temple complexes, and that the culture was goddess-centered." Furthermore, she states that the temple complexes were "administrative as well as religious centers."[57]

The central iconographic representation of this powerful female-centered remnant of Goddess culture was the Double Axe, which was "most conspicuous, the real sign of Minoan religion, as omnipresent as the cross in Christianity and the crescent in Islam."[58] They are painted on beautiful Kamaresware vases and later Minoan pots looking like flowers or anthropomorphized as female, incised on a sealstone from eastern Crete showing a crowned Goddess "with the wings of an eyed butterfly"[59] rising from between the horns of a bovine animal, and in other instances depicted on top of "bucrania" and ritual horns. A precursor could be the Double Axe or "butterfly sign" seen next to a bull's (or cow's) head in a wall painting from Catal Höyük dated to the seventh millennium B.C.E.[60]

Bases for standing Double Axes are to be found at all the so-called palaces, where the huge Double Axes functioned as protection in front of the pillar crypts and storage rooms. The undeciphered Linear A script includes a Double Axe sign, and Double Axes are incised on stone

Fig. 1.32. These miniature gold Double Axes from Crete were deposited as offerings in cave sanctuaries. Double Axes, as the code sign for female rule, are discovered on altars and stuffed into crevices and cracks in cave walls and rocky mountain top shrines.

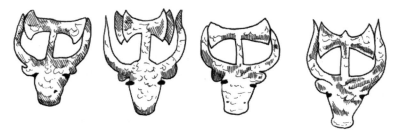

Fig. 1.33. These Double Axes from Bronze Age Mycenae, mounted on heads of the sacred Cow Goddess—no doubt Hera or Rhea herself—and called "bucrania," are always *assumed by archaeologists (often wrongly) to be male (bulls). But female cows with long or imposing horns can be found suckling their young in meadows all over the world, like the entire herd I saw grazing near an Etruscan shrine I visited in Italy a few years ago.*

pillars and walls at many places, including Knossos and Phaistos. There was a "House of the Double Axe" at Knossos, which Gimbutas says was both a tomb and a shrine,[61] and Double Axe stands functioned as "cult furnishings like large candlesticks in various Christian rites."[62] Near the cave of the birthing Goddess, Artemis-Eiliethyia, with its natural rock formation in the shape of a Double Goddess, huge bronze Double Axes on tall stands (three meters high) were discovered at the site of Nirou Khani and can be seen on display today in the Heraklion archaeological museum, giving us a general idea of the power of the icon and its multivalent meaning.

This "popular attribute of the Minoan female deity" has frequently been found in cave sanctuaries, such as at Psychro (the Dictaean Cave), where tiny gold ones were stuck into crevices of stalagmites and stalactites as "cult offerings and fetishes." Twenty-six exquisite Double Axes of gold, six of silver, and nineteen of bronze were found in the cave of Prophitis Ilias near Arkalokhori (one of the gold ones marked with undeciphered Linear A script), along with "a number of bronze rapier blades . . . recalling weapons in Grave Circles A and B at Mycenae."[63] These ceremonial swords, more than a meter in length, are among the longest found in Crete, and in all except one, the blades were too thin to be used in fighting.[64] Some of the silver and gold Double Axes were found lying on a small altar, whereas others were "thrust into the earth, or fixed onto pieces of wood."[65] It would seem that our Minoan fore-mothers were practicing some intense magic with these ceremonial weapons.

The mountain peak and cave sanctuaries seem to have focused more on rituals of death and regeneration, such as those depicted in murals, seal stones, and on the Hagia Triada sarcophagus. (More on this special sar-cophagus in chapter four.) In one often-reproduced scene on the sar-cophagus, an obelisk topped by a Double Axe on which a bird sits appears behind the priestesses pouring libations. In another scene, a priestess pours liquid into a vessel between two poles with Double Axes on top.

Bogdan Rutkowski—one of the most thorough scholars on *The Cult Places of the Aegean*—points out that a change took place between the Middle Minoan and Late Minoan periods regarding the "cult of the Double Axe" on Crete. It always symbolized the "presence of a divin-ity" (female) but "may have become a symbol of secular authority," par-ticularly accruing to kingship and a "new concept of divinity" (male) in the later times.[66] Rutkowski also believes a Goddess on the mountain shown with her scepter (or spear) and two lionesses facing each other at her sides is conferring kingship (endowing royal powers) on the man standing in front of her wearing only a loincloth.[67] This would be very similar to other places where the Goddess was worshipped for eons: female priestesses facilitated her ancient religion, and—during the tran-sition times—the newly installed kings received their confirmation by virtue of the ancient theacracy of priestesses impersonating the Goddess. Naturally the new institution of kingship would usurp for itself the essential emblem of authority to rule, in many cases, the Double Axe. (See chapter four for the same phenomenon in Thrace.) Perhaps the many so-called "hoards" of female accoutrements (boars' tusks, necklaces, rings, bracelets, and other jewels) unearthed in so many places from the Bronze and Iron Ages were buried in order to hide them from invaders. Robert Graves's suggestion that the priestesses fled with the artifacts of their ancient religion to the Greek Islands holds up well under scrutiny. It is quite likely that the caves and mountain shrines in Mediterranean areas were the repositories of religious objects and icons saved by priestesses of the old religion from the mainland cultures that were being destroyed around 2100 B.C.E., after which the first peak sanctuaries began to be active in Crete. The oval "cult place" on Mount Jouktas, for example, was "used as a refuge for the local people in times of danger."[68] It is the site of a "hoard of thirty cult double axes," two of which were large and the others small.[69] Both Mount Jouktas and Mount Karphi produced the "Gazi type" statues with raised arms and poppies or birds on their crowns, "such as were probably generally used as cult statues,"[70] meaning that even though the place had been overrun with invaders in the late Bronze Age times (1200 B.C.E.), the Cretans were still making every effort to retain their sacred objects of worship (the Double Axes) and continued to use their difficult-to-access mountain shrines.

LONG FEMALE LINEAGE OF THE DOUBLE AXE

At Alvastra in southern Sweden at the foot of a mountain range, a unique open-air sanctuary from 3000 B.C.E. (contemporaneous with the female-centered religion in the Aegean area) was discovered with more than a hundred fireplaces, where forty stone Double Axes and miniature axes of amber and bone were found. One extraordinary Double Axe made of amber was drilled with perforations "for seven strands of an amber-bead necklace" to attach through it.[71] Gimbutas suggests this place was an outdoor site of spring renewal rituals.

A fabulous Double Axe necklace made of Baltic amber was displayed in an exhibit at the Smithsonian in 1997. The necklace was made of beautifully carved Double Axes in graduated sizes from small to quite large, perhaps two and a half inches for the one at the center, dating to 3000 B.C.E. from Jutland, an island off the coast of Sweden. I photographed the Double Axe necklace when I saw it at the exhibit, and—

as I was preparing to leave on my trip to southern Russia with Jeannine Davis-Kimball in the fall of that year—intuitively stuck the photo in with my papers. Our trip consisted of traveling to one museum after another along the Volga River, where we were invited into basements to view archival treasures from Amazon graves from the fifth century B.C.E. (Sauromatian and Sarmatian women) and to speak with the archaeologists who excavated the remains.

In the museum at Saratov, as we were being shown artifacts from high-status female burials in the area, the archaeologist handed us a small amber necklace of what looked vaguely like Double Axes. He referred to them as "anthropomorphic figures," and it's true that their hourglass shape was not distinct, but still it reminded me of the amber necklace I had seen at the museum and whose photo I had fortuitously brought with me. When I showed him the necklace in the photo from the Smithsonian, he understood my excitement and agreed there might be a connection. Across the span of 2,500 years and a fair geographic distance, the resemblance could be seen, even though the axes on his necklace were more rounded in shape, similar to figure-of-8 shields, such as those on a fifth-century B.C.E. bracelet from Greece.

From the island Cyprus off the coast of Syria, another interesting necklace was created in the late Bronze Age out of beads of cornelian and gold, including sixteen in the shape of Double Shields placed side-by-side.[72] Similar necklaces—in which the Double Axes are rounded to form figure-of-8 shields—have been found in a variety of sites, such as one made of glass beads found at Thebes (Greece) from the thirteenth

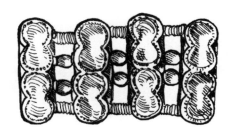

Fig. 1.34. This gold bracelet was made in the shape of pairs of figure-of-8 Shield Goddesses, in Greece, during the fifth century B.C.E., and shows an unbroken tradition from the earlier Bronze Age. Burials of powerful priestesses are documented in Greece until at least the third century B.C.E.

Fig. 1.35. This gold necklace of double figure-of-8 Shield Goddesses hails from the island of Cyprus, during Bronze Age Mycenaean times, dating to the fourteenth century B.C.E. Necklaces in the shape of figure-of-8 shields are numerous from the Bronze and Iron Ages, some made of gold, others carved from amethyst and other gemstones.

century B.C.E. and another made of amethyst found in a "rich child's burial" in an early Mycenaean cyst grave at Argos (fifteenth century B.C.E.). In the sixth century B.C.E. in northern Greece, an elegant gold necklace of Double Axes was created using the filigree and granulation techniques that made Greek gold work famous.

In Egypt, significantly, the same word for axe ("Netert") also meant Goddess.[73] Although established scholars find many of Martin Bernal's theories disturbing and sometimes inaccurate, he does make some interesting intuitive connections when he discusses a "cult of a double-axe which flourished in Lower Egypt during the Old Kingdom and which has deeper roots still in Upper Egypt."[74] Referring back to an earlier "mysterious" Upper Egyptian sign dating to at least 3400 B.C.E., which scholars describe as "two fossil belemnites," Bernal points out that "the earliest (examples) resemble a double-headed arrow."[75] This is especially interesting in regard to Egyptian Neith's early symbol of two arrows crossed. The corresponding name glyph for the early queen, Neith-hotep, is linked with the beginnings of the First Dynasty in

Fig. 1.36. This beautiful necklace of hammered gold Double Axes was worked in the famous filigree and granulation techniques popular in northern Greece during the sixth century B.C.E.

Egypt and is also believed to be the forerunner of the Greek Goddess Athena. Furthermore, Bernal (a linguist whose intuitive leaps have been challenged by other linguists) synthesizes signs and words for "shrine," "uterus," and "sacred," and concludes that "the 'two belemnites' as a sign of divine power was used more as a general symbol of sanctity rather in the way the double-axe was used in Crete."[76]

Even though the Double Axe, as we have seen, dates from the Neolithic and is found extensively throughout the Bronze and Iron Ages in the Mediterranean area and all across the steppes (to Mongolia), mainstream scholars seem to have paid unusually little attention to it. This oversight was made especially clear when a conference at Harvard in the spring of 2001 featured the discoveries of an archaeologist who recently found an important "seal stone" from one of many BMAC (Bactria Margiana Archaeology Complex) sites along the Silk Road. The huge urban sites in Uzbekistan and Turkmenistan date from around 2300 to 1700 B.C.E.—a key five-hundred-year period in the study of the Amazon Queens who ruled in Dual Queenship. Dr. Fredrik T. Hiebert, who was interviewed by the *New York Times,* enthusiastically reported his "most recent and provocative discovery," a small black stone object that, according to him, depicts letters ("proto-writing") that "apparently bear no resemblance to any other writing system of the time."[77] The stone (pictured in the newspaper article) shows a clearly incised Double Axe, along with three other symbols that appear to be variations on the sign *E* (a symbol for rain in early Chinese and a glyph for "yoni" in the Vajrayogini rituals of Tibetan Buddhism).[78]

Contemporary feminists, on the other hand, have picked up the Double Axe image and worn it as an adornment and political statement for twenty-five years. The ancient abstract symbol has become a modern glyph of lesbianism and female power. Of all the symbols available to modern women from the past, the Labyris seems to most vividly encompass the meaning of the ancient Great Goddess and point to the long-standing female lineage of matriarchal sovereignty and personal spiritual autonomy.

TWO

Authentic Female Sovereignty: Chains and Doubles

The Double Goddess motif is essentially one of grounded collaborative female government and sovereignty, pointing us in a visionary direction to both our ancient past and our only viable future. The much-glorified linear thinking and its one-directional orientation—underlying the basic idea of "progress" and evolution that has led us at this moment to the brink of ecological disaster—are proving to be untenable. There is wisdom, then, in revisiting ancient societies that lived in harmony with nature, and with one another, in order to investigate the core thinking that might have contributed to such a peaceful way of life. Archaeologists ardently seek to find evidence of war in earlier societies, but there is actually no proof whatsoever of violence or war before the middle of the fifth millennium B.C.E. Although people built houses close together and lived in fairly high population density in the early urban centers, they had apparently developed ways of resolving conflict and living in harmony with their environments that allowed them to share food and resources, irrigate fields, and participate in large ritual and artistic endeavors, such as the building of stone temples in Malta or the burial chambers all over Old Europe. Goddess scholars believe that content and form cannot be separated and that the reason for the lack of violence and conflict in early societies is the presence of active worship of the Great Mother.

In societies that worship a Great Mother, priestesses fulfill the religious and ceremonial functions and almost certainly would have governed as well. An analysis of the earliest burials found under the floors of Old European houses reveals that 1) the burials were almost always women, and 2) the women were usually of an older age.[1] Old Europeans didn't begin to dispose of their dead outside of the settlements in extramural cemeteries until 5000 B.C.E., and even then "older women in cemeteries continued to be accorded high status . . . attested by the high concentration of symbolic items in their graves."[2] Blood types studied in cemeteries in Hungary belonging to the Lengyel culture showed that the "adult females and children were found to have been related by blood group, but the adult males of the same cemetery were found to be unrelated,"[3] demonstrating matrilineal descent and matrifocal location.

What if, as I have been suggesting in my writing for the last twenty years, the peaceful ancient agricultural civilizations were literally organized around the collective female menstrual cycle?[4] We have to assume that the whole community of women would have bled at the same time, since they lived together without the disruption of electric lights or isolated family units to throw their cycles off. And let's assume that their synchronized bleeding took place in tandem with the lunar cycle, so that they ovulated with the Full Moon and bled as a community with the Dark Moon, and that they were able to harness and align with the power of the waxing and waning Moon in their rituals and ceremonial life. Using the lunar model but applying it to the solar year, they might have constructed rituals and rites of passage for the seasonal cycle of dark (winter) and light (summer), planting (spring), and harvest (summer).

For a woman having her period, there is a psychic opening that leads—at the very least—to emotional sensitivity and a feeling of vulnerability. Multiply this experience by a whole community of adult women, stage it naturally at the times of greatest planetary power (Dark and Full Moons are when solar and lunar eclipses happen, for example), and you have the makings of a serious "Council of Women." As Monica Sjöö and Barbara Mor wrote "women were everywhere the original mantics."[5] The lunar connection brings with it the gift of prophecy and divination, still practiced by many women around the world. Perhaps the women's council made their most important governing decisions during the time when they were bleeding together, like an early form of monthly tribal council, the way certain Tibetan Buddhist groups still secretly work with the collective power of menstrual blood today.

Now what if these councils of women—perhaps our earliest form of tribal or clan government—were facilitated by a pair of women (shaman-priestesses) in the position of leadership? Perhaps in order to insure egalitarianism and equality, they decided very early to install two presiding leaders, maybe blood sisters, rather than one woman with unlimited power. The early choice to elect two women, rather than one, as leaders of female-centered societies appears to have remained standard practice at least until the classical age. If we take the evidence from these highly evolved civilizations seriously, then we have to recognize that they worshipped a Mother Goddess and frequently portrayed her as a Double Goddess.

Lineage—the ruling power being passed down through the blood lines from mother to daughter—is another possibility for understanding the Double Goddess figures as early, primordial rulers. The word *matriarchy*, although currently out of fashion because of being understood as connoting female rule, *literally* means "beginning with the mother," and suggests the birth-giving function as the method for passing along the right to rule. In even the most limited personal sense, all women in a matriarchy have personal sovereignty in that they are allowed to rule over themselves. No man commands them, no father or husband owns them, and they experience the liberating effect of knowing themselves to be the *subject* of their own realities (rather than the object or appendage of someone else's). In early societies in which ownership of property was almost certainly collective (represented by the communal granary or storehouse in Goddess civilizations), then the matriarchal concept is extended to include the whole tribe of women passing down the inheritance to the next generation of women born to the tribe.

In the modern world there are almost no places on earth where matriarchy is a reality, making it difficult to imagine (let alone prove) how women would handle such authentic sovereignty and power to rule. And what kind of men would "allow" it? However, a professor at the University of Beijing recently published a book on the Na of China who live in a matrilineal culture, "where women and men freely engage in sexual relations with several partners and exchange them whenever they so desire."[6] *A Society Without Fathers or Husbands* documents this society* in the Himalayas near Tibet, where "The transmission of inheritance is carried out, from one generation to the next, collectively."[7] There is no term in their language for "the notion of father," no economic bond between partners, and women are free to have lovers as they please. Like the Na, the matriarchal residents of Çatalhöyük would have "recognize(d) the mother but [would] not know of the existence of the father."[8]

---

*The Cultural Revolution in China seriously inhibited the customs of the Na by requiring monogamous marriage and the registration of paternity.

THE DOUBLE GODDESS SHRINES OF ÇATALHÖYÜK

Many of the earliest images of the Double Goddess were sketched in color by archaeologist James Mellaart from wall paintings he uncovered in shrine rooms at Çatalhöyük, a site whose importance with regard to the Double Goddess cannot be overstated. Even with only the one acre that James Mellaart excavated in the 1960s (out of thirty acres still to be examined), the numerous and diverse representations of the Double Goddess unearthed there already provide a kind of universal template for the Double Goddesses that show up everywhere else after that. Not only was matrilineal descent undoubtedly practiced, as in other Neolithic (agricultural) civilizations around the world, but it was expressed as a divine foundational formula through a variety of artistic media.

A magnificent sculpture of the Great Goddess can be seen in the monumental enthroned Queen Mother of Çatalhöyük with her flanking leopards as armrests—a variation of the Two-in-One Double Goddess that continued to be portrayed in Anatolia for the next several thousand years. Mellaart and others have described this now-famous figure as giving birth, as there is something between her legs that could *possibly* be taken as an emerging child. I have never personally thought

Fig. 2.1. This regal enthroned female figure from Çatalhöyük, seventh millennium B.C.E. *Anatolia (ancient Turkey), represents the ancestral Great Mother with her flanking leopards or lionesses, perhaps ancient Artemis herself. Early inhabitants of this important site brought their Mountain Goddess with them, along with the shamanistic rites used in her ongoing worship, and like the mural shown in fig. 2.2, she functions as a template for all the other Goddesses-with-leopards to follow.*

it looked anything like a birth scene (surely the baby would be squashed) and prefer to think of her as an enthroned Female Ancestress, her fleshy corpulence representing the round fertile Earth itself. Surely in the largest sense this figure represents Mother Nature, the Mistress of the Beasts, ruling the world in tandem with her special shamanistic animal familiars. The leopards bespeak her awesome authority. One has only to think of the Strength card in a tarot deck, traditionally portrayed by a woman who—gently, through her magical will alone—is in the act of subduing a lion or leopard.

Like Marshack's concept of the "Clan-Mother" or "sovereign mistress," she was originally the "owner of the elements of nature."[9] In the long transition from hunter-gatherer cultures to the beginnings of agriculture, the ancient Goddess of the Paleolithic became the keeper of the abundance for the whole Neolithic community, protecting and blessing the harvest by her magical presence in the granary. That this sculpture was found in the community grain bin suggests that she represents the collective female ownership of the agricultural production of "surplus," an expression of the abundance of Mother Earth that made it possible for humans to settle in one place, cultivate food, and create civilization. Many of the shrines and altars that Mellaart uncovered in the early excavations probably relate to the sacredness and gratitude expressed by the newly settled agricultural community.

In a long horizontal wall painting from Shrine A.III/11 at Çatalhöyük, a variety of Goddesses are centered in cave niches with various flanking animals that could be taken almost as prototypes of the later Goddess-with-Animals figures so popular in Greece and Anatolia. One of the paintings replicates the sculpted Great Mother with her leopards, showing a Goddess sitting within a cave niche with two spotted cats in front of her facing in opposite directions, their tails creating a sense of her legs as being in a crossed-leg yoga posture. A second thinner Goddess stands holding two leopards out to her sides by the scruff of their necks. Next to her, in another cave niche, stands another thin figure who seems to wear a belt or skirt and perhaps a hat, holding two vultures by their necks. Mellaart calls this one Artemis, perhaps partly because of the resemblance to much later Artemis figures in Greece during the archaic period (eighth century B.C.E.). As ancient female shamanism (a collective rather than individual phenomenon) was connected to the Great Bear constellation in the sky known as "Arktos" (Bear) or Artemis, the ancient derivation supports this name.[10] In between each of these scenes are pairs of Double Axes, symbolizing—along with the leopards—female power, sovereignty, and rank.[11]

Wall murals painted in bright colors—looking unmistakably like flat-woven kilims—depict a variety of Double Goddess images (both figurative and stylized) that have one (or more than one) woman on top of, next to, or underneath the other. Numerous sketches of these Double Goddesses by James Mellaart are reproduced in a four-volume art set that shows the chain of mothers and daughters in every possible aspect. Two Goddesses, each giving birth to a visible baby, stand upside down in mirror relation to one another; fat Buddha-women sitting with leopards and bears in a cave niche are reflected, one upside down to the other; Goddesses grasping totemic animals on either side are also shown in mirror reflection upside down; and sometimes the two upside-down mirror images of the Double Goddess are shown inside a cave niche, at the center of which is a Double Axe. In one painting, the niches in mirror image actually form imposing Double Axes themselves. Goddesses on top of holy mountains are also shown upside down to each other, as are groups of trees and ibexes. Another wall painting shows the Goddess (or central woman) wearing a skirt or dress created in the style of an hourglass (related to the Double Axe), repeated several times vertically with the ubiquitous flanking leopards in each repeated image.

All of the motifs seen in the murals at Çatalhöyük can be clearly seen in stylized form in tribal rugs from Turkey today. And since it is still (and always) women who weave the rugs (except recently in a few urban commercial workshops where the patterns are changing to please the Western clientele), one could conclude that the kilims are explicit vehicles for the matrilineal chain or unbroken female lineage referred to by textile expert Mary Kelly in her discussion of Ukrainian embroideries. Kelly emphasizes the "repetition of pattern to engender power" that is clearly expressed in the mirror images, as well as birthing images, and even four-part figures that double the already Double Goddess.[12] She focuses on the cult power and talismanic magic of the textiles and women's weaving practices, reminding us that kilims, for example, were used in religious ceremonies rather than simply as decorative floor or wall coverings. This is important to remember, since the whole idea of "shrines" at Çatalhöyük is now under scrutiny in the archaeological community.

Kelly's observation that the cumulative effect of the repetition of images on the borders of embroidered cloths "intensifies the efficacy of the protection" granted by the image[13] is reminiscent of the power of repeated mantras (vocalizations or incantations) used in Eastern religions and clearly understood to be magical spells. Emphasizing the female lineage depicted in the mirror images, Kelly describes "chains of mothers and daughters" establishing a "matrilineal chain" that can still be seen on belts made by Ukrainian weavers today.[14]

A striking example (and perhaps prototype) of this form comes from a complex Çatalhöyük wall painting that depicts several pairs of Goddesses side by side; two pairs, one beneath another as if (metaphorically) being birthed, and one small Goddess emerging from the crown of the larger one in the center of the whole composition, which takes the form of an artist's triptych. Mellaart describes this as "three niches with Goddesses giving birth."[15] The archetypal birthing Goddess in the form of a leopard actually takes the shape of—and is symbolically interchangeable with—a frog, with her arms and legs out to the sides and curled up. This is the complex image that greets the viewer in the shrine room that is reproduced inside the Museum in Ankara, the capital of Turkey, which houses so many of the original finds from Çatalhöyük (including the enthroned Goddess with leopards).

In a disturbing about-face from traditional archaeological assessment,

Fig. 2.2. Wall mural from Çatalhöyük, Anatolia (ancient Turkey), Neolithic period, seventh millennium B.C.E. In this painting, six pairs of Double Goddesses are depicted in a variety of forms, three pairs vertically and three pairs horizontally, along with one pair of flanking leopards or lionesses. In this one inspired image, a template is created, foretelling the diversity of Double Goddess images that would be found throughout the Aegean region during the next several thousand years.

the current excavation team at Çatalhöyük, headed by Ian Hodder at Stanford University, formerly of Cambridge, England, is referring to the birthing image as a "splayed animal" and calling into doubt its status as a "Goddess." Yet the frog is linked to birthing and fertility all over the world, and this abstract image of the woman-as-leopard, stylized as a frog—the alter ego of the birthing woman—is widely recognized by experts in the field.[16] It is these frog-shaped "splayed" leopard Goddesses that are reproduced in duplicate repeated images in this powerful triptych. On the left panel, additionally a pair of leopards is shown eye to eye; and on the right panel—the only singular image in the whole piece—a black bird like a raven is portrayed.

None of these Goddesses actually appears to be in the act of giving birth (as compared with other images at the site, in which clearly a baby is emerging from between the legs of a birthing Goddess), which is why, like Kelly, I feel that in the most basic sense these are images of matrilineal descent (chains of mothers and daughters) rather than representing strictly physical fertility. And because they are found at the same site as two sculpted images of Double Goddesses that share a girdle, or are close enough to be Siamese twins (see fig. 1.25), I would go even further and posit that they represent matriarchy, authentic female sovereignty (what feminist theologian Mary Daly calls "gynocracy").[17]

In the recently opened visitor's center at the site in central Turkey, Hodder—along with Ruth Tringham of University of California, Berkeley, and other scholars practicing what they call "New Archaeology"—is creating a virtual reality (with CD-ROM and other visual representations) in an effort to replace the prior scholarly interpretations of Çatalhöyük as the earliest intact Goddess site in the ancient world. Still, Çatalhöyük remains the most important Goddess site (and early city) in the world, as I hope will become clearer now that the site is once more open for excavation. In his 1960s dig, Mellaart unearthed dozens of exquisite female statuettes. The figurines (mostly housed in the Museum of Anatolian Civilizations in Ankara, Turkey) are carved from alabaster and stone, many of them in meditation or yoga postures, others wearing tall headdresses. If these images had been found in India or Tibet, they would automatically be taken as sacred or religious icons of a female deity. In the West these implications are often dismissed or ignored, especially nowadays.

Mellaart also unearthed the burial of an old woman with a convex polished obsidian mirror. It was *only* women who were buried with mirrors, which are known to be the oracular tools of shaman women and priestesses throughout the centuries. In a huge shrine he found the "rich burial of a woman, interred with three tusked lower jaws of wild boars arranged around her head."[18] Just the ritualistic arrangement of the boar's jaws suggests the high status reserved for those holding an office of importance, but beyond that, the boar's tusk was a female accoutrement down through the ages, found buried with women in Central Europe, Crete, and along the steppes down to the Iron Age Amazons recently unearthed in Russia. The mirrors, boars' tusks, wall paintings, and female figurines from the site can be seen beautifully displayed in the National Archaeological Museum in Ankara. Clearly, in these shrines to the Goddess, the people of the time created artistic ritual and food offerings for her, adorned her statues with woven and naturally dyed gowns, performed rituals of birthing and prophecy in her temples, and used mirrors for healing and "skrying" (clairvoyance), which, when they died, were buried with them.

WOMEN SHARING POWER: THE QUEENS RULED TOGETHER

Another form of Double Goddess found at Çatalhöyük is a tiny side-by-side figure (see fig. 0.9) displayed at one time in the Metropolitan Museum in New York. It bears a strong resemblance to another of the earliest side-by-side Double Goddess figures. The prehistoric Sesklo Double Goddess comes from eight thousand years ago in northern Greece, at Achilleion in Thessaly, where Marija Gimbutas leaned down and picked up the first of the many Goddess figures she would come to examine so carefully. The sixth-millennium Sesklo culture in northern Greece contained artifacts that would remain consistent in Goddess sites over the next several thousand years, such as portable offering tables, bird-shaped vases with breasts, miniature clay temple models, bread ovens, grinding stones, and female figurines wearing headgear indicative of their special rank or office. The Dimini culture that followed in the same place (fifth millennium B.C.E.) contained figurines "that may suggest a hierarchical order among temple priestesses or other ritual performers."[19]

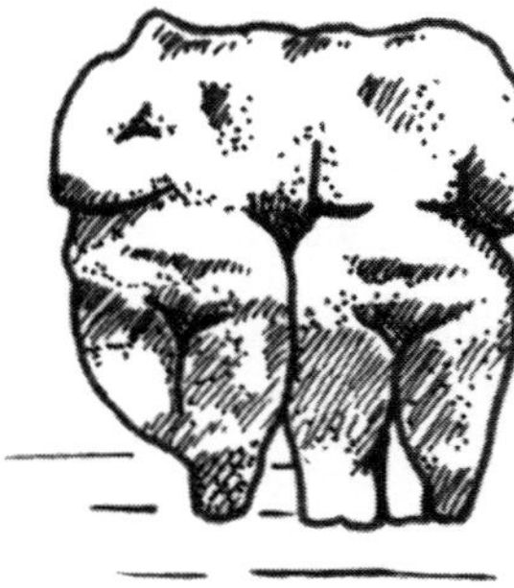

Fig. 2.3. This early Double Goddess is from the Sesklo culture in Thessaly, northern Greece, dating to the sixth millennium B.C.E. It shows strong affinities to the similar pair from Çatalhöyük (fig. 0.9) from around the same time period, suggesting certain cultural contacts and shared understandings.

The Çatalhöyük figurine comes from the same time period, although it is softer and rounder than the more robust, angular one from Achilleion. Both sculptures show two fleshy Goddesses with their arms around each other's shoulders, like dear friends or equals, comrades in some enterprise, Divine Twin Deities modeling a profound sharing of power.

Like the Siamese-twin figures from the last chapter, side-by-side Double Goddesses may have metaphorically expressed the duality we have come to expect of the feminine archetype, such as opposite seasons (winter and summer, spring and fall); the alternating rhythm of day and night; the integration of death and life; or the female twin deities of Moon and Earth. But rather than a merged pair, these two almost-identical women sit or stand side by side more like equal comrades in a work project, coleaders in government, or blood sisters (perhaps demonstrating a kinship connection). Of course, the image could still be used to express the relationship of lovers, but without the psychic fusion we saw in the two women sharing a girdle or one body. Psychologist Christine Downing discusses Athene and the "friendly rivalry" she maintained with her dear friend Pallas as "emblematic of a connection between women where women challenge one another to achieve, bless one another's creative accomplishments, encourage one another's power." In Downing's view of this more detached partnership, the relationship focuses, "on the work women help one another do."[20] It is the work of running the government that the standing and enthroned side-by-side Double Goddess figures most likely represent. They radiate authority.

Perhaps the most potent enthroned Double Goddess comes to us from the Mediterranean islands of Malta and Gozo, from the early period between the Neolithic and the Bronze Ages, around 4000 B.C.E. The small sculpture of two monumental Goddesses shows them sitting together on a platform or throne, painted with red ochre, wearing the fluted skirts we have come to expect, and each holding something different and precious in her lap. One appears to be holding a smaller

Fig. 2.4. This Double Goddess from the tiny island of Gozo, near Malta, shows Two Queens enthroned on a couch or platform of some kind. The figure was found near Gigantija ("giantess"), a double temple built in the shape of two women, dating from the fifth millennium B.C.E.

version of herself, and the other seems to hold a ritual cup or vessel. Like later murals at the Aegean site of Akrotiri (on the island of Santorini) or the frescoes at Mycenae, this pictorial display of a ritual or ceremonial performance ensures that the viewer will appreciate precisely how the statues and ritual objects might have been used by the very queen-priestesses who are portrayed holding the objects.

Also important, perhaps, in our consideration of the Double Goddess is that in Gozo first, and Malta shortly after, the temples themselves are built in the form of two women. When compared with the corpulent female figurines found there, the temples bear a striking (and even somewhat jarring) resemblance to the statues. Clearly the similarity is no accident. The first double temple, Gigantija (meaning "female giant") is very near where the enthroned Double Goddess was found by archaeologists. Gimbutas describes a legend: that the female giant with a baby at her breast, strengthened by a meal of magical beans, took great blocks of stone to the site in a single day and built the walls by night. Veronica Veen, who lives on the island of Gozo, reiterates that "up to recently stories could be heard about a Giantess and her children, who became the foremother and the ancestors of the first Gozitans and Maltese."[21] Even the two islands themselves, Malta and Gozo, can be taken as a Double Goddess, making me wonder if the early inhabitants perceived them that way. Did they see the double islands as implicit representations of the Double Goddess or Double Queens, or did the two islands stimulate them to express the concept?

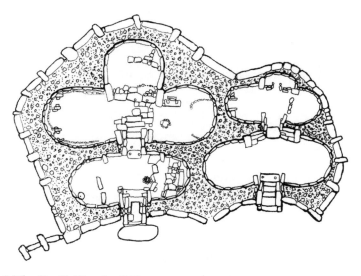

Fig. 2.5. The Double Temple of Gigantija, on the Maltese island of Gozo, was the earliest of many temple complexes in the Maltese Islands that take the shape of women. Malta is known for its underground Hypogeum, a communal burial chamber three stories deep and carved without metal tools, with acoustics that allow the smallest sound to be heard perfectly throughout the entire structure.

A number of sculptures and figurines from Maltese sites strongly resemble the yogic women from two thousand years earlier unearthed at Çatalhöyük, leading some scholars to suggest that there was a migration at some point from the site in central Turkey to the Maltese Islands south of Sicily in the Mediterranean Sea. Most traditional scholars have refused to believe that such a migration could have taken place, the assumption being that a settled agricultural people wouldn't have any reason to pack up and leave their traditional home. However, the recent illuminating research of two geologists revealing a catastrophic flood of the Aegean Sea into the Black Sea during the seventh millennium B.C.E. sheds new light on the whole subject of migrations.[22] Scholars are beginning to understand that the spread of agriculture into Greece and other parts of Old Europe may be related to this enormous natural disaster and the impact it had on settled peoples around what had been a lush and fertile inland freshwater sea. If the geologists are right, the Black Sea—in little more than an instant—became a huge inland sea of salt water, and people had to scatter in every direction. That some of them may have eventually arrived in the Maltese Islands is not really so surprising.

The artifacts and temples of Malta still hold tremendous power today and demonstrate what island sanctuaries and great ceremonial or pilgrimage centers of the transitional time must have looked like. Two hundred miles from Africa and only about forty miles from Sicily, Malta and Gozo were the seat of the oldest known free-standing stone temples and the home of the awesome three-story underground Hypogeum carved by Malta's Stone Age inhabitants, apparently without the use of metal tools. In the Hypogeum—a burial chamber where rituals were performed and the remains of the dead housed for more than a thousand years—one sees the quintessential integration of death and life expressed by ancient civilizations through the icon of the Double Goddess.

Of the corpulent female figurines found at sites on Malta, especially Hagar Qim and Mnajdra (two impressive temples near the ocean on the south side of the island), many were pregnant and birth-giving figures, leading Gimbutas to suggest that these were sites of rituals for healing and childbirth. In the midst of the bones of the dead, shaman-priestesses and midwives might have conducted rites such as those in which a pregnant woman would sleep in the crypt (like the famous figurine called the "Sleeping Lady of Malta") in order to incarnate the spirit of an ancestor into her pregnancy. Similarly, an oracular priestess might sleep in the tomb to incubate a healing dream for a needy petitioner, as was done in later dream incubation temples in Greece. The so-called oracle hole in one of the underground rooms suggests the strong voices of singing, prophetic priestesses, as we know existed in other places around the Mediterranean. Even tantric-type sexual rites might have been performed there by ecstatic priestesses, as in much later times when highly evolved Tibetan and Indian yoginis performed their sacred magical practices in cemeteries and charnel grounds, and sang ecstatic songs of realization for one another (see chapter five).

The ceilings of the Hypogeum were painted with red spiraling plantlike images that Cristina Biaggi has suggested might be pomegranates,[23] which could link to the mystery religion of Demeter and Persephone in Greece. (Persephone was supposed to have eaten several seeds of the pomegranate while she was in the land of Hades, thereby obliging herself to stay there half of every year.) Connections with Malta to the Eleusinian Mysteries of Greece are numerous, and Gimbutas pointed out the womb symbolism linking the Hypogeum to the later oracular sites like Delphi (whose name in Greek, *delphys*, means "womb"). If all of these hypothesized connections bear fruit, then eventually it will be possible to trace a direct unbroken lineage of the ancient female mysteries of the Double Goddess from Çatalhöyük in the seventh millennium B.C.E. to the Eleusinian Mysteries that took place in classical Athens during the "flowering of Western civilization."

THE "TWO LADIES": A EUPHEMISM FOR RULING QUEENS

Bronze Age archives from the "palace" of Pylos, in what is now southern Greece (the Peloponnese), report that offerings were made there to the *wanasso*, or the "two queens."[24] The word being translated as "queen" is interchangeable with the word for "lady," but scholars have for the most part chosen to translate the title as "lady" rather than "queen" (if they mention it at all). In Crete the Two Ladies were similarly assumed to mean Ariadne and her sister Pasiphae, from the Minoan mythology of a King Minos and his daughters. Archaeological studies reflect that the "Two Ladies" was an epithet widely used in both Crete and Egypt. Imagine how it might change our sense of history if the phrase were always translated as the "Two Queens."

In the seventeenth century B.C.E.—during the height of the civilization in nearby Crete—what are referred to as "royal shaft graves"

Fig. 2.6 a and b. Author photos of the "royal shaft graves" at Mycenae, Grave Circle A, from the seventeenth century B.C.E. *It is this grave circle that contained the fabulous Tomb of the Women (burials of three women and two infants covered in gold). Mycenae is a wonderful site to visit, because the "citadel" and "cult centre" with the famous "lion[ess] gate" still partially stand, along with these open grave circles with their impressive Bronze Age cyclopean masonry. If Medea lived, she may have been familiar with Mycenae, with its plethora of female-centered ritual wall paintings, as well as nearby Midea and Tiryns where so many female artifacts have been found.*

were built in Mycenae. Believed to signal the entry of a new people into the Greek Peloponnese, scholars have debated whether the people buried in the shaft graves can be identified as the first Greek-speakers. The graves were lavish and rich, filled with gold and other precious artifacts like the Double Lioness sword hilt, and they have been labeled "princely" and called the graves of "chieftains." For that reason, one's first visit to the Mycenaean Room at the National Museum in Athens can be kind of a shock, since the most important cases in the center of the room are completely taken up with the massive amount of gold and precious objects unearthed from the "Tomb of the Women."

Fig. 2.7. What an amazing sword this must have been, with the Double Goddess expressed as two gold lionesses facing one another on the sword hilt, found in the royal shaft graves at Mycenae, dating to 1700 B.C.E. The spiral design engraved on the gold foil confirms the long, continuous tradition of the Double Goddess and her protective alter egos.

In this fabulous tomb were buried three high-status women and two infants, the infants literally covered in gold. Besides a miniature gold set of scales and several crystal-topped "dress pins" (why not scepters?), the most impressive artifacts are large gold objects that have been labeled "diadems," even though scholars admit that they are much too big to have been worn on someone's head. If you turn the mysterious objects upside down however, they could easily be taken for an Amazon's legendary belt or girdle. Until I visited Athens the first time and saw these archaeological finds for myself, I had only the scholars' interpretations of this early Mycenaean civilization as being patriarchal and ruled by chieftains. These concepts were construed partly from much later "citadels" built at Mycenae and Tiryns during the fourteenth century B.C.E., but mostly from the Homeric stories about the Trojan War with its legendary kings and heroes. These mythological themes were then projected backward onto the owners of the magnificent tombs of this unknown people from the seventeenth century. One *tholos* (round "beehive") tomb on the site is called Agamemnon's Treasury, and the women's tomb has been dubbed Clytemnestra's Tomb, the infants thought to be Cassandra's twins—even though the Trojan War was fought in 1250 B.C.E. (four or even five centuries later than the royal shaft graves). In all fairness to history, these discrepancies need correcting.

An exquisite Double Goddess ivory sculpture from Mycenae found at the foot of the archaic temple includes a child climbing on the laps of the two Goddesses. Their arms are flung around each other's shoulders,

Fig. 2.8. This appealing ivory carving could be called "the Mothers" (or "the Queens") of Mycenae, Greece, in their fluted skirts and Minoan-style bodices. The sculpture, dating to the late Bronze Age, shows the women wrapped together in a giant serpent shawl, while a child crawls over their laps.

and they are slim waisted and dressed in fluted pantaloons in the Minoan-Mycenaean tradition (with a certain undeniable Syrian influence). As Gimbutas reminds us, the Mycenaean civilization, with its thousands of Goddess figurines, "demonstrates that significant worship of the goddess persisted in Bronze Age Europe, even within heavily Indo-Europeanized cultures . . . (representing) an important transitional phase between Old European gynocentric culture and the Classical Greek culture, where the male element came to dominate almost completely."[20] I suggest we go even further and investigate the Indo-European cultures with a new eye as well. My research suggests that women in Indo-European cultures, far from having lower status as has been claimed by scholars since Herodotus, were much more equal to the men of their tribes and still held offices of great importance at times in history when Greek and Roman women were losing all their rights.

The two Mycenaean Goddesses depicted in the figurine under discussion are casually (and sensually) bound together by an article of clothing that appears, from the back, to be a great snake, perhaps linking them to the tradition of the oracular priestesses and making them precursors to the Pythoness at Delphi or

Fig. 2.9. Back view of the "Two Ladies," showing the snake shawl in more detail.

the legendary Cassandra of Troy. The snakelike shawl may have "tassles," which Homer mentions as characterizing Hera's girdle. As in some of the other Double Goddess statues, these women could be lovers if we judged them at face value by the intimacy and emotional ambience contained in the carved image. In the present day, when so many Western women are single mothers, with or without a lesbian partner, many are choosing to become pregnant, give birth, and coparent without the active presence of a dad, and their families resemble this ancient figurine.

There is an important mural at Akrotiri (Thera, ancient Santorini) depicting what look to be the Two Queens in a viewing box set high above all the other houses in the so-called Miniature Frieze considered to be of great importance. These gorgeous "Minoan" paintings were done early in the second mil-lennium around the same time that the Snake Goddesses of Knossos were sculpted (see fig. 4.25 in chapter four). Christos Doumas, who provides the commentary on the murals in a beautiful book, *The Wall-Paintings of Thera,* establishes a connection of "mutual influences" between Thera and the famous site of Mari in

Fig. 2.10. This Double Goddess, or this pair of Double Queens, are shown in a viewing box at the Minoan ceremonial center of Akrotiri, on the volcanic island of Thera (Santorini), watching a procession of ships. This image is part of a larger important mural from the site, preserved by the volcanic explosion that destroyed the island center in the early second millennium B.C.E. Murals from this site document the active facilitation of religious ceremonies by priestesses in the organized theacratic religion of the Great Goddess, called "Potnia Theron," or the Goddess of the Animals (Lady of the Beasts).

the Middle Euphrates (Syria near the border of Iraq).[26] Amélie Kuhrt describes Mari, a trade-route city and a supplier of tin to the West (including Crete), as especially powerful politically from 2600–2300 B.C.E. (This time period coincides with the height of the Yortan, Troy, and Alaca Höyük cultures in Anatolia, the Cycladic Island cultures in the Aegean, and the BMAC civilizations along the Silk Road, all of which are important to the thesis of this book.) At Mari archaeologists found "brilliantly colored frescoes" depicting the "investiture" of the king "by a warrior-goddess, very probably Ishtar." The queens of Mari actively participated in running "a major palace industry" of the "production of textiles."[27] The great palace at Mari was destroyed by the patriarch Hammurabi in the eighteenth century B.C.E. The frieze from Akrotiri under discussion shows a storied tradition of some kind of oral history, involving several ships in a flotilla on a mythic voyage or ritualized journey around the Aegean, with the homecoming celebration taking place in this particular (south wall) area of the large room that housed the mural. The Two Queens are bare breasted and shown in silhouette, in a convention very similar to the depiction of a hugebreasted priestess in a later mural called "the Women's Frieze" at Tiryns (near Mycenae). Other women are shown in other viewing areas, one of them waving at the homecoming ships, but the Two Queens are clearly set apart and have status. The importance of these queens is contextualized by the strong emphasis of female imagery and ritual themes in the place as a whole. The so-called House of the Ladies (a three-storied building that was probably an important cult center) has murals depicting women's religious rituals, as does a second three-story building (Xeste 3) that houses "the largest representation of the Nature Goddess in the Aegean world."[28] This impressive Goddess, "a majestic female figure seated on a stepped structure," wears necklaces, has snakes in her hair, and is accompanied by a peacock-griffin like those flanking the throne at Knossos in Crete.[29]

AFRICAN QUEEN-MOTHER AND
QUEEN-SISTER: EGYPT'S "MIGHTY ONES"

There are a number of pairs of Two Ladies in Egyptian history as well, along with a widespread tradition of Double Queens in Africa as a whole, such as the ancient tradition of the Queen-Mother and the Queen-Sister. I imagine that in its earliest incarnation, the African Double Goddess represented a female-centered civilization as in so many other parts of the world. Robert Briffault speaks of "gynaeco-cratic monarchies" in both Asia and Africa that lived by a system of Dual Queenship, for example in Uganda: "But by their side reign two women, the Queen-Mother ('Namasole') and the Queen ('Lubuga'); the latter is the king's sister. Each of these women bears the title of 'Kabaka,' that is, King; each has her court and extensive estates in various parts of the kingdom which she administers, appointing her own officials. The Queen-Mother lives in a separate enclosure at some distance from that of the king, and separated from it by a stream of running water, 'because it was said that she also was a king, and that two kings could not live on the same hill.'"[30] Maybe the same tradition explains why Egypt's most famous queen, Hatshepsut, felt the need to wear a beard and call herself "king," disassociating herself from the increasingly powerless position of queenship in patriarchy during the Bronze Age.

In another African tribe the "Queen-Sister was chosen by the Queen-Mother. She sat on the same throne as the king at coronation ceremonies, and took the same oath."[31] These customs, according to

Fig. 2.11. This African Double Goddess, from an unknown provenance, shows two Goddesses (or priestesses) wearing the high headdresses that belong to a widely shared tradition of sacred women in leadership positions, ruling, as the Amazons were said to do, in Dual Queenship.

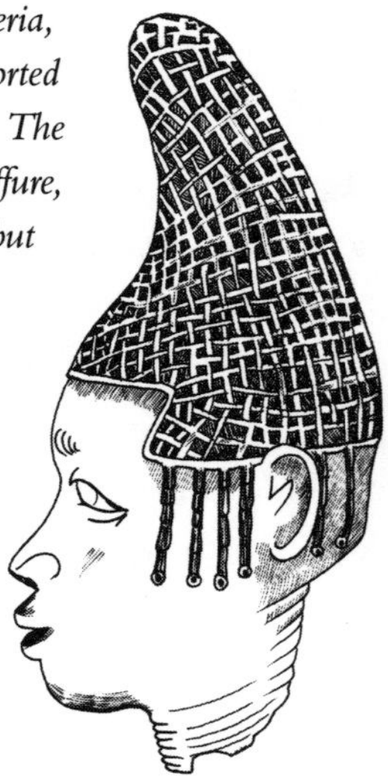

Fig. 2.12. This beautifully sculpted brass head from Benin, Nigeria, dated to the sixteenth century, shows Queen-Mother, who is reported to have ruled along with a Queen-Sister in Dual Queenship. The Queen-Mother was the only one to wear this unique pointy coiffure, which appears to utilize a hair net, perhaps linking to similar, but earlier, beaded hair nets found at Neolithic Jericho.

Briffault, existed widely in Africa until Christianization in the twentieth century, when "the status of the royal women, as Queen-Sister or as Queen-Mother, has come to consist of little more than empty ceremonial and hollow titles . . . archaic forms of the (earlier) institution."[32]

In Egypt "all princesses were by birthright, and from the moment of their birth, 'Royal Wives.'" Rather than marrying to power, as contemporary scholars would have it, the women of pharaonic Egypt were already "wives of the gods" and were therefore themselves the (matrilineal) means for acquiring the throne.[33] In later times, the Two Queens are associated with one man, the king (and finally pharaoh) of two great lands of Upper and Lower Egypt. Even Ramses II, whose gigantic statues at Karnak depict him as the most self-aggrandizing pharaoh of all time, "married two of his sisters . . . and is everywhere represented in association with the Queen-Mother or with one of the queens."[34]

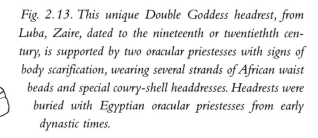

Fig. 2.13. This unique Double Goddess headrest, from Luba, Zaire, dated to the nineteenth or twentiethth century, is supported by two oracular priestesses with signs of body scarification, wearing several strands of African waist beads and special cowry-shell headdresses. Headrests were buried with Egyptian oracular priestesses from early dynastic times.

Fig. 2.14. This Egyptian Pharaoh shown with Two Queens, is one of eight known triads showing a queen and the Goddess Hathor with the identified Pharaoh, Menkaura, from the fourth dynasty, in Giza, about the time of the building of the pyramids there. The convention of the Two Queens was clearly absorbed into the newly created male system at a fairly early date (mid-third millennium B.C.E.).

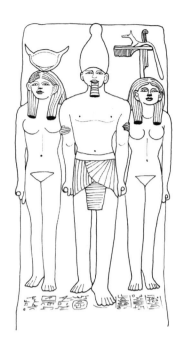

Briffault discusses this tradition at length in his three-volume work, *The Mothers*, arguing that it was a queen who started the First Dynasty. In the "oldest inscription in Egyptian writing . . . is the name of a queen." This powerful female, Queen Neit-hotep, bore the "Ka" name and "transmitted the crown of Egypt from pre-dynastic times to the first dynasty."[35] Many scholars believe that the Greek Athena was a late derivation of the "Libyan" (or North African) Neith, a creator Goddess complete within herself, whose name translates as "that which is," referring to her primeval quality, and "the terrifying," signifying the wrathful aspect of her ancient Two-in-Oneness. The two-headed Double

Fig. 2.15. This African Double Goddess with two heads, provenance and date unknown, holds her belly in her hands as if she (they) might be pregnant. But her powerful stance, like that of a martial artist, bespeaks the fierce strength for which African warrior women have been known through the centuries, even into modern times when whole armies of women form military cadres under the aegis of African kings.

Goddess illustrated here could be a representation of the self-created intactness of the fierce Neith.

In Egypt two distinct parts of the country—"Lower Egypt" (the northern Delta region bordering on the Mediterranean) and "Upper Egypt" (the southern Nubian portion)—were forcibly "unified" under one ruler around the end of the fourth millennium B.C.E. when the First Dynasty was established. It was Neith's dynasty that originally ruled over the "unified" Egypt but then, as always, we are supposed to believe that she handed over her executive power to her consort, the first king of Egypt. Neith's "early dominance" shows up in her name glyph being "clearly associated with both male and female royalty."[36] Her emblem, "two bows bound in a package" is connected with Queen Neith-hotep, shown in a hieroglyph that includes two crossed arrows, and Queen Merenith, whose tomb artifacts record that she founded a "religious sanctuary of the goddess Neith, probably at her later centre of Sais in the Delta."[37] A text from a wooden label for a jar of oil records a visit to a sanctuary of Neith dated to the First Dynasty.[38]

I went to Egypt in 1995 eager to see for myself this strong, predynastic Goddess civilization, intending to trace its potent signs and symbols down through the intervening ages. I was dumbfounded to see almost nothing matriarchal left anywhere in the Egyptian foreground, where men speak freely and engage in public commerce and conversation, while women hide, shyly veiled, in the background. Along the Nile are huge sculpted figures of pharaohs, male warrior kings, priests, and slaves, and hieroglyphic inscriptions glorifying the exploits of men and gods. The few women portrayed at all are shown as profoundly submissive, in supportive roles at best, as slaves and dancing girls or wives of the pharaohs. When a "wife" is shown with her hand on the king's shoulder, she is always described as "supporting" him, even though in fact she is probably conferring the kingship on him as a stand-in for the Goddess Isis, whose very name means "throne" and whose lap represents the seat of power.

I flew into Egypt two days early for a women's pilgrimage tour I was coleading so that I could take my time in the archaeological museum before our trip started. I stayed overnight in Cairo's Hilton Hotel, built for the convenience of travelers like me who want to be a stone's throw from the museum. On waking just before dawn my first morning, I was drawn out onto the balcony by the haunting sound of deep male voices chanting from every direction, a resonant first call to Allah carrying far and wide over loudspeakers to the whole city. Cairo is full of mosques, and the men pray five times daily facing Mecca. I wondered if the singing or chanting derived from chants addressed to the ancient female deity, Allat, whose black meteorite stone at Mecca now belongs to her successor, the Islamic Allah. The Islamic flag still contains Allat's crescent Moon and star.[39]

As I toured the Cairo museum, I watched with fascination as a group of veiled young women students with drawing tablets sat and stood in artistic concentration throughout the various rooms, drawing what they observed in the display cases. Outside of urban Cairo, the women in Egypt—mostly orthodox Islamic—are covered from head to toe in voluminous black tents, even though the heat is extreme, while the men are free to wear light-colored, thin, practical garments. Five thousand years of unmitigated patriarchal rule have similarly veiled most of Egyptian prehistory, and I was sad to learn that many of the most ancient Goddess figures have been taken out of Egypt to be displayed or stored in other places such as the Metropolitan Museum in New York or the British Museum in London.

Even after the establishment of the First Dynasty, however, the Double Goddess theme stayed strong in Egypt for the more than three thousand years of the mostly male rulers, although they tended to take a more symbolic, even abstracted, form. The Two Ladies required to be worn on every Egyptian pharaoh's crown represent the ancient Cobra Goddess of Lower Egypt and the Vulture Goddess of Upper Egypt. Nekhbet, the vulture, is portrayed by the beautiful predynastic bird Goddesses with their arms raised to the sky, and Wadjet, the raised cobra, remained essential in the "Uraeus" image, literally meaning

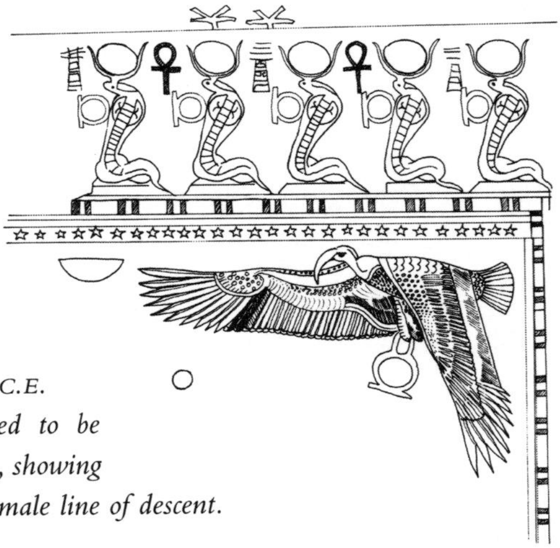

Fig. 2.16. In Egypt, the Two Ladies, representing the Cobra Goddess of Lower Egypt (Nile Delta) and the Vulture Goddess of Upper Egypt (Nubia), have long been representational of the so-called "Great Unification" that brought the two parts of the country together under one ruler around the end of the fourth millennium B.C.E. *These two Goddesses were required to be worn on the crown of every pharaoh, showing authorization through the ancient female line of descent.*

"goddess" and always associated with Egyptian royalty. Together these Two Ladies were called the two "Mighty Ones," embodying the White Crown and Red Crown of the two regions and thus requiring homage. This continuous sovereignty of the Two-in-One, the ancient Bird and Snake Goddess, harks back to Old Europe and the images found in the extensive work of Marija Gimbutas.

Another common pairing of Goddesses in Egypt is the Vulture Goddess Mut, the hieroglyph whose name means "mother," with the Hippopotamus Taweret, "the Great One," whose image was worn as an amulet especially by pregnant women and women in childbirth. An inscribed stone stele (pillar or monument) incorporating "powerful magical and medical symbols appropriate for the protection of a pregnant or newly delivered woman" was dedicated to the two of them, "Taweret, the Great One," and "Mut, the Great One," by a woman who served as a "Chantress of Amen."[40] Chantress was the name given to priestesses during the later dynastic times, a diminution of powers but still a recognition of the woman's sacred role. This particular twinning reminds me of Erich Neumann's differentiation of the "elementary" and "transformative" feminine, as articulated in his classic book, *The Great Mother* (see fig. 1.10).

THE TWO HERAS

A sculpted image of two enthroned queens, called the "Two Heras," was found in mainland Greece after the so-called Dark Ages, during the archaic period. The figures are reminiscent of the much earlier Maltese Double Goddess, although these queens are thinner and wear fez-style hats more in keeping with their counterparts in nearby Turkey. The similarity with the Malta figurine is in the royal way they are seated, enthroned side by side, as if to say, "These two women still share the capacity and responsibility of governing this community." Like the Maltese queens, this identical twin Double Goddess suggests an integration of the female energy that has come down through the ages since the first images we saw at Çatalhöyük in the seventh millennium. The hats worn by the Two Heras are the round pillbox or fez style seen on earlier Double Goddesses from Anatolia in the third millennium (before the destructions) and similar to later fez-style hats worn by Central Asian steppe women, such as the Scythians (see fig. 4.23 in chapter four).

Several great temples were dedicated to Hera during this time in Greece (the early Iron Age), in the Argolid near Mycenae, in Perachora near Corinth, and on the island of Samos just off the coast of Turkey near Ephesus. The Samos Heraion was the largest temple in Greece in the eighth century B.C.E., an architectural wonder (rebuilt at least four times in the next two centuries) that served as a prototype

Fig. 2.17. This Double Goddess is identified as the "Two Heras," enthroned and wearing headdresses, with faces of animals (perhaps cows or leopards). The figure is from Boeotia, mainland Greece, dating to the eighth century B.C.E., and coincides with the great Hera temples built at Argos and on the island of Samos in this period.

for the temple at Ephesus, as well as later classical temples in Athens. Traditional scholars associate Hera primarily with her stormy marriage to Zeus, the patriarchal usurper of her authority as Queen of Heaven, and she "figures most prominently in myth as a wife and a queen."[41] Yet the crowned Hera is sometimes depicted with a horse face or riding sidesaddle on horseback, and we can see that her devotees were most likely Amazons, judging from votive offerings brought to her Samos temples (like the mainland temple of Artemis at Ephesus) being comprised mainly of horse trappings. You can see the horse artifacts if you visit the museum in Samos town near the famous site. Several crowned and elaborately bejeweled figures of queens or Goddesses can be seen in the museum, sculpted from ivory and clay, with poppy heads and pomegranates, both long connected with priestesses of the Goddess religion. You will also see a case taking up one entire wall filled with hundreds of bronze griffins (mythical bird-animals) in a wide range of styles and sizes. Griffins—quintessential animals of the Great Goddess— are first seen flanking the thrones at Knossos in Crete and Pylos in the Argolid during the second millennium B.C.E. and are later famous as

Fig. 2.18. Mythical griffins flanked the curved throne discovered at the Cretan "palace" of Knossos, where the famous Snake Priestess figurines, from the early second millennium B.C.E., were found buried under a floor stone. Some scholars believe the small throne was made for a woman, who then would likely have been an oracular priestess as well as a queen.

Fig. 2.19. Artists often portrayed the Greek Hera as a powerful queen positioned between her flanking leopards or lions, as in this image, even after she lost her official status as Queen of Heaven and became demoted to the role of nagging wife of Zeus.

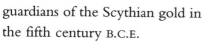

guardians of the Scythian gold in the fifth century B.C.E.

Other Heras exist from this time period, in the form of "plaque Goddesses" found mostly in farmer's fields of mainland Boeotia, as well as sculptures of Hera holding two leopards or lionesses, suggesting that the dual queenship of the earlier civilizations remained alive, at least in a symbolic form, up into the archaic period (the same time as the famous poets, Homer and Sappho). An exquisite gold necklace also from mainland Greece, composed of alternating eggs and acorns, ends in a beautiful horned cow pendant topped by a miniature Double Goddess, the two Heras sharing a hat or crown, with two four-petaled flowers as their bodies. This Double Goddess, with its ancient connection to the Sacred Cow Mother, is a reminder to us that the horned bovine animals depicted all over the ancient Mediterranean area are not necessarily bulls, as they are so often automatically identified. I saw this for myself when I visited the Etruscan site of Vulci (Italy), where mother cows, with imposing sets of horns, were happily nursing their calves in a nearby field. The Cow Goddess is revered in the ancient world, from the hundreds of images of Egypt's Hathor to Homer's "cow-eyed Hera."[42]

As Queen of Heaven, the ancient Hera ruled over the female blood mysteries of menstruation and birth. As an Amazon Queen, she ruled as head of a female lineage of women warriors in the fight for justice

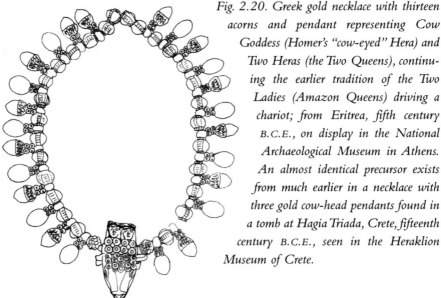

Fig. 2.20. Greek gold necklace with thirteen acorns and pendant representing Cow Goddess (Homer's "cow-eyed" Hera) and Two Heras (the Two Queens), continuing the earlier tradition of the Two Ladies (Amazon Queens) driving a chariot; from Eritrea, fifth century B.C.E., on display in the National Archaeological Museum in Athens. An almost identical precursor exists from much earlier in a necklace with three gold cow-head pendants found in a tomb at Hagia Triada, Crete, fifteenth century B.C.E., seen in the Heraklion Museum of Crete.

during the long patriarchal takeover. Once she was forcibly married to Zeus and installed at Olympus, she was perceived as a raging, bitter shrew of a wife, and she became the Greek Goddess of marriage. Her mythological story reports that after a blowup with her philandering husband, whose raping exploits are the core stuff of Greek origin stories, she would always withdraw to herself and take a renewing bath. After her sacred ritual bath, she would return to the marriage and take up the struggle for equality once again. This story is a form of transition mythology, a tale told by the victors to set in place the new world order of male dominance.

Women's rituals to Hera involved a sacred bath at least as far back as the

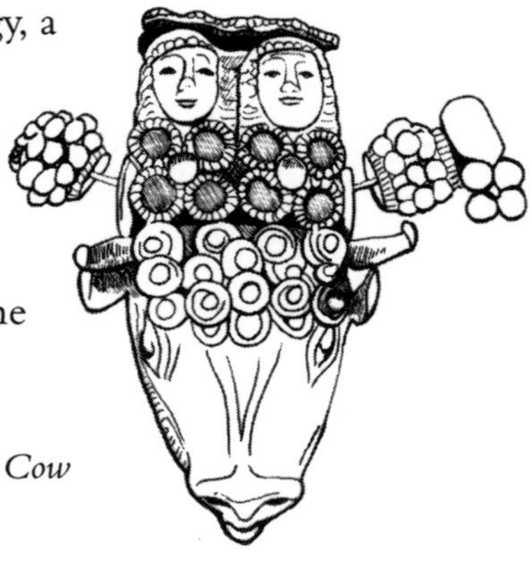

Fig. 2.21. Detail of fig. 2.20, showing the Cow Goddess and her two priestesses.

early Heraion at Perachora on the tip of the peninsula near Corinth. The rites of renewal would have followed any act of menstruation or birth and probably signify the dual poles of the female cycle—the bleeding and birthing, death and life, yin and yang, sacred two-in-one that we have seen in all the Double Goddess motifs. Two thousand metal bowls believed to be used for oracles (water mirrors) were found at the bottom of the sacred spring near the earliest temple at the site. Thus the priestesses at the site were no doubt carrying on the ancient female tradition of reading oracles in the water mirrors that goes back at least to the third millennium B.C.E. in Turkey and the Cycladic Islands.

THREE

Shaman Women
and High Priestesses

In a general way, all the various collectivities of women mentioned by historians and mythologers—from Artemis and her colleges of nymphs and the Maenads, those wild Dionysian women known for their ecstatic frenzies, to the Amazons, Bacchantes, dakinis, yoginis, Valkyries, Vreela, gorgons, Danaïds, Naiads, Raganas, and witches—all are archetypally related and may well be descended from a much earlier stratum of Siberian shamans. Russia (especially Siberia) is the ancient homeland of shamanism, continuous from the Paleolithic era (thirty thousand years ago) and active today even after efforts by the Communist State to eradicate it from the racial memory. Ancient Paleo-Siberian shamanism eventually made its way to Anatolia and Europe, as well as migrating with populations who crossed the land bridge into North America during the last Ice Age.

An early-twentieth-century ethnographic study of Paleo-Siberianism states that "women receive the gift of shamanizing more often than men," and "The woman is by nature a shaman . . . (who) does not need to be specially prepared for the calling."[1] Today there are more women shamans than men, even though they don't always wear special outfits like the men do; nonetheless, "every old woman can shamanize."[2] The oldest word for shaman means "female shaman," and words for male shamans only came into being after the tribes migrated away from the place of origins. Unlike the older female word for shaman that is consistent across a broad region, the male words for shaman are all different. "The men shamans appeared later, when these people [the "Neo-Siberians"] scattered, settling in lands distant from one another, so that the term for man-shaman originated independently in each tribe."[3]

In some dialects the word for female shaman also means "housewife" and "wife," in others "sorcerer" and "cannibal" (epithets of the later Indian yoginis). Connected etymologically to a word for "Earth Goddess" or "Mother Earth," the same word connects "to the two bear constellations."[4] Women who "possess a knowledge of the secret family incantations" often know many others besides, "of which they make use outside the family circle on request." In this way "family shamanism" has developed into "professional shamanism."[5]

This ancient female lineage began in the Neolithic Age (if not earlier) and included priestesses of the Aegean Bronze and Iron Ages (the Maenads); the shaman women of Central Asian tribes, such as the Cimmerians, Scythians, Sauromatians, and Saka (to name only a few); and the cemetery-dwelling yoginis and wandering dakini witches of India and Tibet. Furthermore this lineage includes the Scandinavian Valkyries, Irish Banshees, Iranian and Tocharian mummies of the Tarim Basin, and millions of shaman women murdered as witches during the European "Burning Times."

Josie Blok, writing on the Amazons, reminds us that, "Not only the cult of the Mother Goddess, but also the matriarchal structure, persisted for a long time in certain places, especially on the shores of the Black

Sea—in the immediate neighborhood of the Greeks—among the Sindians, the Maeotians, the Sauromatians, and, in the Crimea, among the Taurians."[6] In a recent Tibetan history (authorized by Lama Namkhai Norbu), John Vincent Bellezza concludes that certain "extinct" Tibetan female sisterhoods provide "evidence suggesting the existence of a matriarchal culture and the supremacy of female deities in prehistory."[7] We can see vestiges of it in Tibetan Buddhist dakini practices—involving chanting, visualization, and prayers—and tantric traditions alive in India today.

The Maenads of sixth century B.C.E. were famous for their "orgiastic" rituals, not only throughout Greece and Turkey, but also in Thrace (Bulgaria), Italy (the Etruscans), and the land of the Scythians. A Thracian vessel depicts a Double Axe, below which is a series of Goddesses and objects that could be either daggers or sheaves of wheat. In a description that matches female images on vessels in ancient Sumer, we're told of Thracian "orgiastic rites which took place in the mountains by night . . . (where) the women, clad in animal skins, and having snakes and daggers in their hands, danced exciting, whirling dances."[8] A mural in Crete shows a woman whirling as far back as the Bronze Age, predating Sufi dancing by more than two millennia. A Greek vase showing pairs of women dancing with lotus flowers in their hands could be a Western counterpart to the Indian yoginis engaged in nocturnal assemblies,

Fig. 3.1. This Thracian silver vessel, dating from the fourth century B.C.E., depicts a series of female images wearing the diadem (headband) of a priestess, each holding up a sword or a sheaf of grain, as in the earlier traditions we have been discussing in this book. In Thrace (Iron Age Bulgaria), this Goddess (a version of Artemis) was known as Bendis.

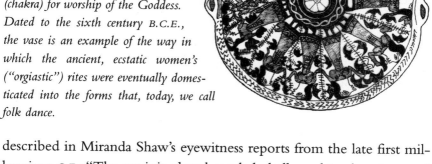

Fig. 3.2. This Greek vase showing pairs of women in dance formation, and holding lotus flowers, suggests to me what in India would be understood as an "assembly of yoginis" who could be participating in a tantric circle (chakra) for worship of the Goddess. Dated to the sixth century B.C.E., the vase is an example of the way in which the ancient, ecstatic women's ("orgiastic") rites were eventually domesticated into the forms that, today, we call folk dance.

described in Miranda Shaw's eyewitness reports from the late first millennium C.E.: "The yoginis played cymbals, bells, and tambourines and danced within a halo of light and a cloud of incense."[9]

Joseph Needham points out that the main connection between the ancient Ural-Altaic and Tungusic words for shaman and the earliest Chinese words for shaman is "the idea of dancing that binds all these words together."[10] Chinese oracle bones depict a dancing "thaumaturgic (wonder-working) shaman holding plumes, feathers, or other ritual objects in his, or her, hands." Chinese shamans—known for their rainmaking magic—could be either male (*hsi*) or female (*wu*), but Needham says "the prominence of women here seems very significant," referring in particular to their sex techniques, ritual nakedness, profuse sweating, and the use of poisonous drugs (perhaps even including an immunization process) up to the end of the Tang Dynasty, after which they were persecuted as witches.[11]

To provide us with an idea of what shaman women might have been doing, we can take a look at a fascinating treatise on the "cult" of Indian yoginis (eighth to twelfth centuries C.E.) whose round stone temples still stand today in remote parts of central and northern India. Vidya Dehejia describes their "extraordinary powers which are often of a magical and yogic nature." Some of these powers include "complete control over breathing and other bodily functions, levitation . . . and control over living creatures."[12] Indian yoginis depicted with animal heads* were famous for inventing and accomplishing the "eight magical siddhis" or shape-shifting abilities in round outdoor temples dedicated to "the Mothers" (Mâtrikâs) as early as the third century B.C.E. Like shaman women elsewhere, the yoginis were skilled in working the weather because of their control over the natural elements. They could produce rain, cause a drought or a flash flood, and induce volcanoes to erupt or earthquakes to occur. "Ritual offerings of food . . . were made to the Mâtrikâs at the crossroads" and "shrines of the Mothers were frequently built at the crossroads."[14]

Miranda Shaw also reports on famous Indian yoginis, who "could become invisible, had mastered the ritual gazes, and had the power of fleetfootedness, the ability to traverse vast distances in a matter of minutes."[15] They had the "power to transform human beings into animals and birds with the aid of a magic thread" (like Ariadne of Crete?).[16] In Indian alchemical literature, Indian supernatural heroes (called Nath Siddhas) have to accomplish feats not unlike Odysseus, Theseus, Hercules, Jason, and the other Greek heroes of the Bronze Age. Often, according to David Gordon White, they were sent to be tested against the powers of certain powerful yoginis. One famous Nath Siddha was freed by another "from sexual bondage in a Kingdom of Women in Assam,"[17] a story reminiscent of Odysseus staying with Calypso or Heracles spending a year in service of the Lydian Amazon queen Omphale, where he was forced to wear women's clothing.

CEMETERIES AND SHAMAN WOMEN

Long before yoga was codified in India or Buddhism was institutionalized in Tibet, women priestesses all across the Silk Road facilitated

---

*A Tibetan version of the Indian yoginis are the "eight queens with human bodies and animal heads" who are "among the obscure 'brog ma goddesses (goddesses of the pastures)" from a "lost cultural tradition which was assimilated and subsumed to some degree by Bon and Buddhism."[13]

shamanistic healing and funerary rites for their communities. Funerary rites as exclusively the province of women must be very ancient, and women's special status in early cultures was no doubt in part based on the facilitation of these practices. In preliterate prepatriarchal cultures, sacred women (often depicted as carrion birds) functioned as regenerative funerary priestesses, providing rituals and facilitating communal ceremonies that took place in shrines and prehistoric cemeteries built above and below the ground. Rites of excarnation (secondary burial) were practiced all over Old Europe and the Mediterranean region for millennia, and in Central Asia as well, and remnants of this practice are carried on in some places today. Gimbutas documents such practices in Italy, the Near East, Anatolia, Greece, and even as far north as the Orkney Islands, with skulls routinely buried separately and skeletons "disarticulated."[18]

Frequently these finds (skulls and disarticulated bones, some with cut marks) have led archaeologists to conclude that cannibalism and human sacrifice were practiced. Yet in Tibet the ancient rite of "sky burial" is still practiced, in which a corpse is taken to a "specially designated area outside the town or village, often at the top of a mountain," and "bodybreakers" (*domdens*) chop the body into pieces and feed it to the vultures who are considered to be incarnate dakinis. Tibetan sky burials take place near sites sacred to pre-Buddhist female deities that are still used as "ritual staging area[s] for the passage of the deceased into the celestial sphere."[19] A pre-Buddhist rock painting at an important site in Tibet sacred to Tara *(bKra shis do)* shows a birdlike female identified as a *khyung*, sacred to Tibetans and precursor to contemporary dakinis or "sky walkers."[20] Recent films about Tibet (e.g., *Seven Years in Tibet*, *Kundun*, and *Himalaya*) show graphic representations of these funerary rites, with pieces of flesh laid out as a banquet and the giant screaming birds coming to feast ravenously on the remains. We in the West tend to view such practices with alarm, judging them as primitive, barbaric, unnatural, or gruesome. Tibetans, on the other hand, view a three-day-old corpse as lifeless, "its purpose fulfilled. The manner of disposal is considered as a final act of generosity, enabling other animals to be nourished by one's remains."[21]

Much the same kind of indigenous tradition probably prevailed in ancient Çatalhöyük in Turkey (seventh millennium B.C.E.), where the enthroned female ancestor or Mother Goddess was found in the communal grain bin. Murals painted on lime-plastered walls in the shrine rooms there show vulture women in flight, attending to the headless bodies of humans laid out on platforms designed for sky burial or excarnation. One such vulture priestess is painted with the Double Axe.

Contemporaneous with Çatalhöyük was Lepenski Vir, a seventh-millennium site on the Danube River (in contemporary Serbia) overlooking a "tumultuous whirlpool"[22] where excarnation rites were practiced for a thousand years. Similarly, the Hal Saflieni Hypogeum on the main island of Malta is a tomb and ritual space where the bones of seven thousand human burials were found, interred over a period of fifteen hundred years. Just as at Çatalhöyük and Lepenski Vir, "the disordered state of the bones may indicate that they underwent excarnation before they were interred in the Hypogeum."[23] In all the British *henge* monuments, "feasting and consumption on a large scale" are suggested, and ritual burials suggesting excarnation are present.[24] The Valkyries of Nordic mythology, who chose and carried away the bodies of the slain in battle, and the shriek of the Banshee in Ireland are late remnants of this ancient widespread funerary tradition.

In parts of Europe where old traditions are still kept, excarnation rites were still being performed by the old women in the late twentieth century. Anthropologist C. Nadia Seremetakis published a detailed record of such practices in the northern Greek province of Inner Mani, where the older women (exclusively) would exhume a corpse three years after a burial in order to deflesh the bones, wash them with vinegar, and lay them out in the sun to dry; from the bones the women could read oracles. Finally the bones were blessed by a priest and reburied. The women who performed this challenging ritual—out of compassion and for the sake of their beloved dead, as well as to protect the community—said: "You can't leave a single bone. It's very bad for you and family if anything is left behind."[25] Similarly, Gimbutas relates an ethnographic report from the 1980s of women in Thessaloniki (also in northern Greece) exhuming a corpse, during which the mother of the dead woman, Eleni, receives the skull into her hands with sobbing and lamenting. "Three times she kisses the skull and touches it to her forehead, then she passes the skull across the grave to be greeted by Eleni's father and the rest of the family."[26]

Diverse ancient people came together in similar ways to bury their dead and celebrate such rites of renewal in cemeteries and ceremonial grounds, probably in much the same way as that remembered by the old women of Inner Mani who say: "In the old days, members of the village used to stream in from all over the countryside and witness the 'opening.' They would wail loudly in memory of their great loss. The dead felt comforted to be mourned by the people who loved them. Nowadays, few people have exhumations, and the old folks think it's a shame."[27]

YOGINIS, BEE PRIESTESSES, AND THE MAGIC SOMA

A number of female figurines from Çatalhöyük, predynastic Egypt, Palestine, Iraq, Malta, and even the Cycladic Islands (e.g., Crete, Naxos) have much in common and appear to be sitting in what we would now call yoga or meditation postures. During the Bronze Age (3000–1250 B.C.E.), an interesting confluence of cultures (African, Asian, and European) came together in the Mediterranean region (perhaps especially in Crete) through trade and cultural exchange. One notable result of this comingling was the development of a legendary female shamanistic priesthood called Maenads ("wild women") who handled snakes, domesticated wild bees, fermented a sacred honey beverage (perhaps the famed *soma* memorialized in the Vedas?), and facilitated ecstatic rituals. Late Bronze Age, Cretan Linear B texts indicate the prominence of "priestesses of the wind,"[28] perhaps the equivalent of

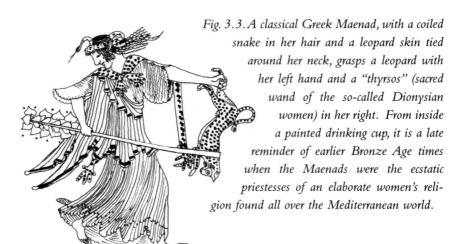

Fig. 3.3. A classical Greek Maenad, with a coiled snake in her hair and a leopard skin tied around her neck, grasps a leopard with her left hand and a "thyrsos" (sacred wand of the so-called Dionysian women) in her right. From inside a painted drinking cup, it is a late reminder of earlier Bronze Age times when the Maenads were the ecstatic priestesses of an elaborate women's religion found all over the Mediterranean world.

sky-walking dakinis. Maenads can be best understood as the Aegean version of yoginis with the same magical, shamanistic practices and ecstatic rituals as their Eastern sisters. Eventually—like them—they became taboo or even illegal, having to conduct their worship outside the boundaries of normal society. Pasiphae of Crete is described by a Cretan archaeologist as "the immortal witch" and "a form of the moon goddess."[29] She and her mythological sister Ariadne may represent these Aegean shaman-priestesses.

The Cretan Maenads were famous for their intoxicating honey brew. Although grains were fermented as early as ten thousand years ago to make beer in Africa, Egypt, Iraq, and South America, the evidence suggests that honey was fermented long before grains, and in Africa bottle gourds were cultivated possibly as early as forty thousand years ago.[30] An early portrait of an Egyptian Maenad occurs in the Old Kingdom, Fourth Dynasty, showing a woman on a lion seat wearing a "ceremonial wig and a closefitting leopardskin dress which leaves her right shoulder bare."[31] In Greek language the word for "bee" *(melissa)* is also a word for "priestess," and the Greek Melissae were the oracular, ecstatic bee priestesses known later at the famous mainland site of Delphi (from which excellent honey is still exported today). The prophetess Pythia herself was called "the Delphic bee."[32] The great antiquity of honey-brewed sacred beverages can be seen in Laszlo Torday's impressive list of cognates that appear in the names of intoxicating liquors brewed from honey: English *mead*, Irish *miodh*, Welsh *medd*, Greek *méthu*, and Sanskrit *mádhu*. Then there are those for honey itself: Lithuanian *medus*, Russian *mëd*, French *miel*, Finnish *mete*, and Hungarian *méz* . . . even the Chinese *myit* is "surely, an extraordinary lexical coincidence."[33]

David Spess adds that, "The secret of soma and its preparation, as well as the secret essence of the Vedas themselves, was called the *madhu-vidyá* or 'honey doctrine,' the oldest references to which are contained in veiled, cryptic religious riddles found in the hymns of the Rg Veda."[34] Spess links mantras and soma to systematized magic and magical techniques that he believes can be traced back to a Vedic "priesthood who had composed a special liturgical language with a potent magical grammar."[35] And from the Rg Veda we know the soma plant ("Moon-plant") was "gathered by moonlight on certain mountains, stripped of its leaves, and then carried to the place of sacrifice" to be prepared by "priests."[36] But before there was a Vedic male priesthood, shaman women like Pasiphae were chanting magical formulae over the gathering and processing of their sacred mind-altering plants. And although the Indian yoginis were "inordinately fond" of wine, we're told that their favorite drink was a honey-brewed beverage made with ginger, lemon, and black peppercorns and fermented for twelve days.[37]

I believe the functions of the oracular shaman priestesses are embedded in the ritual preparation of the soma (or haoma) before it was taken over by male priests. In ancient times, fermented and alcoholic brews were medicinal and nourishing. Their ingestion facilitated a communal religious experience wherein people were liberated through direct (primordial) experiences of the divine. The ingredients in fermented beverages were at once sacred, nutritious, and transformational. For thousands of years the wild honey fermentation process of the "bee priestesses" was a balm to their communities, bringing much-needed antibacterial, antiseptic, antifungal qualities and making people ecstatic. Profoundly mystical rather than merely recreational, the intoxication of the Maenads and yoginis, and the secrets of preparation of their brew, were central to the old religion of the women. "Let us drink soma and become ecstatic, let us drink of the ecstasy that is soma," says the Rg Veda.[38]

In the so-called palaces of Crete (actually ceremonial centers) are rooms plastered entirely in white alabaster or gypsum, where special rituals were performed. This was also true at sites along the Silk Road during the Bronze Age, where a "cult of the White Room" has been documented by archaeologists, having to do with "extracting hallucinogens like opium and hashish" through a ritual of pressing the plants.[39] Ritual vessels and large numbers of cups—often ceremoniously overturned—are found in the Aegean and along the Silk Road as well. The characteristic groups of drinking cups found at cemeteries, kurgans (burial mounds), and temples excavated all across the Silk Road point to widespread systematic use of soma or "ambrosia" by the priestesses. Mummies excavated in China's Tarim Basin at the eastern end of the Silk Road were buried with sprigs of ephedra tied to their shrouds, believed to be somehow part of the soma ceremonies.[40]

A unique gold pendant from Mallia in Crete seems to represent a Double Goddess or two Maenads interacting in some ritual way. A natural history article on bees inadvertently describes the females in char-

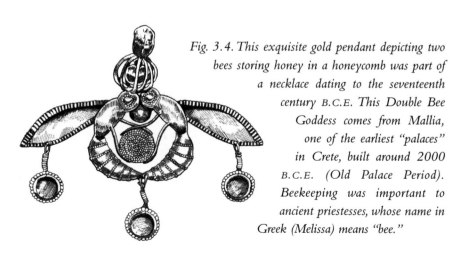

Fig. 3.4. This exquisite gold pendant depicting two bees storing honey in a honeycomb was part of a necklace dating to the seventeenth century B.C.E. This Double Bee Goddess comes from Mallia, one of the earliest "palaces" in Crete, built around 2000 B.C.E. (Old Palace Period). Beekeeping was important to ancient priestesses, whose name in Greek (Melissa) means "bee."

acteristic Double Goddess terminology: "Forager and receiver bees are the yin and yang of honey production. To survive the winter, they must communicate" through a kind of dance that they perform as needed, which was observed and recorded by Thomas D. Seeley, the scientific writer of the piece.[41] Perhaps the Bronze and Iron Age Maenads found a kind of resonance in the various methodologies utilized by the bees, including the central importance of dance and their ability to migrate as a hive when necessary, continuing the matrilineal succession. Modern Pagans or Wiccans organize themselves into covens that function in more or less the same way, "hiving off" when a new High Priestess emerges, thus continuing the ancient matrilineal chain of mothers and daughters.

The buzzing of the bees in the hive is also connected with female oracular prophesy and the use of mantras. Layne Redmond says the sacred mantra OM, considered to be the seed syllable of created existence, if intoned correctly, causes a "sound similar to the humming of bees. This mantra and its sound are linked to the omphalos, the great beehive—the place of sacred utterance and the buzzing vibration of life."[42] Is it any accident that the national site of prophesy and divination was the omphalos at Delphi, and the great Amazon Queen who ruled Lydia in ancient Turkey was named Omphale? Gimbutas mentions a "knob (a head or *omphalos*, a knoblike protrusion, from Greek omphalos, 'navel') on top" of passage graves. "Sometimes the artisan carved hair around this image, perhaps as a metaphor for the goddess' power."[43] In Tibetan Buddhism, this knob or protuberance from the top of the head is called "usnisa" and refers to both enlightenment and the name of a Goddess. The Buddha most notably has such a protuberance on his head, but clearly the concept predates Buddhism by millennia.

MEDEA AND THE GOLDEN FLEECE

Medea of Colchis (Georgia near the Black Sea) is a prototypical shaman-priestess descended from the Paleo-Siberians. An herbalist and sorceress, her story includes all the necessary props to represent an archetypal shaman woman—funerary rites, incantational magic spells (mantra), oracular pronouncements (prophesy), healing performances (epiphany), herbal medicine and regenerating the dead (sorcery). She was also a likely originator of the sacred soma. Her character can stand as a link between Double Goddess cultures documented in Greece, the Aegean Islands, and Anatolia; Amazon priestesses buried in southern Russia along the eastern side of the Black Sea; and Europoid mummies identified as priestesses discovered in the Tarim Basin north of Tibet. Medea's lineage may continue even today in a group of mostly women and girls living in the Caucasus who are "called *messulethe* and described as sorceresses" according to a report by Jeannine Davis-Kimball. They live among tribes considered to be descendants of Scythians and Sarmatians, who lived in southern Russia along the Don and Volga Rivers in the mid-first millennium B.C.E. The *messulethe* "fulfill a role very similar to that of Altaic shamans, falling into trances, escorting the dead to the underworld, or reincarnating them."[44]

In Medea's mythology, she is connected with magic formulae or "incantatory spells, her *carmina*," as a commentary on Medea in Ovid's *Metamorphoses* suggests: "Medea reveals speech as the characteristic source of female power . . . (I whip up the calm seas, I drive away the clouds/and I enshroud the sky with clouds)."[45] In many versions of her mythology, Medea could raise the dead through some form of shamanistic dismemberment and healing practices, what Jacob Rabinowitz refers to as "her participation in the shamanic pattern."[46] Historian Martha Nussbaum perceives Medea as a Maenad, with her "snakelike neck and loosened hair" and defines the central episode of Seneca's version of the play as "the long scene of incantation, in which Medea calls forth all the snakes on earth and in the heavens . . . (and) Out of their bodies she extracts poisons that contain 'hidden seeds of fire.'"[47]

Just as Cretan Ariadne gave Theseus the thread that would lead him out of the Minotaur's Labyrinth, Colchian Medea gave Jason herbs so potent that he was able to get around the giant snake or dragon who guarded her father's Golden Fleece. Strabo linked the myth of the Golden Fleece to the local (Caucasus) practice of panning for gold, wherein a sheep's fleece was dipped in the stream to catch the gold particles in the water.[48] But an equally likely connection with Medea is the one David Spess makes regarding the soma ceremony in which "a special ritual sieve is prepared specifically from the skin and wool removed from a sacrificial ram. This woolen sieve is used in certain parts of the soma ritual to separate liquid soma from its plant parts," in which "the woolen strainer turns a bright golden color when the juice passes through it."*[49] Medea, like the lineage of priestesses before and after her, probably functioned as brewer of this potent magical beverage, using her golden fleece.

Medea, we're told, left her home in Colchis with Jason. Herodotus (fifth century B.C.E.) gives us the unromanticized version of her story, saying that she was abducted like Helen of Troy as were so many royal women of the time. It is Euripides (fifth century B.C.E.), who first makes Medea into an impassioned murderer of her own children; from that time her story begins to include the theme of evil. Ovid connects her with incantatory spells (mantra) and gathering herbs in cemeteries, Seneca slanders her as the "Colchian slut," and Sophocles reports her "by moonlight howling," harvesting her deadly magic herbs. She is said to have regenerated a ram in her magical cauldron, and then to have done the same with Jason's father, but also that she used this magic to murder a rival king. In the final versions of her story, she helps her lover steal the Golden Fleece from her father, the king; kills her brother during their escape; and then—driven mad by jealousy toward her wayward husband, Jason—also kills her innocent children. This process of gradual demonization is a familiar one and part of so many of the transition tales (told by the victor over the vanquished) from around the world.

---

*"By means of this eternal fleece may Surya's Daughter purify Thy Soma that is foaming forth" (Griffith, 1973, Hymn I, line 6). And: "After the way of ancient time, this God, pressed out for Deities, Flows tawny to the straining-cloth" (Griffith, 1973, Hymn III, line 9). (Thanks to Dexter for these references from the Rg Veda.)

In cultures all across the Silk Road for many millennia, the women (like Medea) who performed shamanistic and funerary functions are pervasively documented in images, artifacts, mythologies, abiding traditions, and historical records. If indeed there was an historical Medea, not only was she *not* the murderer of her children, but she probably lived in the fourteenth century B.C.E. in Colchis near the Black Sea, perhaps traveling to northern Greece—to the "witches of Thessaly" renowned for their herbal magic—and to the Peloponnese, where a Cyclopean site named after her (Midea) was built next door to the citadels of Tiryns and Mycenae. Some versions of her story suggest she was the rightful heir to the throne of nearby Corinth and that the Corinthians killed her children to keep them from ascending to the throne.

I like to think she represents a female shamanistic lineage of queen-priestesses from Central Asia, some of whom went west to Turkey and the Greek Islands during the third and second millennia, whereas others went east along the Silk Road. (The Medes were supposedly named for Medea.) Her Goddess Hekate was worshipped with ritual offerings of food at crossroads, perhaps the source of similar practices among India's yoginis. The themes of dismemberment and regeneration in her story bear some resemblance to the tenth-century Tibetan yogini Machig Lapdrom's shamanistic Chöd ritual, wherein (in visualization) the Tibetan Black Dakini cuts off the top of your head, makes a skull-cup out of it, dismembers your body and puts it into the cup, then stirs it into nectar to be fed to demons, ghosts, and other hungry spirit beings. Chöd practitioners (who are reputed to be able to heal epidemics and raise the dead) are urged to practice in scary places like cemeteries and charnel grounds. Such regenerative magic belonged to the wise women of old.

Let's journey back to one of the earliest sites in northern Greece, Nea Nikomedeia, which happens to include the name of our heroine: Nea=new; Nike=victory; Medeia=wise woman.[50] The word *Nike* was a name given (much later) to female figures with a bent-knee dancing posture and wings on their feet that may relate to Tibetan dakinis or "sky-dancers." Perhaps it signifies an early ancestral lineage of shaman women with whom Medea shares a sacred office. Nea Nikomedeia was established around 5500 B.C.E. It is the site of the earliest known temple in Greece and one that may be a prototype of later ones in Crete and Mycenae.[51] Seals found there contain Old European script signs.[52] Other important finds include Bird Goddess sculptures, bird-shaped vases (a tradition still found in the Aegean islands several thousand years later), and large green stone ceremonial axes.[53] This temple building has been referred to as a "large house" of a chief, built to house servants of the "big man." However, as the name Nea Nikomedeia implies, it was much more likely built to house the core family of a lineage who were "members of a kin-related group descended from one female ancestor."[54] The women of the extended family would have maintained the temple-shrine, just as Greek Orthodox women still do today.*

THE ETERNAL POWER AND PRESTIGE OF GOLD

The issue of gold and precious metals must be addressed if we are to understand our Bronze and Iron Age shaman-priestesses. Indian and Tibetan texts mention a "Golden Race" living in the "Western Land of Women" and that "gold was sourced in the Upper Indus Valley."[55] The "golden" Goddess Hathor's ecstatic priestesses were connected to gold mines east of the Nile in the deserts and south into Nubia.[56] Gimbutas cautions that originally "copper and gold metallurgy was used for the manufacture of tools, ornaments, jewelry, and ritual equipment, not for weapons of war" and that "the Copper Age Goddess was the patroness of metallurgical crafts and mining."[57] Ivan Marazov describes gold as having the mythological function of "mediating between worlds,"[58] which would put it squarely in the realm of the female oracular priestess.

Perhaps it will be helpful in reconstructing Medea to go back to Varna, an Old European port on the western coast of the Black Sea

---

*A good deal of this material on Medea can also be found in the paper titled "Medea and the Shaman Women of the Silk Road" (publication forthcoming), which I delivered in Italy at the Bogliasco conference on the Black Sea flood, June 2002.

dating from the end of the fifth millennium and home to the earliest goldsmiths.[59] Varna was "an administrative, cult and trade center of a much larger territory" and a "big production centre for copper and gold articles."[60] The Varna burials are particularly interesting in their diversity, suggesting a mixed population that perhaps formed from population movements after the great flood. Gimbutas suggests that "Varna may have functioned as a center where different cultures came to exchange goods from their respective regions in a form of a free market."[61]

The curator of a Thracian exhibit and editor of the Italian publication *Glorie di Tracia* states that Indo-Europeans entered the territory at the end of the fifth millennium and "ancient Thrace perished in the flames of conflagrations and destructions."[62] He believes that although most of the inhabitants remained and "gradually fused with the strangers," some of the "victims tried to find a shelter down south and joined the centers of then-emerging Cretan-Mycenaean civilizations bringing along [their] own culture and traditions."[63] More gold objects were discovered in the Varna necropolis than "all the other contemporary gold objects put together from all over the world."[64] Gold ram's horn appliques filled a "symbolic grave" (that is, one having no corpse) at the center of the site, which included an "ax-scepter" as well. The scepters are terribly important, described by Marazov as the "earliest power insignia ever discovered in the Mediterranean world."[65] Round clay hieroglyphic tablets were also found in a Hotnitsa temple, similar to those found at a Danubian necropolis and settlement at Lake Dourankoulak. (In Crete, a round clay disc with hieroglyphics was found from the Bronze Age, which archaeologists and linguists have not been able to decipher so far. The famous Phaistos Disc is thought to have been brought to Crete from Anatolia, but could there also be a connection to Varna?)

Some of the burials have clay masks decorated with objects made of gold. The gold "mask burials" have the same attributes as the masks of female figurines found elsewhere in Karanovo cultures, "having round eyes and a long mouth with teeth . . . a diadem, and near the chin were hung round ornaments with a hole in the center and two eyes at the top."[66] Gimbutas identifies the mask deity represented at Varna as the White Goddess of Death and Regeneration, whom she links to the shape-shifting Baba Yaga.[67] Many gold "anthropomorphic amulets" almost identical to ones found later at Alaca Höyük, are found "only on the graves of women or in symbolic female burials." The amulets look like finger rings with breasts, described tactfully by one scholar as having "protruberances."[68] A necklace made of gold rings was found in the walls of a building painted red "which probably served a religious purpose." According to Marazov the necklace "probably belonged to a priestess in the temple of Hotnitsa."[69]

Although the various royal burials tend to be described in patriarchal terminology as housing powerful chieftains and rich kings or princes, whose graves are so legendary that they have been plundered from one end of the Silk Road to the other and all across time, the interesting thing about the gold is that it was so much more often used for women's items rather than men's. *Greek Gold* (Williams and Ogden, 1994), *Scythian Gold* (Reeder, 1999), *Ancient Gold: The Wealth of the Thracians* (Marazov, 1997)—these are the names of awesome exhibitions of gold artifacts that traveled to the United States during the last decade. What do they contain? Ritual artifacts and jewelry. Who used them? Women. Priestesses. Not exclusively, of course, but primarily.

Maikop is the name given to the site where the famous "royal burials" (third millennium B.C.E.) were discovered in the Kuban area of the northwest Caucasus and has been extended to describe Medea's whole region between the Black and Caspian Seas in the early Bronze Age. Offshoots of the Maikop culture persisted in the areas of modern Georgia (Colchis) throughout the second millennium B.C.E. (Medea's time and place).[70] Scholars see connections between Maikop and the Double Goddess site of Alaca Höyük in central Turkey (ca. 2500 B.C.E.), where "outstanding items of personal use" were most plentiful in women's tombs,[71] and five miniature sets of Double Goddesses were hammered out of gold.

Fig. 3.5. Five pairs of miniature Double Goddesses, exquisitely made of hammered gold, were unearthed from the "royal burials" at Alaca Höyük in central Anatolia (Turkey), dating to around 2300 B.C.E., the heyday of the legendary Amazons.

The unique miniature gold Double Goddesses were buried with a high-status woman. In her burial also were bronze standards or animal-style pole tops resembling Scythian ones from two thousand years later. This shaman-priestess was wearing a gold crown (diadem) and gold bracelets, and was buried with a large bronze "water mirror," identified by Jürgen Thimme as the prototype for the so-called "frying pans" found in Cycladic burials of the third millennium.[72] A mirror like this identifies her as a shaman priestess and would have been used for the "skrying" or gazing still performed by mirror women in Tibet, for whom "the mirror is where the deities of the seance reside . . . and where the spirit-medium's consciousness is kept while (she) is possessed by the deity."[73] European "witches" were burned during the Inquisition for their shamanic use of mirrors.

Fig. 3.6. Reindeer standard from Alaca Höyük, rich female burial of priestess or queen, 2300 B.C.E. Similar standards or pole tops excavated from female graves in the Altai Mountains are believed to be part of portable shrine wagons, probably for shamans (see fig. 3.21).

THE TRANCE-INDUCED STARE OF THE EYE GODDESS

Shamanic trance is the central feature of the healing practices found in Siberia and from there extending to other parts of the world. Goddess figures all over the Near and Middle East display the wide-open staring eyes of the shaman woman in trance, suggesting that trance can be considered a core feature of practitioners of the ancient Goddess religion.

At Tell Brak in northern Syria (bordering on ancient Turkey and northern Iraq), Professor M. E. L. Mallowan excavated a Halaf-period (sixth millennium B.C.E.) temple that was used for the next three thousand years, until the beginning of the Bronze Age. Thousands of small figurines with large staring almond-shaped eyes like the earlier life-size plaster statues at Ain Ghazal (see figs. 1.14 and 1.15 in chapter one) were found at this site, many of them merged Double Goddesses and some wearing tall pointed headdresses like those found in murals at Çatalhöyük.

The large staring eyes of these Eye Goddesses emphasize the trance function of the oracular priestess tradition all over the ancient world, carried on through various empires and religious traditions that supplanted the earlier ones. O.G.S. Crawford, in his book *The Eye Goddess*, links the Eye Goddesses of Tell Brak with the decorated skulls of Jericho (seventh millennium B.C.E.), with "objects from Lesbos" resembling "spectacle-idols," and the "face urns" of Troy (third millennium B.C.E.).[74]

Some of the Tell Brak Double Goddesses dating from around 3000 B.C.E. are mother and child, with a smaller version of themselves inside,

Fig. 3.7. These Double Eye Goddesses, one inside another, from the temple at Tell Brak in northern Syria, dating to around 3000 B.C.E., appear to represent mother and child, and perhaps refer to the matrilineal chains of descent described by Mary Kelly.

Fig. 3.8. The Double Eye Goddess on the left, from Tell Brak in northern Syria, resembles the Cycladic Double Goddesses, with one woman emerging out of the head of another. The temple of the Eye Goddess at Tell Brak was in continuous use for more than three thousand years. These Double Eye Goddesses (middle and right), from Tell Brak also, recall the Disc Goddesses from nearby Anatolia during the third millennium B.C.E. They represent the side-by-side, symbiotic Double Goddesses who share a body.

a type seen in later Bronze Age Disc Goddesses found in central Anatolian sites. At least one depicts a woman emerging out of another woman's head, as in the early murals from Çatalhöyük and those from the Cycladic Islands. Of the many sharing a body are these with two faces marked only by eyes, resembling the faces of owls. One wears a very strongly emphasized necklace, which Gimbutas always associates with the Bird Goddess seen all over Europe and the Mediterranean. An even more stylized pair has the same shapeless base with two round

"heads" having only a hole in the center of each—not even actual eyes! The resulting impression is that of a single abstract owl or being with two eyes created by the two heads. Another one, the most

Fig. 3.9. This very stylized Double Goddess from the Eye Goddess temple at Tell Brak in northern Syria, looking almost like an owl, dates from around 3000 B.C.E.

Fig. 3.10. This Double Eye Goddess from the temple at Tell Brak in northern Syria depicts two women sharing a necklace, one with a tall pointy conical "witch's" hat, dating to the early Bronze Age. Tell Brak was on the caravan route connecting the important cities of Anatolia with those farther east in India and China.

interesting for being slightly more elaborated, is one base or body surmounted by two heads, with one wearing a tall conical high hat, related to the oracular priestess tradition and female pointy hats found elsewhere. The two sets of eyebrows have no space in between them, creating one long meander (wavy line) above the eyes and causing the same impression of binding them together as we saw in the girdle of the figure from Çatalhöyük. Abstract as they are, with those odd eyes and their tall pointy hat, they look just like somebody's early idea of witches.

Tell Brak, a site on the trade routes between Anatolia, the Aegean Islands, and the Central Asian sites farther east, presents an intriguing mystery to scholars, as it seems likely that although related to Mesopotamia, it actually belonged to the enigmatic Hurrians (non–Indo-European, non–Semitic, Caucasian language family), who may or may not have originated from the steppes farther east.[75] The Hurrians are known from the rock art at the Hittite shrine of Yazikilaya, near Hattusas (the Hittite capital), where their Goddess Hepat leads a procession that includes a Double Goddess riding on Double Eagles (see fig. 4.17). Hurrians may be related to the Hyksos, also a mystery people, who occupied Egypt briefly during the second millennium B.C.E. and whose murals are linked to Minoan ones in Crete and Thera and include images of bull-leaping. Either or both Hurrians and Hyksos may may be related to the royal burials at Alaca Höyük in central Anatolia, where five miniature Double Goddesses were found from 2300 B.C.E. (see fig. 3.5) and which included the important burial of a woman with a portable shrine wagon (see fig. 3.6). The latest version of the Eye Temple at Tell Brak (eight hundred miles north of Uruk/Sumer) was built around 3000 B.C.E. (according to its excavator), but underneath it lay many earlier versions of the temple, always completely "filled solid with brickwork to make way for yet another temple."[76] Sumerian liturgy prescribed "the pouring of libations, milk and honey over the foundations of an older temple before its successor was built."[77] The inner wall of the temple was decorated with the red, white, and black rosettes with eight petals typical of the ancient Great Goddess, especially Sumerian Ishtar or Inanna. Rosettes are painted in murals at Knossos in Crete and crafted in gold on a woman's belt (or girdle) found in a burial at Midea in the Greek Peloponnese.

The late Bronze Age empire of Ugarit (Ras Shamra) on the coast of Syria is also linked to the Hurrians (Mitanni) from Tell Brak and is the source of one of our favorite Double Goddesses found at the Greek site of Mycenae (see fig. 2.8). Hurrian texts from Nuzi describe Hurrian queens as powerful and autonomous, owning property in their own right and running their own textile industries.[78] Like Tell Brak, Ugarit was occupied since the Neolithic period and was a "substantial town" by 3000 B.C.E., the time of our Syrian Double Bird Goddesses with their matching crowns (see fig. 4.7). During the Bronze Age, a walled town nearby held two palaces, "one belonging to the Queen of Ugarit," as well as ivory carving, quantities of gold and silver, and the fine purple-dyed linen and wool that made the Canaanites (Phoenicians) famous.[79] Another ivory carving found at Mycenae but made in Ugarit depicts a "War Goddess" wearing a boar's tusk helmet (see fig. 4.39) and holding sheaves of wheat like the Goddess at Mycenae (see fig. 4.32). The Ugarit Goddess is flanked by two goats like the Triangle (Goddess) depicted on a Canaanite goblet from Bronze Age Palestine (see fig. 0.6); she's dressed like earlier images of the Mesopotamian high priestess, Enheduanna, whose poetry in honor of the Goddess Ishtar is the first recorded (see page 123).

ISLAND SANCTUARIES OF THE AEGEAN

In the larger scheme of things, all the rampaging groups of wild, prophetic, and ecstatic shaman-priestesses can be seen as members of an ancient worldwide cult of the Goddess, left over from earlier earth-based, matristic civilizations that have broken down and migrated in every direction. Island civilizations—like those of Malta, the Cycladic Islands, Crete, and Cyprus—became the last strongholds of female-centered shamanistic Goddess rites during a time when mainland cultures were being decimated by violent intruders. It is most likely that Cycladic Islands, such as Keros, Naxos, and Delos, were major holy places very early in the Bronze Age (or even late Neolithic). They were at least partly populated by Karians (Carians) from the west coast of Anatolia who worshipped Hekate, mentioned as Medea's Goddess in the later mythologies.[80]

The early Bronze Age Cycladic islanders were astute seafarers and astronomers, having named the constellations of the zodiac by 3000 B.C.E. The Cycladic Islands exhibit a "most unambiguous picture of trade."[81] Artifacts and sculptures found in the Cycladic graves provide visual links and connections to both earlier and later Goddess cultures, from Europe and Anatolia to Central Asia and Tibet. Jürgen Thimme posits an Anatolian origin for the Cycladic Islands, the influence of which, besides Çatalhöyük and nearby Hacilar, would also include Tell Brak, where the amazing Double Eye Goddesses were found.[82] Certainly the unusual plank Double Goddesses found in Cyprus from the third millennium B.C.E. (see fig. 1.7) are visually somewhat similar to the tiny Eye Goddesses from so much earlier at Tell Brak. Equally convincing concrete visual and artifactual connections can be made with predynastic Egypt and ancient Sumer, and Marija Gimbutas noted that Cycladic figurines "have prototypes created three thousand years earlier for burials in southern and southeast Europe."[83]

The oracular shrine on Delos (birthplace of classical Greek twins Artemis and Apollo) was the sacred center of the circle of Cycladic

Islands that gave them their name. There, women were painting their faces and probably performing most (if not all) of the significant religious rituals, including the voicing of oracular prophesies and the facilitation of funerary rites. A Bronze Age shrine on the side of the mountain on Delos created from a natural formation in stone looks like a cave honoring a living Goddess. Cyclopean stones were laid to create a partial roof over the natural site, and an altar stone was set in front of the Goddess. Here the earliest oracles must have been given by shamanistic priestesses of Artemis.

Evidence of women's leadership in the third millennium B.C.E. is unequivocal, although often ignored. Many Cycladic female figures sit on intricately carved chairs, surely meant to represent their oracular seats of power, if not the thrones of temporal ruling queens. More burial goods are found in Cycladic female graves than male ones, clearly suggesting status,[84] and many more Cycladic "idols" are female than male.

The Cycladic Islands have large dance/ritual funerary platforms that have come to be generally equated with women's religious rites of dancing and excarnation, indicating connections to Çatalhöyük, where the vulture murals were painted and textiles found during excavations had been used for wrapping the bones of certain dead people.[85]

Fig. 3.11. This lovely Double Vessel from Tanagra, Greece, is what scholars call a pyxis, a box perceived to be for holding women's cosmetics, but generally found in burials or ritual contexts. Clearly connected with women's "cult ritual" during the Bronze Age, pyxides often held pigments, as well as ritual objects. This one is also beautifully painted.

Fig. 3.12. Like the hundreds of female figurines found there during the third millennium B.C.E., Double Vessels like this were created from the white marble that characterizes the Cycladic Islands. The vessels are marked with the spirals so central to the "language of the Goddess."

Archaeologists have unearthed female "cult" figures (some life-size), rock art showing known constellations, suspension beakers and cups for fermenting ritual beverages, and *pyxides,* special boxes often assumed to be for cosmetics that really must have been containers for ritual objects and pigments (some even look like temple or shrine models), similar to one from Tanagra, Greece. That the concept of the Double Goddess remained central for them can be seen in the numerous Double Vessels they used in their rituals, such as one with spirals incised all around and a miniature alabaster vessel stained with red ochre pigment, indicating its use by priestesses in religious ceremonies. Spirals and red ochre are linked to the ancient religion of the Goddess all over the world.

Fig. 3.13. This Double Vessel of alabaster, stained with red ochre, from the Cycladic Islands, third millennium B.C.E., is miniature in size. Carved of pure white marble, it was stained with red ochre, showing that it contained pigments utilized in ritual by priestesses who might have painted their bodies, faces, or some of the other figurines.

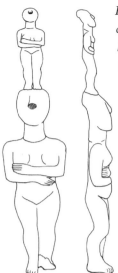

Fig. 3.14. This marble Cycladic Island Double Goddess shows one woman giving birth to a smaller one out of the top of her head, perhaps representing a female matrilineal tradition in the third millennium B.C.E. Several images of the vertical Double Goddess have been found in the Cycladic Islands, suggesting a precursor for the later (unconvincing) story of Athena being born out of her father, Zeus's, head.

The quirky vertical form of the Cycladic Double Goddesses—with one Goddess emerging out of another's head—was seen earlier at Çatalhöyük. Among the hundreds of individual examples, I know of at least three such figures like these made of the white alabaster marble of the Cyclades. Although many of them have strong angular shoulders and broad chests, these fine sculptural masterpieces are almost all female, with breasts and a clearly delineated pubic triangle, causing a certain consternation on the part of scholars. The angular, athletic look of these "butch" women may relate to a lineage of bull-leapers (discussed in chapter four) or experts in some other ritual game of the times.

Perhaps it is some early homophobic anxiety that created the late

Fig. 3.15. Double Goddess from Cycladic Islands in side-by-side type, third millennium B.C.E. These "butch" women of the third millennium could be evocations of horsewomen, athletes, or warrior women, like the heroic Amazons referred to in later legends and poetic narratives. Many Cycladic Goddess figures have an angular, athletic look, in distinct contrast to their rather more "femme" counterparts in other places.

and obviously compensatory myth of the Great Goddess Athena being born out of Zeus's head, the concept itself having come from these Double Goddesses, whose form may have signified that the matrilineal clan structure remained in place and that the chains of mothers and daughters, or the lineage of spiritual knowledge passed from priestess to priestess, had not been damaged. To this day the female chain or lineage is stressed by embroiderers who emphasize that "the knowledge of goddess imagery must be handed down from mother to daughter."[86]

The rich variety of Cycladic Goddess figures can be profoundly experienced by visiting the Goulandis Museum of Cycladic Art in Athens, where the majority of them are stored and brilliantly displayed. The imposing size of some of the "cult" figures (four feet high) is impressive. Their stiff angular quality—even the ones that are pregnant are not really round—led Gimbutas to refer to them as Death Goddesses ("stiff nudes"), although I believe they are just as likely to represent female shamans or meditation experts in the trance state known as samadhi. Some of the faces are marked with pigment, as if to suggest tattoos, which would fit with what we know of yoginis, shamans, and priestesses from other times and places. A few scholars concede that rather than dolls or toys, the "Cycladic idols serve the cult of the Great Goddess and Mother, the Queen of Heaven who descends to the underworld and from it ascends to new life, who possesses a daughter and is occasionally accompanied by musicians: such an interpretation . . . is in complete accord with all the different forms of the canonical idol known to date."[87]

MEDITERRANEAN "WILD WOMEN"

What we know about the flourishing Cycladic period (third millennium) is from burials, since settlements are so few and far between. But the later Bronze Age ruins of Akrotiri on the island of Santorini (ancient Thera) include murals from the second millennium B.C.E. showing high-status women in active positions of religious leadership, pointing to a sustained tradition even after the cultures of the Cycladic Islands receded. The female figurines, precious seal stones, gold rings, and fabulous lime-plaster murals of Crete and Santorini show bare-breasted, snake-handling, entranced women facilitating sacred rituals and ceremonies, wearing headdresses and elegant, probably silk, clothing. Chinese silk was found at Central Asian sites in Bactria (along the Silk Road) dating from 1500 B.C.E.,[88] and it's clear now that East and West were already connected by 2000 B.C.E. (Remember the seal stone with a Double Axe incised on it, discovered at a Central Asian Bronze Age site.) The women of Greece were spinning their own wild silk by at least the fourth century B.C.E. and probably much earlier.[89] Similar Bronze Age Egyptian murals in Minoan style found at the Hyksos capital at Avaris are connected to those in Crete and Thera from around the same time period.[90]

The wall paintings of Thera (ancient Santorini) were preserved intact from the seventeenth century B.C.E., when a violent volcanic eruption buried the town (or ceremonial center) under a layer of dust. In chapter two I discussed the Two Queens depicted in one of the most significant murals found at the site of Akrotiri (see fig. 2.10 in chapter two). In other murals from the site, beautiful women in a variety of clothing and ritual hairdos gather saffron on outdoor rocky hillsides, burn incense, and serve a Great Goddess of the Animals (Potnia Therion), shown seated on an elevated throne in the center of an important shrine with a live snake crawling over her hair, a peacock

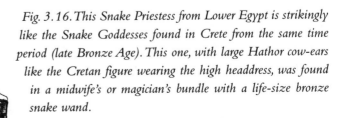

Fig. 3.16. This Snake Priestess from Lower Egypt is strikingly like the Snake Goddesses found in Crete from the same time period (late Bronze Age). This one, with large Hathor cow-ears like the Cretan figure wearing the high headdress, was found in a midwife's or magician's bundle with a life-size bronze snake wand.

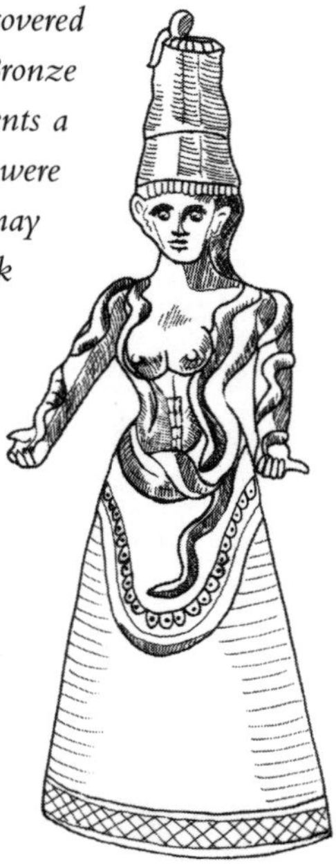

Fig. 3.17. This powerful Snake Goddess (or priestess) was discovered in "Temple Repositories" at Knossos, in Crete, from the late Bronze Age. She wears a high "polos" headdress and probably represents a snake-handling Maenad ("wild woman") whose ecstatic rites were later identified with the wine god Dionysus. Her cow ears may link her to the Egyptian Goddess Hathor as well as the Greek Goddess Hera.

griffin and a blue monkey flanking her.[91] An important tripod offering table (similar to those buried with priestesses all across Central Asia during the Iron Age) points to the presence of high-ranking women whose real titles (priestess, shaman, wise woman, queen) have been obscured by automatic labels of chieftain's wife or noblewoman.

Recorded descriptions of the Egyptian goddess Hathor's priestesses, "practitioners of the sacred arts," sound like they could be Cretan Maenads or Indian yoginis connected with "birthing, magical spells, amulets, and medical prescriptions" and being "called in to perform special incantations and dances, invoking the gods [*sic*] to ensure a safe and speedy delivery."[92] A priestess's tomb excavated from Deir el-Medina (contemporaneous with Bronze Age Minoan sites in Crete and Thera) revealed a midwife's kit with magical ivory knives "for protecting mother and child" and a wooden female figurine holding a bronze snake staff in each hand looking uncannily like one of

Fig. 3.18. This Egyptian mirror no doubt belonged to an oracular priestess of the Goddess Hathor, represented as a Heavenly Cow, whose face (with its exaggerated cow ears) can also be seen sculpted on pillars all over Egypt. Hathor was connected with women's sexuality, ecstatic rites, and birthing, and many of the mammisi (birthing houses) bear her name and her (frequently defaced) image.

the Cretan Snake Goddess figures from the same period and even sharing with her the cow ears of the bovine Hathor,[93] such as the ones on this Egyptian mirror.

Much textual and artifactual evidence points to a continuation of the female shamanistic religious rites throughout the Mycenaean period in Greece, even with the extreme male dominance and militarism that we know held sway over world events. These irrepressible female religious impulses descended through the centuries to unfold into the famous Mystery School of Demeter and Persephone at Eleusis and the powerful site of the Delphic Oracle, where they could still be found into classical times. Gimbutas asserts that the "matrilineal traditions remained strong" even after the arrival of the Indo-European Mycenaeans.[94] Even amongst the Mycenaean "warrior aristocracy," women held high status as shamans who facilitated the religious rituals and ceremonies of the tribe, a commonality between the invaders and the indigenous people that led to a continuation of the shared female-centered religion that had always been practiced by both.

A peculiar stylized Bird Goddess form unique to late Mycenaean sites, known as either *psi, phi,* or *tau* types (depending on which Greek letter it resembles), shows that female-centered religious or "cult" practices continued to exist there side by side with the domination of chieftains and the pervasiveness of war. The *phi* types have their arms close to their bodies, creating a round torso with a column rather than legs, like the

Fig. 3.19. This Double Goddess from Mycenaean Greece shows women made in the shape of the Greek letter, phi, *and belongs to a mass-produced tradition of late Bronze Age Greek Goddesses found by the thousands. Because they were frequently found in shrines, they are considered to be religious; but because they were also found in burials, especially graves of children, they are often referred to as toys.*

Greek letter *phi*, and some of these are merged at the torso like Siamese twins creating a Double Goddess. It's conceivable that many of these small Goddess figurines belonged to women brought to Mycenae from Crete, or from other places nearby, since slave lists from the written records at Mycenae in the thirteenth century B.C.E. document a predominance of women slaves brought from the west coast of Anatolia, where the Amazons once ruled.

On the island of Kea (ancient Keos, just offshore from mainland Greece), the largest temple in the Aegean area (R.L.N. Barber calls it "unparalleled") was built during the Mycenaean period (fifteenth to thirteenth centuries B.C.E.) with large platforms reminiscent of earlier Cycladic cemeteries where rituals were performed.[95] More than fifty unique (some life-size) terra-cotta figurines of dancing women wearing Cretan (Minoan-style) clothing present the most significant Bronze Age evidence yet for Maenads. The group of dancing women clearly expresses as a college of yoginis or ecstatic shaman priestesses. In keeping with what we know of the Maenads and their medicinal honey-fermented beverage,[96] archaeologists found a "predominance of drinking vessels throughout the history of the temple."[97]

The terra-cotta figures from Keos were destroyed in an earthquake that ruined the temple in the fourteenth century B.C.E. and again (after it was rebuilt) in the thirteenth. When excavators began working on the site, they found the head of a "deity" placed lovingly in a "ring-stand" used for worship by people during the eighth century (beginning of the archaic period, after the so-called Dark Ages in Greece). According to Mrs. Caskey (the wife of the excavator), who wrote the commentary: "When the terracotta head was first uncovered, the instant reaction of the excavators was that it represented Dionysos . . ." since a later temple from 500 B.C.E. had an inscription to that famous god of wine, women, and song. She goes on: "The discovery later that the head belonged to one of the [dancing female] statues . . . gave a different perspective to the problem."[98] In later times, as Olympian Greece is taking its patriarchal shape, the god Dionysos would frequently be associated with such a "striking array of dancing women, many of them characterized by the fullness of their breasts and by the wearing of garlands."[99]

Mrs. Caskey (and presumably the late John Caskey as well) believes epiphany to have been the purpose of the cult, which accords well with the religious practices in Crete. "The terracotta statues, in their postures of dancing or standing, appear to await or to celebrate an epiphany of the divinity they served . . . a perpetual liturgy, perhaps for the purpose of inducing the divinity to appear or to play a part in the celebration of the epiphany at the proper times."[100] Terra-cotta beehives were also produced on the island of Keos, suggesting that rather than the wine of Dionysos, the shaman women there were still domesticating bees and brewing their famous honey beverage even in the first millennium B.C.E.

ENHEDUANNA, THE SHAMAN-PRIESTESS OF INANNA

Just as we saw with the Eye Goddess temple in Tell Brak, Betty De Shong Meador points out that the "Neolithic Samarran/Ubaidian lineage (from the sixth millennium) continued directly into Sumerian culture."The Samarrans "used the ubiquitous, earth-hugging snake symbol in their iconography," as well as fabulous images of dancing (dakini) women twirling with their hair flying.[101]

The earliest Sumerian writing was used to create devotional hymns to the Goddess Inanna, narrating tales of her sacred sexuality and her descent and initiation through the aegis of her dark underworld sister, Ereshkigal. These Inanna stories have been central to feminist scholarship and revisioning of history and religion during the last thirty years. Inanna's epithets from the third millennium B.C.E. include "Princely Inanna," "Morning and Evening Inanna" (Inanna was interchangeable with the planet Venus), and "Inanna of the Steppes."[102] She was "guardian of the abundant harvest kept in the communal storehouse" at Uruk (the largest city in Mesopotamia, present-day Iraq), and she received different offerings presented to the different aspects of her divine Self.[103]

Meador, a Jungian scholar, has spent the last decade translating the poems of the Inanna priestess, Enheduanna, who lived in 2300 B.C.E., the period from which so much documentation exists to support the existence of Double Amazon Queens (the "warrior" and the "priestess"). Enheduanna, depicted in a flounced dress and high conical rolled-brimmed hat, represents the end of a long lineage of priestesses who presided over shamanistic rites for several millennia in the area of present-day Iraq. Her origins are bound up with saffron, as her powerful father, Sargon, was born in Saffron Town, where saffron was harvested, linking Enheduanna to the Minoan priestesses shown to be harvesting saffron in murals from Crete and Santorini. Sargon's mother was "a priestess who bore her child in secret" and put him in a basket on the water, to be raised by a gardener.[104]

Enheduanna "and the other en-priestesses were buried in a special cemetery beside the *gipar*" (storehouse and priestess residence building) in Ur. The cemetery was used over a long period of time as a place for communal festivals and funerary rites, just as in the Cycladic Islands. "Offerings of cheese, butter, dates, and oil were made to the dead en-priestesses. Some were worshiped in small shrines . . ."[105] On my first visit to the British Museum in London, I remember being very moved by the display of a High Priestess's gold headdress and jewelry from the famous burials at Ur. The headdress was dated to 2300 B.C.E. (the same date as the Double Axe seal stone found by Dr. Fredrik T. Hiebert at Anau). The elaborate headdress must have been worn by a priestess such as Enheduanna.

IRON AGE SHAMAN WOMEN

For the much later Iron Age nomadic Scythians and Saka tribes, "cemeteries were cultic sites" where religious rites were performed, as we saw earlier in the Cycladic Islands and other parts of Old Europe. And just as in those other cemeteries and tombs, "general tribal rites" were celebrated in Scythian cemeteries, where archaeologists found the usual evidence of "special sanctuaries in the form of raised platforms with ritual performances."[106] The gold-covered shaman-priestesses buried in Scythian sites with so much evidence of high rank within their tribes were surely the facilitators of the ritual performances.

"The religious leaders of the ancient nomads were almost always women" and "were considered among the elite."[107] Female "cultic" items (such as mirrors, special knives, combs, small boxes, portable altars, pots with pebbles, boar's tusks, gold, silver, and other valuable jewelry) are found throughout the ages and across the miles. Tiny gold female images identified as Maenads with their heads thrown back in ecstasy—exactly like those from Greece, Italy, and Thrace—have been found as far east as the Pazyryk burials in the Altai Mountains, which Davis-Kimball describes as having evidence of what she calls a "priestess cult." For example, a high-status Saka Ukok shaman-priestess unearthed from a frozen kurgan, with fantastical animal tattoos on her left arm and shoulder, wore an extremely tall headdress of felt on a wood frame, even more elaborate than the tall pointy headdresses on Goddesses in the murals at Çatalhöyük and Crete, on the sculptures at Tell Brak (see fig. 3.10), and elsewhere in the Aegean region. The amazing headdress was covered with numerous felines and birds crafted of wood and covered in gold, with a deer finial on a bronze pin placed at the very top.[108] A Scythian hat like this was recently excavated

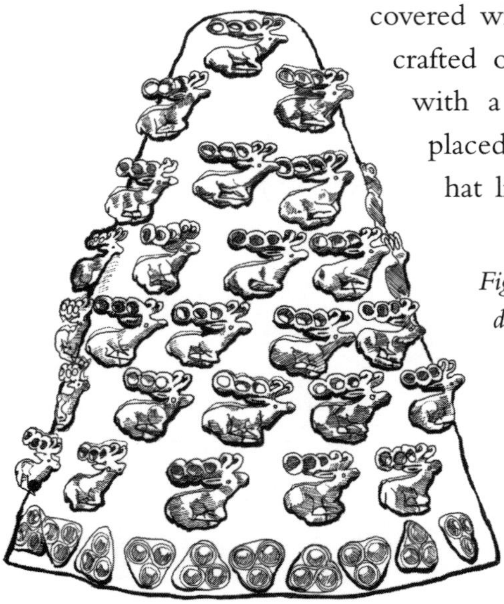

Fig. 3.20. This pointy conical felt headdress decorated with gold reindeer stags (linked by Russian archaeologists to a Siberian Mother Goddess), was found in the extra-high (four meters) burial mound of a high-status Scythian female (shaman-priestess) north of the Black Sea, dating to the late seventh or early sixth century B.C.E.

Fig. 3.21. This reindeer "jingling pole-top finial" with "bell-clapper" would have made sounds as the shrine wagon moved along. The reindeer matches those on the shaman-priestess's hat in fig. 3.20. Movable shrine wagons were buried blocking the entrances to women's tombs.

from a wealthy "special status female" grave in the Ukraine, along with a finial or poletop decorated with exactly the same animal. The remains of mobile shrine wagons upon which archaeologists think the finials were mounted have been found at the entrance to women's tombs; no doubt they belonged to nomadic shaman priestesses.

Davis-Kimball recounts the story of her exciting collaborative discovery of a young warrior-priestess (Amazon) from the burials at Pokrovka near the Kazakhstan border. The young woman was buried with an iron dagger and about forty bronze arrowheads, marking her as a young warrior woman. But there were also seashells (always buried with women, generally priestesses) with a white substance in one of them. The extremely large boar's tusk at her feet—the largest Davis-Kimball had ever seen—would have been "worn as an amulet, probably suspended from her waist on a leather cord . . . " indicating "her prowess as a warrior."[109] Similar large boar's tusks were found in central

Fig. 3.22. This beautiful boar's tusk necklace comes from a prehistoric settlement in northern Greece, dated to the early Bronze Age. Ancient women appreciated the beauty and strength of the crescent-shaped boar's tusk, working it into jewelry that was probably worn by high priestesses when performing religious rituals. In central Europe, the sacred boar's tusks have been found in stunning metal settings, showing signs of having been worn for long periods of time, perhaps at the waist.

Europe from the Bronze Age, a beautiful one from a woman's grave in France that was mounted in a frame of wire.[110] Another one from earlier in the Bronze Age, found in Germany, was mounted in a setting of bound wire "rather complicated and indicative of an advanced level of technical skill." The piece may have been worn for a long period of time (an heirloom?). It is assumed to have been worn at the waist, just as Davis-Kimball assumed the young warrior-priestess to have worn hers.[111]

A Thracian Maenad in a vase painting (depicting the legendary murder of Orpheus by the Maenads) has "a small stag tattooed on her forearm,"[112] corroborated by a "Scythian" (Saka) shaman priestess buried in the Ukok plateau whose "fantastical" deer tattoo was embellished with two griffin heads.[113] Priestesses in the Tarim Basin were also tattooed (blue spirals on the hands, crescent moons on the eyelids), concurring with historical reports of Maenads in Greece and Thrace.[114]

In Tuva (Siberia), homeland of the Finno-Ugrian peoples with a long history of female shamanism, archaeologists found bone female figurines and cult burials of ram's heads from the first millennium B.C.E.[115] Bone knives hung on women's costumes. This should remind us that although daggers are assumed to be male artifacts, they may more often than not have belonged to women, and these were perhaps the special type of knife called *kysmrk* or *kyssk dyakko* still in recent use by shaman women in Siberia for cutting the umbilical cord after childbirth.[116] The archaeologist Wooley unearthed a golden dagger from the burial of Queen Shubat, the owner of the incredible "jewels" and gold high priestess headdress on display in the British Museum mentioned above.[117]

Women in the Tuva burials wore clothing covered in precious beads and gold. Attached to the belts were bags containing "mirrors, combs, needles in cases [for acupuncture or tattooing?], bronze knives and awls." Some women had tall birch-bark hats and "wore high coiffures with iron or bronze, occasionally gold-covered, hairpins, necklaces made from beads of Mediterranean glass and semiprecious types of stone (amber, argillite) and gold pectorals."[118] Tuva shaman women today still use their mirrors for healing. A Pazyryk (Altai) priestess was found wearing a leopard-skin bag on her belt, linking back to leopard skins worn by Maenads as depicted on Greek vases.

A startling sculptural image of an Etruscan woman from 600 B.C.E. wears a high pointy hat and makes the hand "mudra," later known as the classical blessing pose of the Buddha. According to Buddhism, the historical Buddha (Sakyamuni) was born in northern India in the sixth century B.C.E. But there were no visual images made of him until much later, well after Alexander the Great went east with his armies and so-called "Hellenized" images began to appear. Everything about this Iron Age Etruscan woman is similar to the mostly male images of the Bodhisattvas of northern India that appear in the early part of the common era, suggesting a gradual transition from female spiritual authority to male. A young Tibetan friend of mine, Lama Tulku Thubten, says that there are images of Vajrayogini (the Queen of Tibetan Tantric Buddhism) that look just like the Etruscan figure.

As mysterious were the startling iconographic juxtapositions made on Etruscan stone-carved tomb monuments. An Iron Age Amazon is shown flanked by two griffins—the mythical bird-animals that flanked the throne at Knossos in Bronze Age Crete and were said to guard the gold of the Scythians. Other stones were carved with a gorgon flanked by the two griffins, linking the gorgon to the Amazons as I had always suspected. Gorgons are winged women in a

Fig. 3.23. This Cretan seal stone shows a Goddess with large horns and a Double Axe flanked by a pair of mythical winged griffins. Griffins have a long history of relationship to the Great Goddess, as protectors or guardians of the gold so loved by her devotees.

Fig. 3.24. This relief sculpture of griffins flanking the gorgon Medusa comes from an Etruscan tomb, dated to the fifth century B.C.E., from central Italy (Tuscany). Other reliefs include an Amazon warrior flanked by griffins, reiterating the graphic link I have been making between cultures as far apart as Italy, Greece, Turkey, the Balkans, and Central Asia as far east as Mongolia. Snake-haired Medusa-types have also been found in the high mountains of Bolivia at Tihuanaco, challenging antidiffusionist notions of cultural isolation.

bent-knee posture like Tibetan dakinis, suggesting dance or even flight or speed-walking (some with winged feet or shoes) like Indian yoginis. Their fangs are made from boar's tusks. Some gorgon faces look strikingly similar to the so-called ogresses in the narrative murals of the Ajanta Buddhist caves, and there is a bent-knee figure reminiscent of gorgons painted on a wall of the Buddhist monastery at Tabo (western Tibet).

Some of the monuments replaced both Amazon and gorgon with a simple vase in the center, establishing the interchangeability of all three—Amazon, gorgon, and vase. We already know vases to be anthropomorphic women. In the Tibetan practices I adapt for my Western women students, dakinis invoked from the five directions come carrying vases. In a kind of a visualized "soul retrieval," the dakinis gather and pour their precious elixirs into the top of the head and down into the heart center for healing, protection, transformation, and longevity. The

Fig. 3.25. This perfectly calibrated pair of female images was found in an Etruscan sanctuary, dated to the sixth century B.C.E., and graphically expresses the two types of sacred women (or two aspects of the sacred "feminine") through the visual representation of a Maenad (priestess) and a gorgon (warrior).

Black Dakini at the center of the practices is often depicted with a "grunting black pig's head" on top of her own head.

Etruscan female deities are also winged women, called variously "Lasa" or "Vanth." Etruscan priestesses are shown wearing gold crowns or diadems like the Scythian women from the Black Sea. A famous

Fig. 3.26. This Greek vase painting of an Amazon warrior and her counterpart, an ecstatic Maenad, perfectly expresses the underlying archetypes supporting what has come to be understood in modern terms as "butch" and "femme." Classical writers were threatened by such women, who refused to take husbands and who brazenly preferred one another's company over the company of men.

Etruscan tomb painting at Tarquinia depicts two Amazons driving a chariot pulled by four white horses (see fig. 4.40). At another Etruscan sanctuary, a Maenad and a gorgon are shown in perfect Double Queen juxtaposition by the artists. And on a Greek vase from the same period, an Amazon and a Maenad are similarly shown as a pair. A central Goddess of the Etruscans was Scylla, a woman with snakes for legs— there are numerous images of her in Italy. But what a surprise to find her on the gold objects of the Scythians near the Black Sea.

SCYTHIAN SHAMAN-PRIESTESSES AND TIBETAN DAKINIS: IS THERE A DIRECT CONNECTION?

A photo in the center of a book on the "royal" Scythians caught and held my attention more than twenty years ago.[119] The photo shows a female skeleton from a lavish burial north of the Black Sea in the fifth century B.C.E. She wears a tall gold crown (diadem) and is covered with small gold plaques that were once sewn on her clothing. She wears gold bracelets and rings, a gold "torc" (elaborate necklace) still rests around her neck, and there is a bowl near her head and a bronze mirror near her chest—sure signs, we now know, of a priestess.[120] Although described merely as a young Scythian woman, I always believed she was someone powerful in her own right—surely a queen or priestess—an intuition that has been borne out by recent archaeology.

A curious feature of the burial is that one of her legs was deliberately bent at the knee, which reminded me of Tibetan dakinis in their characteristic bent-knee dance posture. When I was privileged to accompany Jeannine Davis-Kimball to Russia in 1997 on an investigatory journey to visit museums along the Don and Volga Rivers, I took a color xerox of the photo with me as well as photos of dancing dakinis for comparison. I wondered if the priestesses from the southern Russia–Black Sea area might have performed some office as funerary shamans. I also wondered if their dances might connect them somehow to the dakini-witches I had read about in texts on pre-Buddhist Tibet or to the codified dakini practices that have filtered into the West today, transmitted by the diaspora of Tibetan lamas since China's invasion of Tibet in 1950. Russian-born Tibetologist George Roerich had "established that an ancient link existed between Tibet and the Scytho-Siberians of Inner Asia."[121] In the reports from Russian excavations of the "Amazons" (Sauromatians) buried along the Volga and Don Rivers, many of the female skeletons, whom Davis-Kimball identified as priestesses, were placed in this interesting position. By the end of our three-week trip, even the two archaeologists were calling it the "dakini pose."

In a cemetery near the Bronze Age site of Archanes, archaeologists unearthed a "larnax" or sarcophagus similar to the one found at Hagia Triada on Crete, a high priestess buried with her horse, an ivory-handled mirror, an ivory pyxis (box) inlaid with ivory figure-of-8 shields, large boar's tusks, lovely necklaces, and a portable altar. The bones of her horse and all the special artifacts that mark her high-ranking office are on display in the Heraklion Museum. Archanes is the earliest and most important of the peak sanctuaries that were established suddenly in Crete around 2000 B.C.E., at the same time the so-called palaces were begun, including the one at Knossos not far away. The cemetery of Phourni near Archanes is "the most impressive early second-millennium B.C. cemetery known on Crete," where several hieroglyphic seals were found, including one depicting a Double Axe.[122] The BMAC site, where the Double Axe seal stone 2300 B.C.E. was discovered, was abandoned in 1800 B.C.E. around the time of these burials in Crete, suggesting potential connections. This particular female burial is considered to be fairly late and probably belongs to a newcomer from the steppes (refugee? Amazon?).

It is in this cemetery that archaeologists have also found what they called a "house of the living," where people whom they assume to be "undertakers" lived for several hundred years and ran a wine press.[123] This could be an important link (among many) to Tibetan and Indian dakinis and yoginis of a later period, who tended to live and practice in cemeteries and charnel grounds. A suggestive inscription from

Gangadhar from 423 C.E. near where yogini temples were built links the place to ". . . female ghouls *(dakinis)* of the divine mothers *(matr)* who utter loud and tremendous shouts in joy, who stir up oceans with the mighty wind rising from the magic rites of their religion (tantra) . . ."[124] This is eerily similar to Medea's lines in Ovid, mentioned earlier in this chapter.

Chögyam Trungpa Rinpoche quotes texts on a ritual practice connected with the Tibetan Vajrayogini, variously called the "Co-Emergent Mother" and the "Great Queen of the Dakinis," who embodies the red element of fire or "psychic heat." One of Tibet's most important sky burial sites (predating Buddhism) is near a place with cave paintings and pits containing the mineral iron oxide (red ochre), a "sanctified substance" known as "the blood of Vajrayogini." Bellezza suggests: "Perhaps as cave painting developed, the red ochre from this mine was used as a ritual face paint and also valued as a medicine in Tibet."[125]

Vajrayogini *sadhanas* (ritual practices) contain a surprising number of motifs found in the Aegean religion facilitated by the yogic priestesses as depicted in the artifacts and murals of Crete and Thera (e.g., mandatory use of mantric formulas, conch shells, bread sculptures as offerings, mirrors, special vases, bowls, saffron, flowers, incense, lamps, feast food, necklaces, and jewels, "loosed hair," red powder, musical instruments, bone ornaments, silk scarves and clothing, and "amrita" to alter consciousness).[126] The text says that Vajrayogini's "terrifying cry 'cuts off the *klesas,'*" which refers to subjugating the "obscurations" or "defilements" of the ego, the neurotic or distorted emotions of our conditioned reality.[127] The powerful shouts point back to the Greek Maenads, who in the classical period were reported running barefoot up snowy mountainsides in wintertime, carrying torches and shouting their great invocational shout to arouse their god of ecstasy: "Evohe!"

It may seem far-fetched to connect Crete in the mid-second millennium B.C.E. with Tibetan Buddhist practices performed in the present day. But this is only because until recently historians did not take into account the profound importance of Central Asia to the unfolding events of history. It is "truly the 'missing link' in Eurasian and even world history."[128] It is now clear that the so-called Silk Road linked the Mediterranean with India and China for *at least* four thousand years, and one thing that stands out is the unique and enduring amalgam of the Afro-Eurasian female shaman priestess.

June Campbell reports that Bön (a pre-Buddhist shamanistic religion still practiced by some Tibetans today) was introduced into Tibet in the fifth century B.C.E., "when there occurred a mass migration of Iranians, from Sogdiana in north-east Iran, to the northern parts of Tibet."[129] This predates Tibetan Buddhism by more than a thousand years. The fifth century B.C.E. is also the date given for the birth of the Buddha himself, Sakyamuni, whose clan (the Saka) were an eastern part of the huge tribal confederation of Central Asian steppe peoples we have been discussing, including the Scythians, Sarmatians, Issyk, and Pazyryk in the Altai Mountains. When Buddhism entered Tibet, the Bön religion had to be "subdued" in order for the monasteries to be built and for Buddhism to become the state religion.

The circles of yoginis whose "songs of realization" led to the development of Tibetan Buddhist tantric practices[130] could be distant relatives of the circles of snake priestesses depicted in Old European artifacts from Romania (fifth millennium B.C.E.).[131] Rock art on cliff walls of the Tarim Basin, depicting what scholars believe to be a fertility ritual from the second millennium B.C.E., has been identified as belonging to Old European Cucuteni-Karanovo tribes once living near the Black Sea (see fig. 1.30 in chapter one). In village India, women designated as snake priestesses still tend shrines that are actively used to this day, and all over India women (who in so many other ways are clearly second-class citizens) still perform the ancient rituals of their ancestors—and perhaps our ancestors as well? Could a so-called winged Nike (or Victory) from Delphi have been informed by contact with the fleet-footed yoginis of the northern Indian state of Orissa? The griffins on a cauldron at Delphi suggest that such a link is not so far-fetched as we might once have thought.

When I perform my Tibetan Buddhist chanting practice in honor of Throma, the Black Dakini (Khrodi Kali), surely I am indebted to the ancient lineage of shaman women from as far back as the Paleolithic who have continued to express their ecstatic, visionary consciousness into contemporary times. Tulku Thubten Rinpoche, a popular Tibetan Buddhist reincarnated lama and teacher of Western students, translates Throma's name as "angry woman." How different is this from the *Random House Unabridged Dictionary*'s definition of *Maenad* as "any frenzied or raging woman"? This brings the scholarly investigation right into present-day political reality and allows for an immediate recognition of the connections between these ancient shamanistic women and the global resistance movement of contemporary women that we call feminism.

FOUR

Amazons in the Aegean and Beyond: A Bronze Age Female Lineage

On my first visit to the west coast of Turkey, taking a group of women "in search of Artemis and the Amazons," we were told by our Turkish tour guide at Ephesus that an Amazon Queen named Ephesia had founded the city around 2000 B.C.E. Before that, like other Westerners, I basically believed what I had read about the Amazons—that they were a "legendary" race of women who terrorized the Greek imagination to the point of obsession. Classical Greeks depicted Amazons more frequently than any other subject, never tiring of making images of these supposedly "mythical" women harking back to the Bronze ("Heroic") Age. The much-hated Amazons were the most popular subject of the Greek vase-painting period, and at least one far-flung fifth-century B.C.E. Greek vase depicting Amazons fighting Greeks has been

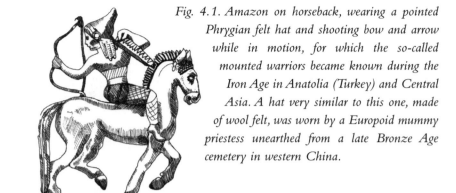

Fig. 4.1. Amazon on horseback, wearing a pointed Phrygian felt hat and shooting bow and arrow while in motion, for which the so-called mounted warriors became known during the Iron Age in Anatolia (Turkey) and Central Asia. A hat very similar to this one, made of wool felt, was worn by a Europoid mummy priestess unearthed from a late Bronze Age cemetery in western China.

unearthed from an Amazon's burial north of the Black Sea. The "Amazonamachy" (an epic visual narrative of Greeks fighting Amazons) took up one whole side of Athena's Parthenon on the Acropolis in Athens, and similar images were carved on the famous mausoleum at Hallicarnasus in Turkey (one of the Seven Wonders of the World). The friezes from the mausoleum, which can be seen today in the British Museum, were powerfully brought to life in Donna Read's award-winning documentary, *Goddess Remembered.* The "Tiryns Shield" shows Heracles stealing the Amazon's girdle, and Homer's *Iliad* states that Amazons were "men's equals."

Ephesus is the site of the famous temple of Artemis of the Thousand

Fig. 4.2. This fifth-century B.C.E. *Greek vase shows Greeks fighting Amazons, their most popular pictorial theme for several centuries of vase-painting and sculpture in relief. This vase shows a variety of fashionable costumes worn by the Amazons, including what look to be metal helmets, headscarves, and perhaps a felt pointed Phrygian-type hat, as well as armor and weapons (battle axes, spears, and bow and arrows), and Persian-style textiles.*

Fig. 4.3. This Greek vase in red-figure style, depicting Greeks fighting mounted Amazons, was unearthed from an Amazon grave in southern Russia, near Sea of Azov, dated to the early fourth century B.C.E. The burial was one of the "royal graves" of the Elizavetovskoye settlement, where the gold-covered, crowned priestess with the bent-knee posture (who first caught my attention in the late 1970s) originated.

Breasts, built in the fifth century B.C.E. Like the Hallicarnasus mausoleum, it is considered one of the Seven Wonders of the World. Tacitus related that Amazons started the custom of asylum there, "and mainly it served them."[1] "Amazons are noted in legends as founders of the shrine and as fugitives claiming its asylum."[2] To visit the Artemis temple at Ephesus today is an exercise in imagination, as only one pillar remains standing from the original structure (which was rebuilt several times over a period of centuries). At the top of the pillar, a pair of storks nest, and down below archaeologists continue excavating the site for posterity. Mainstream tours to Ephesus skip the place and whisk you past it to the Roman town of Ephesus, with its city streets, a library, and giant amphitheater. Our Goddess groups like to visit the site and do rituals around the ancient pillar. Amazons have been treated as a fantasy in the West, as if they erupted out of the collective imagination during the classical period. The truth is they are a remnant of much earlier female-centered cultures and represent the tragic end of a long and glorious her-story. "We may believe then that the tradition of the Amazons preserves memories of a time when women held the important place in state and religion in Aegean lands, and that they reflect the goddess of this civilization."[3] Although authors down through the centuries (beginning with Diodorus Siculus) have erroneously attributed the name Amazon to *a-mazos* ("without a breast"),

Fig. 4.4. Author photo of the temple of Artemis at Ephesus. Only one pillar remains of the ancient temple of Artemis at Ephesus—once one of the Seven Wonders of the World, and a haven of refuge for Amazons during the Bronze Age. A pair of storks nests at the top of the pillar, as archaeologists continue their work on the ground. The author takes groups of women to visit the Artemis temple where they like to do ritual, as in this photo of one such group on pilgrimage, encircling the ancient pillar in homage to Artemis and the Amazons.

referring to a custom of severing the right breast in order to facilitate shooting with a bow, there is no evidence for this. On the contrary, relief sculptures at Ephesus—the great site of Artemis-worship where Paul preached that women should be silent in church—depict Amazons carved with both breasts originally intact, but with the right breasts consistently hacked off of the sculptures by later antagonists. Jeannine Davis-Kimball states in her recent book, *Warrior Women*, that the word actually comes from a Proto-Indo-European term meaning "no-husband one."[4] The idea of autonomous women without husbands conjures up lesbian fears and goes a long way toward explaining the vit-riol with which the classical Greeks approached the Amazons. The implicit and ongoing nature of the threat remains within the suggestion that it could happen anywhere at any time when women rise up in their own defense: "The revolt of women is what transforms them into Amazons."[5]

THE TROJAN WOMEN

Like Ephesus and Sardis (the Lydian city later ruled by the famous Amazon Queen Omphale), the famed city of Troy was also most likely founded by an Amazon Queen. Greek commentators name the Amazon Queen Myrina as an "ancestress of the royal line of Troy,"[6] and according to Homer's *Iliad*, Myrina's tomb is somewhere near Troy.[7] The fabulous discoveries of Henry Schliemann—which he mistakenly believed to belong to the period of the Trojan War (1250 B.C.E.)—were misnamed "Priam's Treasure" for the recorded king of Troy. The artifacts actually come from a much earlier strata, belonging to Troy II, dated to the late third millennium. The jewelry from the Troy II level that Heinrich Schliemann excavated resembles that from Alaca Höyük's royal tombs of approximately the same time period. Troy in the third millennium was almost certainly female centered, with its thousands of spindle whorls, horse trappings, owl-faced pots with breasts, and Double Vessels, echoing those found in Malta, not to mention a mythological

Fig. 4.5. This Double Vessel, reminiscent of one found on the island of Malta dating a thousand years before (see fig. 4.6), is one of many found in early levels of Troy, dating to the third millennium B.C.E.

reputation for the powerful Trojan Women that continues all the way into the classical period.

The early Double Goddesses from the Neolithic period emerged out of nature-based and earth-based religious cultures with women (the Mothers) at the center, sharing power and passing on wisdom through the female lineage, the matrilineal chain of descent. The Amazons were a product of (and response to) male domination and the breakdown of the peaceful farming cultures of the Neolithic. Although we don't know exactly when the queens and shaman priestesses became the Amazon warriors of late legendary fame, there are stories that may mark the transition.

One such story is told about the women of Lemnos (an island off the coast of Troy) who murdered their husbands after the husbands came home with Thracian concubines (that is, slave women as booty) from one of their invasions. The people of Lemnos, an important site

Fig. 4.6. This Double Vessel comes from Malta, where an important Double Goddess was found (see fig. 2.4) near the Gigantija temples arranged in pairs in the shape of two women (Goddesses). The Maltese temples were built from the fifth to the fourth millennium B.C.E., *and this Double Vessel predates the many similar ones found in the Cycladic Islands, Troy, and central Anatolia during the third millennium* B.C.E.

since Neolithic times, supposedly claim their descent from the Amazon Queen Myrina.[8] Later, when Jason and the Argonauts stopped at Lemnos in their travels—according to the story by Apollonius Rhodius ("Argonautica")—they found the island "solely inhabited by women" who appeared in "battle array."[9] This would have been the fourteenth century B.C.E., about a century before the clash between the Mycenaeans and the Trojans took place. What else could this be describing but an army or tribe of Amazons (women without husbands)?

Records from Hittite texts as well as Mycenaean Linear B texts record enormously high counts of female captives brought from various places to be used as slaves, many of them royal women. Elizabeth Barber believes that such raiding practices went on even when there were no wars, because of the need for captive female labor for the mass production of woven cloth. "Being carried off was a constant hazard for women and children during Mycenaean times, especially for those living by the sea," and Lemnos is one of the places mentioned in the Mycenaean texts as a source for slave women.[10] Perhaps larger numbers than we know of such "slave" women rose up whenever they could and murdered the men who brought them home as booty from their wars, and these are remnant stories from that period.

If we investigate Lemnos from an earlier period, however, we find it occupied by powerful archers (the Amazons were considered some of the best!) clothed in marvelous gold jewelry and accessories. This early Bronze Age period—the middle of the third millennium B.C.E.—is famous for fabulous gold treasures found at both Troy and the town of Poliochni on the island of Lemnos.[11] Sixteen prehistoric sites are now known on Lemnos, two of them "almost on a par with Poliochni."[12] One such city, in fact, is named Myrina after the legendary Amazon Queen. Lemnos and Lesbos are both just off the coast near Troy and could be considered part of the confederation of tribes known as Trojan-Yortan. According to one story, Queen Myrina "sallied forth on a career of conquest with a female army of 30,000 infantry and 3,000 cavalry, armed with swords, spears and bows . . . Myrina led her forces through Egypt, Arabia, Syria and Asia Minor to islands of the Aegean Sea, among them Lesbos and Samothrace."[13]

Both Thermi on the island of Lesbos and Poliochni on Lemnos "seem to have been converted into citadels" at about same time as the beginnings of Troy in the third millennium.[14] At Poliochni (still the most impressive site of the period), stone-built walls were five meters high and had "slits for archers."[15] Amazons—whose Goddess was Artemis the archer—may have favored bows and arrows, as seen in later Sauromatian graves along the Don and Volga Rivers (sixth century B.C.E.). In fact scholars believe the name Sauromatian/Sarmatian means something related to "bow and arrows," probably "archer."[16] I'm sure it is no accident that the sixth-century poet Sappho lived on the island of Lesbos, which has been taken as the ancestral namesake of modern Lesbians—surely a tribe of Amazons or husbandless-ones.

There is evidence that powerfully points to a theacracy of women-centered (gynocentric) rule in the Aegean-Mediterranean area throughout the Bronze Age that simply refused to die, even near the end when warrior chiefs were beginning to establish the total male hegemony that would resurface even more powerfully during the classical period a thousand years later. Herodotus reported in his own time that the all-female Thesmophoria celebrations in classical Athens were based on an "extremely ancient festival" providing the "best evidence of pre-Olympian religiosity" from which "men were rigorously excluded." The festival, he said, had been brought to Greece originally by the Danaïds, those "husband-murdering sisters."[17] As the story goes, forty-nine of the fifty Danaïd sisters who were "forced into marriage, killed their husbands on their wedding night" with daggers given to them by their father. (The dagger, as we have seen, has been sacred to the female shaman since the earliest times.) The Danaïd who spared her husband supposedly "conceived by him the ruling dynasty of Argos," whose tribal name was Danaë, pointing to the "matrilineality of the pre-Hellenic settlers of the Peloponnese."[18] The name Danaë links as well to the Goddess Danu (or Donu), whose name blesses all the rivers pouring into the Black Sea in the area where Amazons are known to have lived.[19]

There are hints available to us that aggressive fighting women were not at this point considered to be lacking any of the beauty and allure of the feminine archetype in general. Famous Near Eastern War Goddesses such as Ishtar, Inanna, and Anath, whose reputations reached certainly as far as Crete, were credited with abundant and active sacred sexuality, as well as the capacity for bloodthirsty violence. This blood lust, of course, could be merely a demonization of their primal menstrual power as seen through the eyes of patriarchal scribes. But it also seems to present an integrated model of female power, which I believe must relate to the historical reality of active female resistance in those violent times that developed into armed priestesses who were determined to fight back to save their religion. "The Amazons, then, symbolize woman's desire for freedom."[20]

The final defeat of Troy is believed to have been executed from Mycenae in the middle of the thirteenth century, in which it would appear that even *royal* Trojan women were brought home as slaves and wives for the victors, if we can take seriously the classical plays of Euripides. In *The Trojan Women* and *Hecuba,* he shows us Hecuba, matriarch and queen of Troy, performing a revenge murder on the children of her son's murderer as the Trojan women are waiting to board Greek ships to be carried back to Mycenae. And the same playwright shows Clytemnestra, the wife of Agamemnon, murdering him and Cassandra, High Priestess of Troy, after Cassandra was brought home from the Trojan war as his trophy wife.

EARLY AMAZONS RULED IN DUAL QUEENSHIP

The first historian to mention the fact that the Amazons had "two queens at the same time," was Justinius, who discussed "two sisters . . . who held the government…"; many others have repeated this fact since.[21] In 1926, a Marxist historian named Emanuel Kantor published a book, *The Amazons: A Marxist Study*, in which he analyzed the Amazons as a resistance movement against violent male dominance. "Amazons . . . do not appear until barbarism is firmly established as a system. For it is from the disruption of primitive communist tribes which are on the point of becoming patriarchal in character . . . that they arise."[22] His understanding of their dual system of leadership is very insightful: "This society was ruled democratically by them through the mechanism of a peace 'queen' and a war 'queen,' who were in reality chiefs equivalent to the sachem and war-chief in an Iroquois gens or tribe."[23] This is especially interesting because the Tibetan monastic system is run in a similar way by two lamas whose functions differ, but who share the responsibility in a collaborative way. In his discussion of Tibetan leadership, Geoffrey Samuels mentions "the appointment of two persons, one lay and one monastic . . . the lay monastic relationship is a special case of the principle of division of responsibility."[24] And perhaps this custom relates back even farther to the birth of the Buddha, Siddhartha, and his two mothers. According to a short essay in *Tricycle* magazine, the mother of the Buddha, Maya, had a sister,

Pajapatai. Both were "married to Suddhodana, a chief of the shakyan clan, and went to live with him in the town of Kapilavatthu." Maya became pregnant first and gave birth to the "future Buddha," but she died seven days later, "whereupon Pajapati took Siddhartha and raised him as her own firstborn."[25]

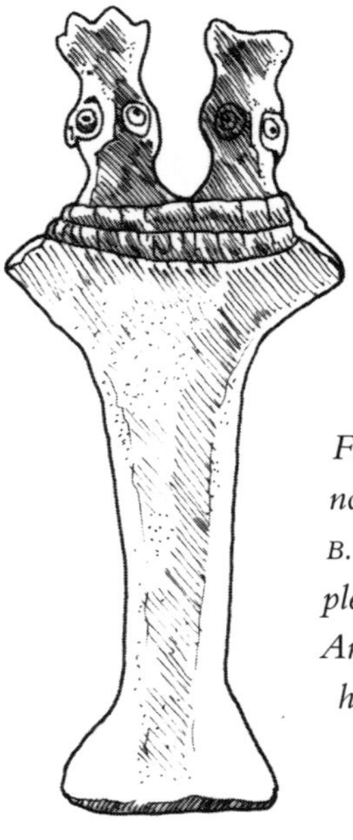

Fig. 4.7. This crowned Double Bird Goddess comes from northern Syria, dating to the early Bronze Age, around 3000 B.C.E. (same time as the nearby Tell Brak Eye Goddess temple). Perhaps the double figure is an early representation of Amazons ruling in Dual Queenship, as they were reported to have done. One of the queens would look after the domestic sphere; the other was a military queen, overseeing the warriors. Together, they shared the leadership.

Ancient gynocratic rule was represented by the marvelous cross-cultural amalgam of the Double Goddess, particularly as perceived in the Two Queens whose images are so especially widespread and diverse in the Bronze Age. Several Double Goddesses have been found in northern Syria (close to Turkey) dating to the early Bronze Age (3000 B.C.E.), one of which is especially significant for us, since both Goddesses wear crowns. I believe we must take seriously any images of two women shown sharing power during the Bronze Age period. If they are wearing crowns, gold diadems, or elaborate headdresses, they should at least theoretically be regarded as representing Amazon Queens (or queen priestesses), until proven otherwise. In this almost whimsical figure, the two Bird Goddesses are winged (rather than having arms) and share one body; they wear a large double-stranded necklace between them. Depicted as identical twins and sharing the power in a completely egalitarian way, they certainly fit the Amazon template of Dual Queens, one ruling military affairs and the other overseeing the domestic sphere. Perhaps their single body suggests a tribe or clan, in which they hold a shared office of leadership.

Although the Amazons of Anatolia (Turkey) are generally believed to have been Iron Age warriors, the actual heyday of the Amazon Queens who founded cities and truly ruled in tandem would most certainly have been in Anatolia during the middle of the third millennium. It is here that the largest number of Double Goddess figures are found in one place at one time (all the Disc Goddesses discussed in the last chapter), and it is here during the third millennium B.C.E. that a significant gap exists in the historical record so that no one really knows what happened. The "empires" and powerful kings that scholars are seeking are simply not to be found. The closest thing to a powerful kingdom would be the royal burials at Alaca Höyük, where miniature gold Double Goddesses were found in the rich grave of a female priestess discussed in the last chapter (see fig. 3.5).

The miniature gold Double Goddesses are highly stylized figures with arms that could be wings, their gender clearly marked by circles

Fig. 4.8. This photo was taken by my student Susan Zuern on a Goddess pilgrimage to Turkey, where we visited Bronze Age sites related to the Amazons. This restaurant sign depicting one of the gold Double Goddesses from Alaca Höyük demonstrates the way contemporary villagers relate to the ancient material.

cut out for breasts, and their heads shaped like anchors or shovels in the consistent style of other female figurines of the same time and place (ca. 2300 B.C.E.). One has gold breasts and wears gold boots. They also resemble the silver and gold ring amulets found all over Thrace, Anatolia, and Greece. The stylized pairs of women holding hands (with their forthright lesbian subtext) have so captivated the Turkish nation that single pairs can be found reproduced in a wide variety of expressions, from jewelry items to the photograph of a restaurant sign taken by one of the women on a recent tour that I led to the place. In the advertisement for the local Kibele Restaurant, the two Goddesses are identified as Kubaba and Kibele.

However, no settlements, towns, or castles have been found to explain these figures—only the graves of an elite group of horse-riding people from the steppes whose entry into Anatolia appears to have been peaceful and integrative with the indigenous Hatti. The peaceful Hatti

Fig. 4.9. The Hittites created this Double Sphinx Gate at the Anatolian site of Alaca Höyük (Turkey), which they occupied during the late second millennium B.C.E. A thousand years earlier, the site had belonged to the Hatti, indigenous non-Indo-European speakers.

(as well as the elite group buried in the shaft graves) predate the arrival of the Hittites by almost a thousand years, and even the Hittites appear to have absorbed the indigenous culture into their own religion and culture when they took over in the eighteenth century B.C.E. The Hittites may have absorbed their tradition of Double Queens from the Hatti or else borrowed from the neighboring non-Indo-European Hurrians, or both, since one Hittite king is known from inscriptions to have married a Hurrian queen who was also probably a priestess. A Double Bird Goddess vase (see fig. 1.1) was discovered at the late Bronze Age (second millennium B.C.E.) Hittite capital of Hattusas. Hittite records refer to the "chiefs" and "kings" of nearby tribes in the western part of Turkey, although a king from the north is explicitly referred to as ruling "after a time when . . . rule by a single man had not existed."[26]

The first king of Hattusas is described as violently seizing the place, then delivering up

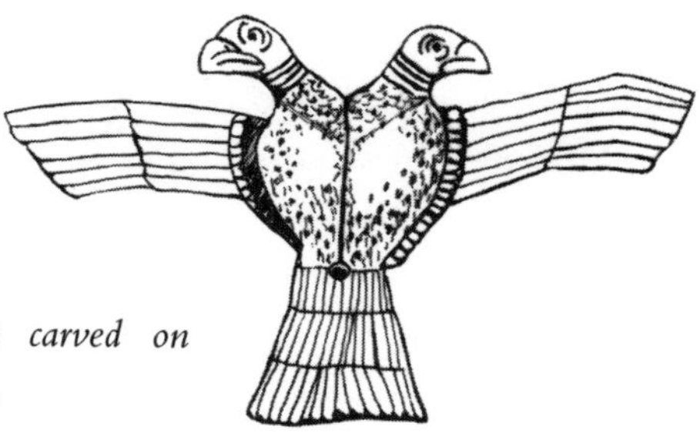

Fig. 4.10. Detail of Double Eagles carved on base of the Sphinx on the left in fig. 4.9.

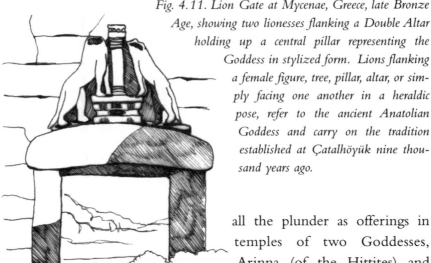

Fig. 4.11. Lion Gate at Mycenae, Greece, late Bronze Age, showing two lionesses flanking a Double Altar holding up a central pillar representing the Goddess in stylized form. Lions flanking a female figure, tree, pillar, altar, or simply facing one another in a heraldic pose, refer to the ancient Anatolian Goddess and carry on the tradition established at Çatalhöyük nine thousand years ago.

all the plunder as offerings in temples of two Goddesses, Arinna (of the Hittites) and Hepat (of the Hurrians), located in the upper part of the city.[27] The Hittites built a Lion Gate at Hattusas and a Sphinx Gate nearby at Alaca Höyük in the late Mycenaean period (fourteenth century B.C.E.), with a Double Eagle carved on one side. Like the famous Lion Gate at Mycenae the Hittite gates clearly carry on the old Anatolian tradition of the Goddess (as pillar in this case) with her flanking animals. This theme goes at least as far back as Çatalhöyük and the enthroned female ancestor so beautifully expressed there in sculpture and murals. There may some kind of ongoing link between Alaca Höyük (2300 B.C.E.), with its gold Double

Fig. 4.12. This Double Eagle necklace of gold comes from the royal shaft graves at Mycenae, dating to about 1700 B.C.E. The necklace was found in a shaft grave that held three men, but the image itself may represent the Double Goddess, as it is found in other contexts with two female deities.

Fig. 4.13. This gold signet ring showing Double Sphinxes (winged lion women with human faces), crowned and facing a Pillar Goddess in the center, was discovered at Mycenae in Greece, dating to the late Bronze Age.

Goddesses and the early shaft graves of Mycenae (seventeenth century B.C.E.), where a gold necklace of Double Eagles was found in a male grave as well as a gold sword hilt shaped as a Double Lioness (see fig. 2.7 in chapter two) presaging the Lion Gates. Similar images can be seen on a signet ring from Mycenae and a cauldron stand from Cyprus, both from the late Bronze Age. The Double Lioness image was also found at Harappa, India, dating to the third millennium B.C.E. All these doubles are echoed by later images from Thrace (Bulgaria), such as a small gold plaque of double Eagles shown in fig. 4.16 on page 150.

Impressive rock art in the

Fig. 4.14. This bronze-wheeled cauldron stand (or mobile shrine wagon?) from Cyprus, with detail showing two pairs of crowned sphinxes facing into central Goddess column, recalls the gold Mycenaean signet ring with crowned Double Sphinxes (see 4.13) from about the same time period (late Bronze Age). The cauldron, always of central importance in Bronze Age women's religion, is found in all the areas under discussion in this book and of course is archetypally linked with European witches from the Middle Ages.

Fig. 4.15. The Double Lionesses so often depicted as alter egos of the Great Mother, either flanking her image or facing one another in a heraldic formula, or facing out like this one, can be found all over the ancient world. This image comes from the Harappa culture, India, an impressive pre-Indo-European civilization (third millennium B.C.E.) with definite cultural contacts and exchange as far west as the Aegean.

Fig. 4.16. This gold pair of eagles, one of six appliqués for clothing, comes from Thrace (Bulgaria), dating to the fourth century B.C.E. The legendary tattooed Thracian women were still famous for their orgiastic rituals, even at this late date.

Fig. 4.17. This outdoor rock shrine at Yazilikaya, near the Hittite capital of Hattusas, was carved with elaborate processions of deities during the late second millennium B.C.E. One much-studied image of the Hurrian Goddess Hepat meeting the Hittite Storm God is shown here, with an interesting Double Goddess standing on the heads of Double Eagles.

open-air sanctuary of Yazilikaya near Hattusas clearly depicts two high-crowned queens standing on a double-headed eagle, suggesting a powerful correlation to the Dual Queenship of the Amazons. They stand behind a larger, even more important figure of a high-hatted queen, in a procession of male and female "deities" coming from two different directions, for a ceremony that one scholar recently described in a popular archaeological magazine as "Sacred Sex in the Hittite Temple of Yazilikaya."[28] The queen at the front of the female procession shown in the rock carvings is generally identified as the Hurrian (non-Indo-European) Goddess Hepat standing on her leopard.[29] Her son, depicted behind her, also stands on a leopard, emphasizing a matrilineal connection to his mother (rather than the lineage of his father, the Indo-European Hittite Storm God, shown on the left).

Hurrian literary works are archived at the Hittite capital, and a "strong Hurrian cultic/religious influence is also definitely perceptible . . . at the great open-air shrine of Yazilikaya," because of the "marriage of Hattusilis III to Pudehepa," a Hurrian queen.[30] Non-Indo-European Hurrian society had some interesting legal customs governing women, according to texts that discuss the "estates of queens, embracing whole villages, [that] appear to have had their own administration; the palace ran an extensive textile-production centre, staffed by slaves and female-palace servants."[31] The center of Tell Brak, where the Double Eye Goddesses (see figs. 3.7–3.10) were found, may have been Hurrian.[32] One fascinating custom recorded for the Hurrians is the "formal adoption of daughters, in the absence of male offspring, as 'sons' by their fathers. . . . In this position they could act legally like male heads of families: they arranged their own marriages; they cared for domestic gods which symbolized a family's identity; their husbands moved into the homes of their wives."[33]

This explains why Hittite queens had a special name (*tawanannas*) and ruled on their own power and not just because they were married to kings. "It appears that the position of *tawananna* was handed down separately from the kingship . . . (and) where the king's wife was not

Fig. 4.18. This vase in the shape of a boar comes from Hacilar (sixth millennium B.C.E.) and expresses a reverent attitude toward the wild pig, shown here with its tusks intact. In Chinese astrology, the boar is one of the most positive animal signs, known for its loving-kindness, sincerity, honesty, and resilience.

tawananna, she held instead the title of 'great princess.'"[34] The *tawananna* continued to rule after the death of a husband, and she often took part in governing the country. This may have been a vestige of "ancient matriarchy, later joined by marriage to an Indo-European system of kingship," or it may simply have been their "religious duties" originally belonging to a system of "brother-sister marriage within a closed royal family."[35] In one Hittite text, Hattusilis, the first king, is named "the Tawananna's brother's son."[36] This emphasis stresses *her* lineage, rather than his, and refers to the ancient widespread matrilineal custom of favoring the mother's brother. Significantly, the queens had special "*tawananna-seals*," in a completely different script from those of the kings.[37]

It is possible—even quite likely—that the Hatti represent a remnant of the earlier farming people who once settled at places like Çatalhöyük and nearby Hacilar, plus some admixture of Hurrian, and that the incoming Hittites

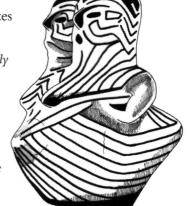

Fig. 4.19. This Double Goddess Vessel, which clearly means to represent two divine women—mothers, sisters, corulers, or lovers—hails from Neolithic Hacilar (a site near Çatalhöyük) and dates to the early Neolithic (sixth millennium B.C.E.). Perhaps the implied sexual preference in the name Amazon ("no-husband one") was already in place eight thousand years ago.

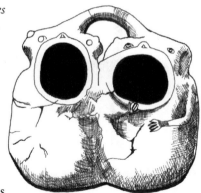

Fig. 4.20. This quirky Double Goddess takes the form of anthropomorphized animals, perhaps leopards, from Kültepe, Anatolia, dating to the late third or early second millennium B.C.E. Surely they must represent a tradition of vocal singing, similar to that found in the nearby Balkan region.

intermarried with their priestesses. We have discussed the Double Goddess images so pervasive at Çatalhöyük—one buried with the jaw of a wild boar, whose influence can be seen down through the millennia in faraway places like Crete and Malta. A painted ceramic pot from Hacilar in the form of two crowned women was unearthed from the sixth millennium. It could be a prototype for similar vessels made in Anatolia during the third millennium and even a double vessel from the Assyrian capital Kültepe (very early second millennium B.C.E.), in which the two Goddesses appear to be stylized leopards.

It is fitting somehow that the great Neolithic (matristic) centers of Çatalhöyük and Hacilar would have bequeathed to later descendants in the area the ancient and powerful legacy of the peaceful Double Goddess that represented female sovereignty (women sharing power) to be revisioned and upgraded to fit the unfortunate transition to a violent Bronze Age experience of the Goddess-worshipping people. Whatever the counterpart was originally to the domestic queen, it is in the Bronze Age that the military queen emerges and the concept of Amazon warrior women is born. They may not have been mythic (as in imaginary), but they were certainly larger than life!

MELLAART'S DOUBLE AMAZON QUEENS

The most explicit visual example of an early distinct pair of Amazon Queens turns out to be some "disappeared" figurines from a place called Dorak in the northwest near matriarchal Troy, belonging to the "dimly-known" Yortan culture. The figurines were shown to James Mellaart in 1958 by a woman from Izmir (ancient Smyrna, a city founded by Amazons), along with daggers, bracelets, and a "delicately wrought" gold cup (all items that show up in later female Mycenaean graves). According to his story, she let him sketch images of the figurines, which were presented in a 1967 *Horizon* magazine article telling the story of his being shown the objects, then being accused of forgery or fraud when he couldn't later produce them, and what the authors and editors of the magazine believed to be a deliberate "frame-up" done to him.[38]

The figurines were never seen again, but his sketches are profoundly significant in the context of our Dual Queenship investigation, and it's very unlikely he could have invented them. Along with the artifacts, he was shown photos of two skeletons from two royal tombs unearthed in a neighboring district to Troy. Mellaart dated his missing figurines to approximately 2500 B.C.E., a time from which almost no

Fig. 4.21. These unique Trojan-Yortan figures from northwest Turkey, dating to the third millennium B.C.E., may be an overt representation of Amazons ruling in Dual Queenship. One figure of gold (electrum) holds her breasts, while the other of silver (an attendant or coruler?) holds a horsewhip and something that appears to be a musical instrument. Sketched by James Mellaart.

habitation sites have yet been found in the Yortan area of Turkey to elaborate on what was found in the burials. He felt he had been shown, in the Dorak treasure, evidence of a "large seafaring nation, ruled by a warrior aristocracy, immediately east of Troy."[39] The two figurines he sketched may represent high-status queens in a confederacy of Anatolian tribes that worked gold, wove cloth, and bred and trained horses.

The Yortan cemetery on the mainland had a "lifespan of well over 1000 years," with a "striking absence of metal weapons in Yortan tombs."[40] Their burials included razors with spiral tips, whose purpose is undetermined, but may very well be connected with the art of tattooing, which would link the women to ecstatic Bronze Age priestesses of the Cycladic Islands from the same period, as well as the later Iron Age Maenads, Etruscans, and Amazons (including the nomadic Pazyryks of the Altai Mountains). Mellaart describes the Yortan figure on the right as a "Goddess." She is made of gold—actually electrum, a combination of silver and gold—and wears the high "polos" hat that represents both spiritual and political authority, with her long hair bound in a single braid down the middle of her back. Her hands cup her breasts in what has become a universalized Goddess gesture, particularly in similar Ishtar, Inanna, and Astarte figures. He calls the other figure made of silver with a pillbox hat and long hair one of "her attendants." (Why not her sister? Lover? Coruler?) Significantly, the main "attendant" (there was at least one other similar one, with her hands behind her back) holds in her left hand a gold-covered horsewhip strikingly similar to the type found in "wealthy female" Scythian and Saka graves of the first millennium B.C.E. unearthed in the Ukraine and Kazakhstan.[41]

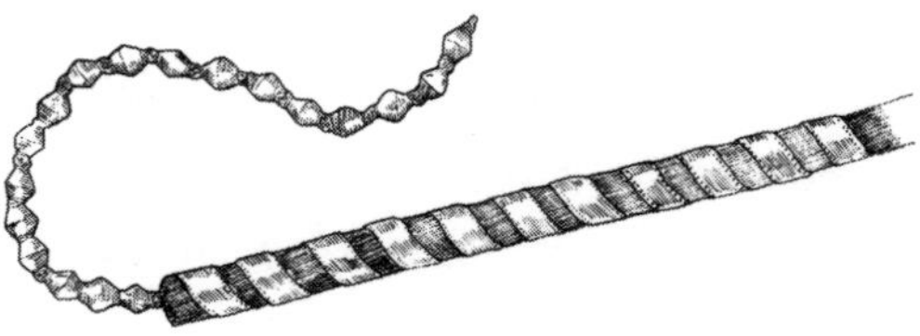

Fig. 4.22. This whip was wound with gold and buried with a Scythian woman (priestess) north of the Black Sea during the fifth century B.C.E. It is similar to the sketched whip held in the hand of the Trojan-Yortan figurine from third millennium B.C.E. (see fig. 4.21).

The two figures wear similar gold belts (Amazon girdles?) engraved with flowers (the ubiquitous rosettes). The horse-woman's belt holds in place a kind of apron or loincloth, and the other wears a string-skirt engraved onto the figurine. The loincloth and belt bear a strong resemblance to the codpiece outfits worn by both men and women for bull-leaping ceremonies in Crete, which are frequently depicted in frescoes and sculptures of that island (see figs. 4.28 and 4.29). The belt with dangly attachments might have produced a tinkling sound, as was true with many of the later Scythian women's gold ornaments. A gold belt not unlike these is displayed in a central case in the Mycenaean room in the Athens archaeological museum, where it appears to have had similar tassels hanging from it, recalling tasseled belts described by Homer as being worn by Goddesses. Another gold belt with rosettes was found, tellingly, in the graves near fourteenth century Midea (possibly named for our heroine, Medea).

THE AMAZONS ENTER HISTORY

At some point during the Bronze or Iron Age, women definitely began to fight battles and even lead armies into war. Jessica Amanda Salmonson, in her *Encyclopedia of Amazons*, describes Bronze Age Penthesilea as "coruler of Amazonia with her sister . . . Hippolyte,"[42] and Antiope as "Queen of the Amazons when Theseus attacked their nation" before she murdered him with "her two-headed ax drawn."[43] Emmanuel Kantor, a Marxist scholar writing in 1926, was apparently correct in reporting that, "They [Scythian Amazons] had two queens, Marpesia and Lambedo, who being considerable for their wealth and power, divided their troops into two bodies, carrying on war and defending their frontiers by turn, and to produce the greater authority for their victories they gave out that they were the daughters of Mars."[44] Amazons down through the ages continued to be "martial by nature, skilled with weapons and/or hand-to-hand combat."[45]

Herodotus tells a harrowing story about Tomyris, "queen of the

Fig. 4.23. Scythian woman's fez-style hat, attached to gold diadem, covered with seventy-six gold ornaments, fifth century B.C.E. Also buried with this woman was a conical woolen hat-headdress, covered with gold gorgons and rosettes, and a pair of woolen shoes decorated with gold plaques.

Massagetae," one of the tribes in the great Saka confederation covering a vast steppe territory all the way from Thrace to Siberia.[46] The Saka are the people who built the frozen Pazyryk Tombs in Siberia, whose famous contents on display in the Hermitage Museum in St. Petersburg corroborate Herodotus's descriptions of their "head-dresses, girdles and bands decorated with gold," like the fez-style hat pictured here. When Cyrus the Great of Persia asked for the hand of Tomyris, she knew he wanted only her "dominions" and refused him. After he attacked and murdered her son, her army, under her command, destroyed the Persian army and killed Cyrus. After the battle she ordered a search for his body, and when it was found, she "flung his severed head into a skin which she had filled with human blood," in revenge for the death of her son.[47]

We're explicitly told that Penthesilea and her troops provided aid in the Trojan War, so that obviously, by the time of late Mycenaean Greece, Amazon warriors had definitely emerged. Strabo describes a battle in which Amazon armies came all the way to Athens and sacked the Acropolis, because Hercules had abducted Queen Hippolyte. Her sister Antiope brought an army to retrieve her, and according to one version of the story, they held the Acropolis for seven months. This would explain why the classical Greeks were obsessed with depicting the battle between themselves and the Amazons, who directly threatened their own hegemony. Amazon tombs at the foot of the Acropolis in Athens and at other sites along the route, as well as four hundred black-figure vases painted with this theme, suggest the story may be true. The

Roman historian, Justinius, tells a version of the story in which Hercules took Menalippe and Theseus her sister Hippolyta. Another version says that Hippolyta, leading the survivors home in defeat, died of grief in Megara, where her tomb there is shaped like the Double Crescent shields of the Amazons[48] depicted in relief sculptures of Amazons that can be seen in the museum at Ephesus.

It is essential to remember that historians who wrote about the Amazons, beginning with the Homeric epics and continuing with Herodotus in the fifth century B.C.E., were often narrating events that had taken place much earlier—sometimes as many as two thousand years before their lifetimes. This is why so many of the stories have a mythic or legendary quality. From the particular time of the Amazon Queens' active real existence, there is unfortunately no writing to document their lives. The scripts from that time period (such as Linear A or the hieroglyphics on the Phaistos Disc) are all extinct or have not yet been deciphered, and therefore we are required to use artifactual and iconographic evidence to read the history of the time.

A ceramic Double Goddess from Bronze Age Anatolia, for example, has heads shaped as if wearing squared-off hats or headdresses of some kind, reminiscent of the fez-type hats depicted on some earlier figurines from the Neolithic culture in Greece. It is heavily marked with what Gimbutas called the

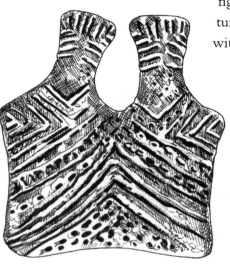

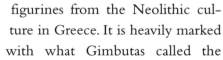

Fig. 4.24. This inscribed Anatolian Double Goddess, made of clay, dates to around 2600 B.C.E. from somewhere in central Turkey, a time when Amazon Queens were founding cities and ruling in Dual Queenship. Marija Gimbutas thought this Double Goddess represented "two divine sisters, and not necessarily mother and daughter."[49]

"language of the Goddess," an ancient visual script found on thousands of figurines and pots in Old Europe. This particular Double Goddess is abstract, flat, and slightly geometric, with what might be called honeycomb patterns as part of a huge chevron that links the two bodies together the way a girdle or belt might. Although the exact area where this Double Goddess comes from is unknown, it is from the late third millennium in Turkey, which is where the Amazon Queens may have made one of their strongest stands. In around 2150 B.C.E., the whole place was burned to the ground by invading patriarchal hordes, and anyone not murdered or enslaved almost certainly fled, perhaps migrating to the islands like Crete, whose female-centered culture received a creative influx at that time.

DESTRUCTION ON THE MAINLAND AND MIGRATION TO THE ISLANDS

The terrible mainland destructions of 2150 B.C.E. erased the history of Anatolian cities as well as important Greek sites such as Lerna, with its beautiful House of Tiles. The House of Tiles was actually a temple and well remembered by the next generation who settled there and lovingly buried the structure under a mound, as if it were a beloved ancestor. The famous seal stones of Lerna disappeared, but may be precursors of those found in sites along the Silk Road beginning around the time of the destruction. The BMAC seal stone featured in the *New York Times* piece mentioned in chapter one is an example, with its important Double Axe sign. The production of seal stones on the island of Crete begins just after 2000 B.C.E., suggesting a migration there as well.

As Josie Blok, author of *The Early Amazons: Modern and Ancient Perspectives on a Persistent Myth*, points out: "The Amazons are localized wherever there was a cult of the ancient Mother-Goddess; where that cult was connected, as it regularly was, with a social and political organization of matriarchal type; where women were not only mothers and nurses, but warriors and chieftains as well. The matriarchal stratum and

Fig. 4.25. This Snake Goddess (or priestess) from Crete, dating to the late Bronze Age, is shown clearly handling live snakes. She has large staring trancelike eyes and a Cretan wild cat on her head. The Snake Priestess figurines were sealed in a stone pit under the floor by the earthquake that devastated Crete in the early second millennium B.C.E.

the cult of the Mother Goddess are very ancient in Asia Minor…"[50] But Amazons in Crete? By the end of her career, Gimbutas was certain that Crete was a theacracy of priestesses residing in ceremonial centers (called "palaces" by scholars). Let's look at some of the evidence for the presence of Amazon Queens (and perhaps even women warriors) during the Minoan-Mycenaean period of the second millennium B.C.E.

There are many so-far-undeciphered clues pointing to the rule of Amazon Queens in Crete. Even the Minoan mythology focuses somewhat on the two daughters of Minos, Ariadne ("shining one") and her sister Pasiphae, whose coupling with a bull supposedly gave birth to the Minotaur in the Labyrinth. The famous bare-breasted faience Snake Goddesses trapped under the floor stones near the throne room (in the earthquake of 1700 B.C.E.) take the form of two basic types (although at least three figurines were actually found and are on display in the museum at

Fig. 4.26. This figure-of-8 shield is one of a series depicted in a wall mural at Knossos, Crete, and very similar to those found at Mycenae, in the late Bronze Age. The shield, helmet, and possibly breastplate were considered symbols of the Goddess, usually identified as Athene or as her nonfigurative manifestation, according to scholars such as Cretan archaeologist Stylanos Alexiou.

Fig. 4.27. This Shield Goddess flanked by two worshipping priestesses, from a wall plaque at late Bronze Age Mycenae, is known as the "Palladion," relating to Pallas Athene. A portable altar, like those found earlier in Crete and later in Russian and Central Asian Amazon burials, can be seen nearby. Figure-of-8 shields, crafted as beads or as decorative elements on jewelry and furniture, were found in women's tombs (such as Archanes in Crete) and indicate priestesses who served this Goddess.

Heraklion). Figure-of-8 shields, painted in murals at Knossos, show up a little later in Mycenaean frescoes identified as the Goddess Athene in her war aspect being worshipped by two priestesses with a Double Axe nearby.

Women Taking the Bull by the Horns

Besides the religious power of the priestess, it seems clear that women in Crete and other Bronze Age centers held religious status derived from (or supported by) bull-leaping and a general athletic prowess of the physical body, as well as horse-training and perhaps battle courage. When Sir Arthur Evans excavated the "palace" of Knossos, he was so enthralled with his own ideas about the place (taken from Homer's epics) that he went way beyond the bounds of what is considered appropriate reconstruction in the field of archaeology today. One of the

Fig. 4.28. This figure from the "palace" at Knossos in Crete was part of an elaborate restoration performed by the excavator, Sir Arthur Evans, in the early part of the twentieth century. He mistakenly imagined (and reconstructed) this personage as a great Priest-King, called the Prince of the Lilies, an epithet that has been called into serious question now that some scholars believe this to be a girl bull-leaper!

frescoes that he restored—and perhaps altered significantly—is the so-called Priest King that he believed to be an image of a young (mythical) King Minos. Although the image is unarguably beautiful, its identification as a king or god is problematic and has been "on good grounds . . . totally rejected."[51]

Mark Cameron instead ("cautiously") suggests that the figure depicts a "girl bull-leaper, striding along in some procession in honour of the goddess of ritual games, or the goddess herself in the role of 'Mistress of the Games.'"[52] The white-skinned bull-leaper (labeled "priest king") should have been identified as female in the first place to be consistent with the convention used in Aegean fresco-painting that depicts men in terra-cotta (red-brown) and women in white. Perhaps because she's portrayed as such a totally different type of woman from the priestesses with their open bodices and voluptuous exposed breasts, she is essentially not even recognized. She's what, in modern lesbian parlance, might be described as "butch." She's a jock, an athlete, an Amazon. She's prepared to risk her life, "taking the bull by the horns" and leaping over its head and onto its back while it is moving.

The female bull-leapers in the main bull-leaping fresco from Knossos (in which one man, clearly painted in brown, and two women in white are shown) wear the same arm bands and bracelets that we saw on Mellaart's Trojan-Yortan figurines from the mainland. There are other images of bull-leaping women from Knossos, and similar frescoes

Fig. 4.29. Bull-leapers from a mural at Knossos in Bronze Age Crete include two women in white and one man in brown, following the painting convention popular in the Aegean area. One of the women is actively "taking the bull by the horns," while the man is depicted in the act of leaping over the bull's back.

at Tiryns showing women in the process of their amazing acrobatics over the bull's back. A bronze sculpture from the sixteenth century B.C.E. shows a bull-leaper similarly in the process of hand-springing onto the bull's back. The leaper, described as "he" in photo captions, is caught in a beautiful moving backward arc, hands still on the horns of the bull while "his" long hair touches the bull's forehead. The only thing is, "he" appears to have breasts, which in the athletic pose are deemphasized and therefore, apparently, unnoticed.[53]

Bull-leaping took place in the central courtyards of the temple-palaces, and some scholars think bullfighting traditions might all derive from Minoan bull games, although it doesn't appear that the bulls were sacrificed in Crete before Mycenaean times (ca. 1400 B.C.E.). The bull-leaping sport must have grown up out of a deep, visceral connectedness to these animals that were some of the earliest domesticates; in India the cattle are still sacred and adorned for ritual events. There is a fantastic wall mural at Çatalhöyük ("Cattle Hill") showing a larger-than-life (mythic) bull, perhaps the earliest version of the Dionysus archetype, around which men in animal skins and naked women dance and cavort

Fig. 4.30. Author photo of the Horns of Consecration, Palace of Knossos, Bronze Age Crete. These Horns of Consecration were restored by Sir Arthur Evans at the beginning of the twentieth century. Similar horns are believed to have adorned the rooftops of the "palace" (or ceremonial center) and to have been aligned with mountaintops in the distance. The horned animals—both male and female—were significant to the ancient religion of the Goddess, as can be seen in Crete by the cow-eared priestesses and the legends of the "minotaur," or bull-headed man, who lived in the labyrinth.

with a Mother Goddess at the center. Certainly a people who domesticated cattle would have an understanding of the power of fertility, the means of reproduction, and the sheer physical force of the bull. The so-called Horns of Consecration honoring the bovine deities (male and female) are ubiquitous at Knossos, adorning the roofs of buildings and carved from huge standing stones.

Fig. 4.31. Two lesser known images from either end of the sarcophagus found at the site of Hagia Triada showing "high-ranking females" driving chariots. On the left, the Two Queens drive an ox-hide chariot pulled by griffins. On the right, they drive an ox-hide chariot pulled by horses.

Chariots Driven by Pairs of Amazon Queens

The most telling evidence comes from the south of the island and a sarcophagus ("larnax") discovered at Hagia Triada, a site near Phaistos where the famous disc was found. The long panels on either side of the fifteenth-century sarcophagus have been much discussed by scholars and apparently portray a funerary ceremony over which priestesses preside; it may include the first instance of a bull sacrifice seen in Crete. A Double Axe on a tall stand is central to the tableau. What hasn't been discussed by scholars are the two narrow ends of the box, which are painted with clear images of pairs of queens driving chariots made of patterned ox or cowhide, just like figure-of-8 shields, with equal-armed four-spoked wheels. Ox-hide chariots are mentioned in Homer's epics and are rare and extremely special in murals as far as I know. To have these images of the famed chariots, "the occupants of which are high-ranked women,"[54] and then not to find it noteworthy shows a staggering lack of general scholarly interest in the roles of women.

One pair of queens holds the reins to a pair of magical winged griffins who are pulling their chariot, and one of these queens wears a high, narrow, pointed conical hat, reminding us of a European witch. The other pair holds double reins to a pair of horses, and one of them carries a whip wrapped with gold—the kind held in the hand of the Yortan figure (2300 B.C.E.) and buried with high-status steppe women almost two thousand years later (see fig. 4.22).

AMAZONS IN THE GREEK ARGOLID: THE WARRIOR GODDESS EMERGES

Let's look at the connections between the two chariot-driving queens with the griffins on the Hagia Triada sarcophagus (see fig. 4.31), one of whom wears a high, pointed, conical, wide-brimmed hat, and the so-called Goddess with the Sheaves from "The Room of the Frescoes" in Mycenae. The second queen in the image on the sarcophagus wears a flatter ceremonial hat identical to that worn by the two female personages in a fresco at Pylos (near Mycenae and from the same time) referred to as the "White Goddess" and "her Priestess." The seated

Fig. 4.32. In an image reminiscent of the Amazons from the Hagia Triada sarcophagus (see fig. 4.31), this late Bronze Age Mycenaean mural, called "The Goddess with the Sheaves," was found in the important "Room of the Frescoes." It shows a female figure wearing a headdress with horns that ends in a tall, conical point and an animal skin tied over her shoulder; she holds up sheaves of grain in a concentrated ritual gesture.

Goddess with the Sheaves wears an animal skin over her dress (later associated with Greek Maenads) and a tall pointed headdress like the queen driving the chariot in Crete. Two life-sized women stand behind or above her, facing each other and wearing two different types of dress (one a Minoan flounced skirt, the other a blue straight dress with tassels and fringed borders), and they hold respectively *a scepter* and "*a big sword* with its midrib pointing downward" [my italics]. One Greek scholar, interpreting the Mycenaean scene as a Double Goddess, perfectly expresses the theme of the Amazon warrior and priestess queens associated with their two "different types or aspects of the female divinity—a warlike goddess associated with the sword and a fertility goddess in the woman with the sheaves."[55]

It is also in Mycenae that the Shield Goddess, Athene, comes into her own. The Shield Goddess motif is "not merely decorative amulets, but . . . also a kind of emblem, denoting a priestess who served the goddess with that shield"[56] (see fig. 4.26). She appears on a gold signet

Fig. 4.33. A Cretan-inspired gold signet ring, from late Bronze Age Mycenae, shows a seated Goddess with three poppies under a sacred tree, with a Double Axe and two priestesses (the Two Ladies) performing ritual. In the background a Shield Goddess floats as if overlooking the whole scene, suggesting this may be a ritual to Athena.

ring, floating above a scene of worship. In the "Palladion," a fresco found at the Cult Center of Mycenae, the shield in the center is identified as an image of the War Goddess, with her two priestesses on either side (see fig. 4.27), and is considered a precursor of the later Greek Athena; many frescoes depicting such shields are found in Minoan-Mycenaean sites. A frieze of shields (the Shield Fresco) at nearby Tiryns "must be interpreted as a 'special symbol of the Goddess of War, worshipped in the Cult Centre, a protective emblem of the State.'"[57]

Also from Tiryns, along with a number of exceptionally beautiful Goddess figurines, is a large wall painting of two pairs of Amazons driving chariots toward one another. The fresco, which can be seen in the National Museum in Athens, is related conceptually to the sarcophagus at Hagia Triada, with its two pairs of Amazons (or Double Queens) driving their chariots toward each other from opposite directions. In the Tiryns fresco, the central scene toward which the chariots are arriving involves a cow or bull (in preparation for bull-games?). One particularly interesting motif is the women's hairstyles, which are almost completely identical to the hairstyles worn by the female bull-leapers

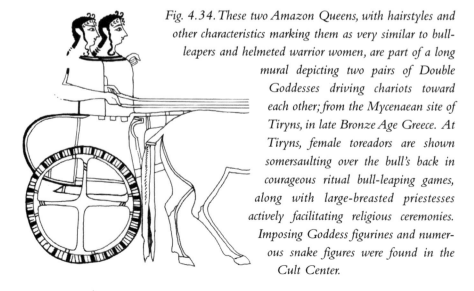

Fig. 4.34. These two Amazon Queens, with hairstyles and other characteristics marking them as very similar to bull-leapers and helmeted warrior women, are part of a long mural depicting two pairs of Double Goddesses driving chariots toward each other; from the Mycenaean site of Tiryns, in late Bronze Age Greece. At Tiryns, female toreadors are shown somersaulting over the bull's back in courageous ritual bull-leaping games, along with large-breasted priestesses actively facilitating religious ceremonies. Imposing Goddess figurines and numerous snake figures were found in the Cult Center.

Fig. 4.35. An intricately carved seal stone from Mycenae (mainland Greece) shows a helmeted priestess, naked from the waist up, wearing a flounced Minoan-type costume, raising a sword (or possibly a staff) over her head in what looks distinctly like an African dance. As such, she is likely a representation of the Goddess Athene, whose antecedents go back to North Africa and the predynastic Egyptian Goddess Neith.

in earlier frescoes from Knossos (see fig. 4.29), with fringed bangs and long locks of wavy hair hanging down on the sides in front of the ears. The only noticeable difference is that the queens in the chariot have the rest of their long hair pulled back into a tail and bound with cloth or rings, whereas the bull-leaper's long wavy hair is loose in back.

Mycenaean seal stones carved with battle and hunting scenes came *not only* from men's graves, as one might expect, but from the burials of women and children. Some were found in the awesome "Women's Tomb" (Shaft Grave III) with the three royal women and their golden Amazon girdles, "the women's most famous treasure, their golden belt of queenship."[58] In a display case in the Mycenaean room of the Athens

Fig. 4.36. This seal stone from Knossos, Crete, depicts a Minoan War Goddess (or her armed priestess) raising a sword over her head, possibly in a ceremonial dance. She appears to also carry a large snake, which is wrapped around her body, marking her as one of the famous Maenads ("mad women") who performed various magical feats, such as handling venomous snakes and walking on hot coals.

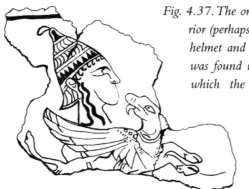

Fig. 4.37. The only for-certain female image of a warrior (perhaps Athena) wearing a famed boar's tusk helmet and carrying a griffin, this unique mural was found in the same Mycenaean temple from which the "Palladion" (see fig. 4.27) was unearthed, dating to the late second millennium B.C.E.

National Museum, one can see a tiny Mycenaean seal stone carved with the figure of a helmeted, bare-breasted priestess wearing a fluted or feathered skirt and holding up a sword (or possibly a staff) over her head in a ritual dance that looks African. A very similar seal stone from Knossos depicts a Minoan War Goddess raising a sword over her head.

A most incredible fresco from the Cult Center at Mycenae shows a female warrior wearing a boar's tusk helmet and carrying a miniature griffin with wings. The boar's tusk helmets are famous from Homer's stories of Bronze Age Greek warriors who wore them in hunting and battle; several are preserved in museum displays and always assumed to belong to men. As we have seen, a long history of the boar's tusk as a female adornment and status symbol precedes the invention of the helmets for use in battle. The helmeted woman with the griffin has been

Fig. 4.38. The boar's tusk helmet, from the late Bronze Age, mentioned by Homer, is usually assumed to be the prerogative of male warriors. But boar's tusks have been found buried with an important woman at Çatalhöyük (seventh millennium B.C.E.) and also with Russian Amazons near the Black Sea (fifth century B.C.E.), and the helmet can also be seen depicted on Bronze Age Goddess images from Mycenae and Syria.

Fig. 4.39. This War Goddess flanked by goats is wearing a boar's tusk helmet, a fluted Minoan-type skirt, and carrying sheaves of wheat, like the "Goddess with the Sheaves" from Mycenae (see fig. 4.32). She is one of several similar figures, carved of ivory, from Ugarit (Ras Shamra), Syria, dating to the late Bronze Age. (This particular figure was actually found at the site of Mycenae.)

interpreted variously as a war deity and a priestess. Under her helmet, she wears a hairstyle almost identical to many of the queens and priestesses we've already discussed, such as the Tiryns Amazons (see fig. 4.34) driving the chariot—except that instead of one long wavy lock hanging down on each side, the warrior figure has two. We know none of the motifs painted and sculpted by these ancient ritualistic people was accidental, so the confluence of these motifs is significant. The priestesses, queens, bull-leapers, and warriors, at least in some instances, wear the same intentional (ritual?) hairstyle.

An ivory figure from Ugarit (Ras Shamra) on the west coast of Syria from the Mycenaean period depicts a Goddess in a fluted skirt wearing a boar's tusk helmet, flanked by two goats. She could represent the Goddess Anath, a slightly different version of the Greek Athene, who expressed love and war (evening and morning star), and she carries wheat as in the Mycenaean fresco, "Goddess with the Sheaves." The wealthy Syrian city of Ugarit was destroyed in 1200 B.C.E. when the whole Minoan-Mycenaean period came to an end with strong earthquakes and massive invasions. Although in the past scholars have blamed the "Sea Peoples" for the defeat of all the major empires of the day, it is not clear who they were, and perhaps the destruction was the result, more loosely, of pirates or "runaway peasants and outlaws banding together to form marauding groups of bandits . . . symptomatic of an underlying, long-term, socio-economic malaise."[59] Whatever the causes, they managed to destroy the Hittites, Egyptians, Mycenaeans, and the people of Ugarit—everyone in the Mediterranean. The destruction was followed by four hundred years of Dark Ages in Greece.

Remnants of our Double Queens can be seen later in Italy and Greece, however, and the presence of the Amazons seems assured in the first millennium B.C.E. even before the life of Herodotus, who documented so many of their customs and traditions in the fifth century B.C.E. A well-known fresco from an Etruscan tomb of the eighth century B.C.E. in Tarquinia distinctly shows (what commentaries describe as) two Iron Age Amazons driving a chariot wildly pulled by four horses. A wonderful Greek vase from Eleusis (site of the Eleusinian Mysteries) shows two Amazons in a chariot (the original Demeter and Persephone?), along with a male musician playing an instrument, pulled by four winged black horses, in front of which, striding toward them, is the huntress Goddess Artemis, holding a stag by the antlers. Artemis

Fig. 4.40. Two Iron Age Amazons are shown driving a chariot pulled by four horses in this tomb painting from Tarquinia, an Etruscan site from the eighth century B.C.E. The Etruscans are thought by linguists to be related to the earlier Lemnian women, famed for killing their husbands and perhaps living as an all-female (warrior) tribe; their interesting script also links to Nordic runes.

Fig. 4.41. What a composite narrative this is: Two Amazon Queens, accompanied by a male musician, drive a chariot pulled by four winged horses, in front of which the huntress Goddess Artemis faces them, with bow and arrows, holding out a stag (her mythic alter ego) in front of her. A griffin, a falcon, and a series of water birds adorn the image, along with many familiar signs of the Old European script. From Eleusis, Iron Age.

wears a crown or diadem exactly replicated on the heads of the two Amazon Queens, although her hairstyle is slightly different.

Given the extraordinary number of visual representations of Amazons fighting during the Greek classical period, as well as the mention of Amazons by name in Homer's *Iliad* and *Odyssey* (two epics that although written in the eighth century, are believed to be describing the late Bronze Age period in which the Hagia Triada sarcophagus was made, around 1400 B.C.E.), it seems quite astonishing that these images of women brandishing swords and driving chariots haven't rung any bells with scholars. Since the male warriors painted on walls or vases, or featured in "heroic" stories, are treated as having really existed, why have we been so slow to believe in the reality of the women warriors? Imagine what we might learn from a full investigation of archaeological sites if one were looking for Amazons in the way that Heinrich Schliemann once went looking for Homer's Troy.

It's not that I think women in Medea's time—fourteenth century

B.C.E.—were still holding their ancient power as ruling queens governing their societies. Clearly the balance of power had shifted to a structure of male dominance by this time almost everywhere in the ancient Western world. Homer's tales make it clear that the Goddess Athena was even adopted by the "heroes" as their patron and guide, and this could partly explain her visible significance during the Mycenaean period. But the presence of so much female imagery, some of them shaman-priestesses and others warrior queens, tells us that the women of the late Bronze Age—even if they were royal women brought as booty from other places—continued to express their ancient customs of Goddess worship and personal sovereignty.

Artemis and Athena

The ancient (non-Greek) Artemis—Goddess of the Mountain and Lady of the Beasts—comes from Anatolia, where her origins are possibly much older. We've seen that her roots go back to the Paleolithic era (thirty thousand years ago) and to original Siberian shamanism, which was linked with the female collective and connected to Ursa Major—Arktos, the Great Bear—perceived as Artemis herself.[60] Certainly at some point the ancient Artemis became more personalized as the Greek Artemis, huntress, midwife, and Goddess of the Amazons. Armed with a bow and arrow, and traveling with her colleges of nymphs, the Greek Artemis roamed the forests and wild places, disdaining the company of men. In some ways, she sounds eerily similar to later tales of Indian tantric yoginis with matted, uncombed hair, wandering in wild places with their Chöd drums and bells, performing their meditations and rituals in caves, cemeteries, and charnel grounds, and meeting together in nocturnal congresses and women-only gatherings outside the boundaries of civilized society.

Southwestern Turkey is covered with ruined temples to Artemis from the period of Greek colonization, built on sites of even earlier temples to the Great Goddess. The latest Ephesus temple had a horseshoe-shaped altar, and a temple of Hestia near the "town hall" was adorned with a mosaic "composed of Amazon shields and whirls," plus several beautiful statues of Artemis Ephesia (the founder of the city), one of which was found by the excavators buried tenderly under the soil of one of the rooms in the temple.[61] Many (perhaps most) of the ruined temples of the period displayed friezes of Amazons fighting Greeks, and the Artemis temple at Didyma (the name itself means "twins") displayed two winged gorgons from the sixth century B.C.E., one at each end of the pediment, and "two splendid female heads" from a century later.[62]

The Goddess Athena was a "direct descendant of the Minoan palace goddess," and "the distant heir of Old Europe" (with her attributes of bird and snake). Gimbutas noted that her town, Athens ("Athenai"), is a pre-Greek name.[63] MacKenzie said Athena's "8-form shield" was from North Africa and belonged to the Great Mother, Neith, and her "fatherless son," signifying her parthenogenic status and matrilineal

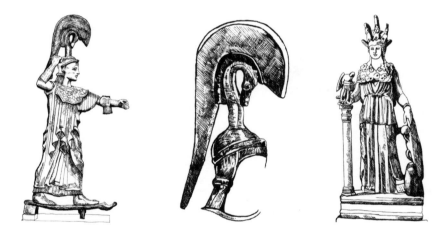

Fig. 4.42. Greek Athena. The Greek image of Athena in horse helmet and warrior posture, shows her in her martial aspect as head of state in Athens in the 5th century B.C.E. The central image shows a Greek horse helmet in more detail. The image on the right shows Athena as a representative of oracular healing and female snake power. In that guise she is related to her Trojan sister, Cassandra. Athena's small temple on the Acropolis, the Erechtheum, had maiden columns holding up the roof and a special pit for the live python to whom recorded offerings were brought.

tradition.[64] And Kerényi connects Athena to Ares, the Greek god of war from whom Amazons claimed to be descended. In a typical doubling motif, the classical Greeks worshipped the warlike Athena, who was (paradoxically) chosen over Poseidon as ruler of Athens because of her olive branch of peace (and the olive fruit itself, according to Miriam Robbins Dexter).[65] Her marvelous statues after the sixth century B.C.E. show her in horse helmet, with owls, snakes, and shields, often taking aim at her enemy with a sword or spear. Even as late as the classical period in Greece, Athena Parthenos ("maiden") was the religious head of state.

AMAZON HOARDS IN BRONZE AGE EUROPE?

Further evidence of the connection between Neolithic Goddess worship and the Amazons of the late Bronze Age can be seen in Goddess representations found buried in Amazon "hoards." According to Pliny it was the Bronze Age Amazon Queen Penthesilea who first invented the Double Axe, which can't be literally true, since the axe appears (also as butterfly and hourglass) so much earlier. But perhaps she developed the axe into a battle-axe, initiating the Amazon epoch when women began to fight back during the Bronze Age of armed priestesses. The ubiquitousness of the Double Axe—from Africa, the Greek mainland,

Fig. 4.43. These Double Axes are worn by oracular priestesses of Yoruba deity Shango, whose consort is Oya, the Great Goddess of change. African scholars link the Double Axe to earlier symbols of the thunderbolt, but these female figures are Yoruba priestesses in trance states performing the function of an oracle (a psychic or visionary, whose mediumistic abilities allow her to receive and transmit messages from the beyond).

the Aegean Islands, Anatolia (greater Turkey), and Thrace (greater Bulgaria)—provides a visual motif that functions as a code for Amazon women and the serious ongoing resistance to patriarchy that they continuously demonstrated over the course of at least three millennia.

In some stories Penthesilea—the Amazon Queen who came with her army of women warriors to fight with the Trojans against the Greeks—is said to have come from Thrace (Bulgaria). (In other stories she hails from North Africa.) One author quoting from classical writers reports that carrying her Double Axe, Penthesilea fought at Troy with her "twelve warriors,"[66] which is significant in regard to a postcard I received from Turkey (provenance unknown) that shows a helmeted Amazon in the center with twelve others holding shields beside her (caption reads: "Artemis and 12 'gods'").

Amazons are consistently described as calling themselves "daughters of Ares (or Mars)," and "[s]tarting with Homer, they (written sources) considered Thrace the birthplace of Ares."[67] Furthermore, the astrological sign for Aries (ruled by Mars) is the ram's horns (which also looks like a uterus and fallopian tubes). Small ram's horns made of gold and sewn onto clothing were part of the original treasure trove in the ancient symbolic burials found at Varna on the Black Sea coast from seven thousand years ago; and they were still present in the much later Amazon graves along the Volga River (fifth century B.C.E.). Famous gold hoards, such as the Vulchitrun treasure found in Thrace, dating to the mid-second millennium B.C.E. (late Bronze Age) "demonstrate not only the considerable sophistication of their work, but also their knowledge of the techniques and styles of their contemporaries from Central Europe to Asia Minor to Mycenae."[68] The closest analogues of the objects in the Vulchitrun hoard are in Bronze Age Mycenae and north of the Black Sea around Odessa (broadly linking Medea's Western and Eastern homes).[69]

The late Bronze Age is the time the Orphic Mysteries began in Thrace. Orpheus corresponds to the Greek Dionysos, and in an eerily familiar story, we learn that the women of a Thracian tribe murdered

Orpheus "by hacking him to pieces." (In Greece it was the classical Maenads who did the same with Dionysos.) Like the late Greek Maenads, the Ciconian women "reversed their social position by leaving their homes, drinking wine, and taking up the weapons of men. . . . After killing Orpheus, the Ciconian women are marked with tattoos, after which their husbands return to them and they become the mothers of their clans."[70] Now surely—as with the Greek Maenads and their acts of resistance—there is more to this transition story that meets the eye. It turns out that—according to Thracian expert, Ivan Marazov—the knowledge of the Mysteries had become "one of the chief secrets of the ruling family . . . to be passed on through the sacred drink. Orpheus made that knowledge accessible only to men, and perhaps [it was] in retribution for this"[71] that the women murdered him. Indeed.

Thracian Double Axes of bronze from the second millennium B.C.E. are described, similarly to those in Crete, as "cult axes" decorated with horned animals. "The shape, the dimensions, and the material of these axes clearly indicate that they were not used for utilitarian purposes. Rather, they are cult objects, symbols of royal or divine power."[72] Since the Double Axe is so consistently connected with female sovereignty, we must assume the presence of still powerful queens and priestesses in Bronze and Iron Age Thrace, an assumption which seems justified by the sheer volume of potent Goddess imagery. Thracian

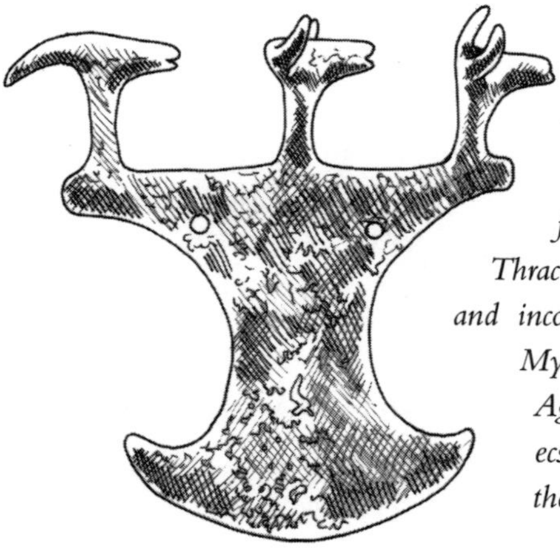

Fig. 4.44. This Thracian bronze Double Axe ("cult axe") with animal heads (goat, bull, ram) from Bulgaria dates from the early first millennium B.C.E. The Thracians were an amalgam of Old Europeans and incoming Indo-Europeans, showing a strong Mycenaean influence at the end of the Bronze Age. Their gold work was renowned, and their ecstatic tattooed Maenads were famous for their orgiastic rituals.

Maenads are described as participating in "nocturnal orgies" in which they "ran barefoot, with snakes hissing in their hair, carrying a *thyrsos*— a mystic staff surmounted by a pine cone and entwined with ivy or vine leaves—in one hand and an ax in the other."[73] Another tantalizing hint about a link to the Aegean Amazons comes in a report that the "sacred language of their (Cabiri) mysteries on Lemnos [where the women killed their husbands] was the tongue of the Thracian Sintioi tribe."[74]

The Thracian Goddess appears in two guises: a virgin who is always a huntress and a matron who has "gone through the female experiences of marriage and motherhood," representing fertility and presenting heroes with the "insignia of power."[75] The virgin is not only a huntress, like Artemis, but also, like Vesta or Hestia, a "goddess of the hearth . . . (who) vowed never to marry, and was isolated from the rest of the world through a number of symbolic attributes," including her invariable association with a snake (a "no-husband one"). "She also symbolizes the continuity of the clan," and had as her central role the king-making rites.[76] In other words, we are seeing here another expression of the usual Double Queens, representing the shaman-priestess and the warrior-woman.

The exhibit of Thracian gold that traveled throughout the United States in 1998 demonstrated, among other things, that the Double Axe was central to the Thracian civilization, whose extraordinary gold and silver pieces rival those of their early contemporaries, the Bronze Age Mycenaeans, and their later contemporaries, the Iron Age Scythians. Exquisite vessels

Fig. 4.45. Gold earring (one of a pair) depicting enthroned Goddess with headdress, flanked by winged sphinxes on either side, from the burial of a young Scythian woman north of the Black Sea, fifth century B.C.E. *Also buried with her was a gold-plated silver "torc" (elaborate necklace), bracelet, quiver, and a leather pouch containing bits of bark, leaves of grass, the bud of an unidentified plant, two beetles, a centipede, and a cherry stone.*

depicting Amazons and Goddesses (inscriptions name them), female charioteers, griffins, eagles, and snakes were found in Iron Age graves along with ritual Goddess headdresses, diadems, jewelry, and clothing appliques—all made out of gold. Gold rhytons (drinking vessels) in the shape of Amazon heads, a female sphinx, a silver pine cone (Maenads carried pinecone staffs), a fantastic silver and gold bowl showing multiple faces of Amazon Goddesses with a Double Axe at the top (see fig. 3.1 in chapter three): all suggest an active religion of the Great Goddess in the face of male domination and violence in the Iron Age world.

The most stunning piece in the exhibit was a greave or warrior's shin guard, made of silver and gold gilt in combination, depicting a Goddess with snakes for hair and snakes climbing on her body (reminiscent of Medusa and the Cretan Snake Goddesses), and what look to be snake staffs making up her arms and legs. Thirteen gold stripes (the Goddess lunar number) cross the right half of her face as if signifying tattoos. "The abundance of serpentine elements emphasizes the goddess's role as an embodiment of autochthonicity, or indigenousness . . . of particular importance to the royal family, because it implied the right of the king to rule the territory of his kingdom."[77] Although it was mentioned neither in the exhibit or the catalogue, I was fortunate to learn from the curator himself that this important shin greave was found in the burial of a sixteen-year-old female warrior.[78]

Not only objects but apparently even the women themselves were deliberately hidden underground during the Iron Age. A famous *tholos* (beehive) tomb like those in Mycenae and Crete was discovered in southern Bulgaria (Thrace) from the fourth century B.C.E. "While the *tholos* gradually disappeared in Greece after the twelfth century B.C., it continued in use in Thrace for more than a thousand years after that date."[79] The totally relevant thing about this particular tomb is that it contained the *secret* burials of two women. "A second, older floor was discovered about thirty centimeters below the upper one. Between the two floors the bodies of the two women had been buried" with gold and silver artifacts.[80]

Kingship in Thrace, as in so many other places, depended on the king coming to "marry" (almost certainly by force) the princess or queen of the indigenous land. "Marriage to the daughter of the Goddess, who personifies a given territory, consecrates the hero–outsider as its *lawful* ruler. The *marriage* is a necessary condition for his *legitimate* possession of the land"[81] (my emphasis). Given these conditions of male dominance and usurpation of female ownership and sovereignty, which were also being played out in the rest of the world during the Bronze Age, we are not surprised to learn that "the burial of sacred treasure seems to have been one of the most important royal rituals in Thrace," and that, "Remarkably, more than fifty buried hoards of precious metal objects *with no archaeological context* have been discovered there . . . and ample evidence for the practice of similar treasure burial in Europe from earlier times, as well"[82] (my emphasis).

Similarly, four unique and absolutely amazing hoards from the middle and late Bronze Age were discovered in areas of Germany and Switzerland. Four different high, pointed witches' hats were discovered separately and by accident and are viewed as hoards from the Bronze Age. "The four known conical hats resemble each other in their form, symbolism, technique, and above all the circumstances of their discovery."[83] All four hats "were hammered up whole from a single piece of gold, an achievement that presupposes extraordinary metallurgical skill and craftsmanship" and were "buried upright" underground as individual objects. "When, why and how the gold cones were consigned to the earth remains a mystery. The artifacts from this entire corpus, embracing not only the gold cones but also gold caps, gold vessels and gold disks— all with similar circular ornamentation—were generally buried as individual objects."[84]

When I read this piece—ironically, in a book called *Gods and Heroes of Bronze Age Europe*—I wept. The curators suggest that the hoards are "cult objects" rather than personal ones and that their burial "took place at the end of the period during which they were used, concurrent with the decline of associated religious beliefs. . . . A considerable

Fig. 4.46. These fabulous "Gold Cones," as they have been dubbed by archaeologists, are understood to be important Bronze Age religious headdresses but patently misunderstood as belonging to male priests or god-kings, rather than, obviously, female priestesses in a worldwide tradition of wearing tall, pointed hats for performing ecstatic, shamanistic rituals. The hats sketched here are two of the four that have been discovered so far, all in central Europe from the late Bronze Age.

span of time may still have elapsed between the manufacture of these objects and their burial."[85] I imagine our dazzling Bronze Age queens and priestesses in what we so casually call "migrations" and "cross-cultural contact." I see them riding their beloved horses in a desperate flight from one place to another, to the islands, then all across Europe, and finally even the Central Asian steppes and all along the Silk Road—in a wild, sustained effort to save the lineage of what they loved. When defeat was inevitable, they buried their precious heirlooms wherever they could—perhaps in hopes that they might be able to return, or maybe just to keep them from being profaned.

EURASIAN AMAZONS

When Jeannine Davis-Kimball announced the results of her Russian excavations of Amazon burials at the border between Russia and Kazakhstan, the whole world was transfixed. Newspapers, magazines, and television teams around the world carried the story of the excavations of warrior women, and Davis-Kimball has since proceeded to unmask other burials in various places that had earlier been misidentified as male simply because of weapons found with the skeletons. The renowned "Gold Man" of Issyk, according to Davis-Kimball's very convincing documentation, is actually one of the legendary gold-clad *women* warriors of the Russian steppes.[86] Russian excavations of burial mounds (kurgans) housing priestesses and warrior women have been taking place for fifty years; in the 1950s and 1960s, Russian archaeologists discovered the skeleton of a young Sauromatian/Sarmatian woman buried near the Sea of Azov with a bronze mirror, beads, and a Greek vase, plus "two iron lance blades were found close to her skull," with a quiver of twenty arrows and a suit of iron-scale armor next to her. Near the Dnieper River, they found a female skeleton "surrounded by a bronze mirror, bronze ear-rings, a glass-bead necklace, an iron sword and the remains of a quiver with 36 arrows," and in the foothills of the Caucasus Mountains, a "woman buried in a crouching position, surrounded by weapons," while another female skeleton "lay with a bronze mirror and iron lance-heads at her side and the skeleton of an attendant at her feet."[87] These findings corroborate most of what Herodotus wrote about the Amazons in the fifth century B.C.E. But we in the West—having been told repeatedly by historians that the Amazons were a mythic race, a legend, nothing more—are flabbergasted to learn of their bona fide existence.

A Russian scholar, T.V. Miroshina, reports on an "iron scaly girdle" found in the burial mounds on the banks of the Kuban River, which he equates with the legendary Thermodon River of the fabled Amazons. He links this war girdle to stories of an Amazon, Tirgatao ("Powerful Arrow")—a most-revered tribal queen who lived on the

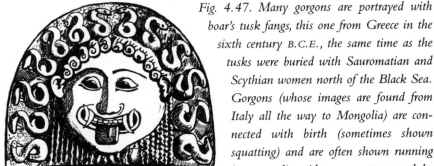

Fig. 4.47. Many gorgons are portrayed with boar's tusk fangs, this one from Greece in the sixth century B.C.E., *the same time as the tusks were buried with Sauromatian and Scythian women north of the Black Sea. Gorgons (whose images are found from Italy all the way to Mongolia) are connected with birth (sometimes shown squatting) and are often shown running in a peculiar sideways posture used by female athletes; they frequently have wings. In Africa, gorgons (like Medusa) wore dreadlocks and snakeskins, or in a variation on the theme, the skins of crocodiles.*

right bank of the Kuban—saying that she wore such a famed girdle, as did forest steppe Scythians north of the Black Sea in the sixth century B.C.E.[88] A Greek reference to gorgons describes them as having similar scaly armor, as well as "heads twined about with the scales of dragons, and great tusks like swine's,"[89] linking to the boars' tusks found in female burials of the Russian steppes. Gold plaques sewn on clothing of nomadic people from Greece all the way across the Russian steppes, as well as gold diadems and sword scabbards, were decorated with gorgon faces. Is gorgon really just another name for Amazon or warrior woman?

In the late 1970s—during the time I was creating the Motherpeace drawings with Karen Vogel—I fell in love with an Amazon Queen pictured in the center foldout of a book on the Scythians. My beloved queen's skeleton was covered with small gold Artemis plaques that had been sewn onto her clothing, a bronze mirror lay nearby, and on her skull she wore an elaborate gold crown. In the narrow canon that so often plagues academic scholarship, all this was ignored in the typical jargon that identified her merely as a "noblewoman" (in other words, someone's wife). When I heard Jeannine Davis-Kimball lecturing at University of California at Berkeley in the mid-1990s about a similar burial of a sixth century B.C.E. Sauromatian priestess, with her bronze mirror, portable altar, and other "cultic equipment," I was thrilled. And when she added that priestesses were one of two special types of women found in Sauromatian burials—the other being female "warriors" buried with long iron swords and daggers and bronze arrowheads—I knew for sure establishment scholarship would never be the same. The Russian excavations suggest that Iron Age tribes continued to have some form of the ancient female (religious?) leadership model, with two women ruling in Dual Queenship, as can be seen in the two female types described by Davis-Kimball and her Russian colleagues.

AMAZONS IN CHINA?

The connection noted in the last chapter between the shaman priestesses from one end of the Silk Road to another can also be seen between the chariot-driving Double Queens from Hagia Triada in Crete, their counterparts in Mycenae from slightly later, and three female mummies unearthed in the Tarim Basin from the sixth century B.C.E. Although the distance across the Silk Road is more than four thousand miles, steppe people have always had the advantage of the horse and the amazing mobility it provides.

The Double Queens on the Hagia Triada sarcophagus wore them (see fig. 4.31), the "Goddess with the Sheaves" in Mycenae wore one (see fig. 4.32), and at least one of the gold hats from central Europe is constructed in a very

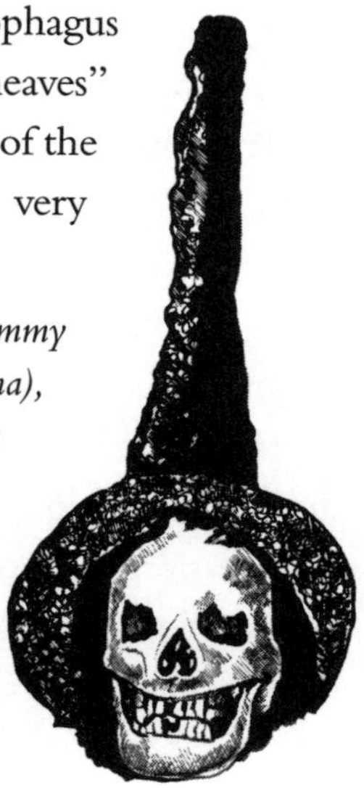

Fig. 4.48. This image is the head of a Europoid female mummy unearthed at the Subeshi cemetery in the Tarim Basin (China), from around 500 B.C.E. She wears a tall, conical black hat whose shape resembles the high pointed hat seen on one end of the Hagia Triada sarcophagus (see fig. 4.31), the so-called Goddess with the Sheaves mural from Mycenae (see fig. 4.32), as well as the "Gold Cones" discovered in central Europe (see fig. 4.46), and the hats of European witches from the Middle Ages.

similar way (see fig. 4.46). The type of hat that we have seen so much—with the odd, very thin, high pointed middle cone—looks like hat worn by at least one of the three mummy priestesses unearthed in China's Tarim Basin at the site of Subeshi from the fifth century B.C.E. "All three women, tall and elegant, were crowned with enormous pointed hats." One had two peaks, and another one was so large it couldn't fit in her grave; it was removed and placed next to her chest with sticks inside to keep the peaks intact.[90] One of the so-called Witches of Subeshi (all three are acknowledged to be "either priestesses or royalty or both") wore a sheepskin coat, the tall funnel-shaped hat, a "magnificent, eye-catching woolen skirt," and a "leather mitten on her left hand while her right was bare" (leading to the conclusion that the leather mitten was for falconry).[91]

Earlier mummies found in the Tarim Basin have other remarkable and unexpected characteristics, like blue eyes, blonde or red hair, and blue tattoos on their wrists. Some of them (from 1200 B.C.E.) were buried in wool tartan plaid twill fabrics (like the material in a Scottish kilt) that were preserved by the sand and salt of the desert climate. Their language, Tocharian, is closer to Celtic than anything and was used to write later Buddhist texts found in the Tarim Basin, potentially linking them to the origins of Tibetan Buddhism. One female mummy wore a "false braid" and had blue tattoos on her face and hands.[92] "Her face was painted with a red triangle on her cheek, and yellow spirals both inside the triangle and climbing over the bridge of her nose."[93] Similar spiral motifs are to be found on spindle whorls and textiles from the same cemetery at Cherchen.[94] Colorful textiles woven with rams and hourglass figures are found there, looking similar to the textiles at Pazyryk in the Altai (where other priestesses were buried).

The textiles worn by the mummies found at Cherchen tell the story of migrations from West to East during the Bronze Age, and the preservation of both the humans and their clothing by the dry desert salt and sand provides us with uncontestable datable proof for the story. (The cemetery at Cherchen up on a salt flat remained in use into the early centuries of this era.) Spool-shaped objects used for plaiting the belts worn by Cherchen mummies document the connection between Greece and the Tarim Basin. An overcoat of dark brown wool twill worn by one of the mummies, the so-called Cherchen Man (1000 B.C.E.), is similar to Tibetan men's homespun woolen coats today.[95]

The origins of these textiles—provided by world textile expert Elizabeth Wayland Barber—neatly link them to most of the Amazon cultures we've been discussing in this chapter. According to Barber, the first evidence for twill weave comes from central Turkey around 3000 B.C.E., where fragments of the cloth "still clung to a jawbone and to pieces of animal skin in a child's burial" at the site of Alishar. Another scrap of woolen twill comes from Georgia (Medea's territory) on the south slope of the Caucasus mountains, also from the third millennium. "About the same time, weavers in the famed city of Troy set up a warp-weighted loom specifically to weave twill patterns; the loom's remains were preserved for us when the city burned to the ground around 2600 B.C." Archaeologists found tiny gold beads "by the dozens" that "must have adorned the cloth that burned unfinished in the room." And shortly after that, "the Minoans of Crete began modifying their warp-weighted looms to accommodate the twill." Then came the twills from Hami (in the Tarim Basin) and Hallstatt in Europe, around 1000 B.C.E.[96] Barber thinks the weavers ("proto-Indo-Europeans") went out from a central spot in the western Caucasus and migrated in two directions starting around 3000 B.C.E. (This identification has served inadvertently to bring closure to the long argument about the mysterious homeland of the Indo-Europeans.)

The Tocharian speakers in their wool twill clothing brought "later and more sophisticated techniques of weaving and dyeing" that clearly suggest their "ancient knowledge of weaving."[97] It was apparently the even earlier immigrants into the area at Loulan (2000 B.C.E.) who "seem to have *introduced* weaving into the Tarim Basin." The so-called Beauty of Loulan, a female mummy wearing dyed woolen cloth, was buried with combs used for weaving wool and a "neatly woven bag or soft basket" that held grains of wheat, along with a large winnowing tray. Both the wheat and the sheep for weaving wool were domesticated in Anatolia in the fourth millennium B.C.E.[98] In other words, the immigrants were not nomadic people, but had been a settled agricultural people living somewhere in central Turkey before their migrations.

This provides startling and profoundly satisfying documentation for the connections I have been showing between the Old European and Anatolian Goddess cultures, the Amazon Queens of the Aegean region in the Bronze Age, Central Asian shaman women, and Silk Road links to the beginnings of Tibetan Buddhism. The High Priestess buried in the cemetery in Archanes, Crete, and the Beauty of Loulan could be relatives! The "Gold Cones" (pointed hats) that were buried in Hallstatt territory at the end of the Bronze Age could potentially be linked to the Tocharian speakers who migrated to the Tarim Basin. The Witches of Subeshi could be descendants of the Double Amazon Queens depicted driving chariots on the ends of the sarcophagus at Hagia Triada, and the Hami woman wearing woolen twill with the wheat and winnowing basket could be descended from the "Goddess with the Sheaves" in Mycenae.

AFRICAN AMAZON WARRIORS

Historians claim African Amazons came to fight for Troy against the Greeks. Herodotus mentioned the Libyan Amazons, and Diodorus Siculus (first century C.E.) described ancient African Amazons as "the warlike women of Libya" who, supposedly predating those from Asia, were "bedecked in snakeskins."[99] Certainly there are interesting legends about African women of power. "Libyan Amazonia was a gynecocracy: women alone did military service and held all political and judicial offices. Men kept house, reared children and obeyed their consorts."[100]

Martin Bernal—whose controversial theories revolve around the idea of Egyptian colonizations of Greece before the arrival of Indo-Europeans—points to a fragment from a lost epic, "the *Danaïs*, which describes the daughters of Danaos arming themselves by the banks of the Nile."[101] Given our earlier story about the Danaïds (the "husband-murdering sisters"), this reference to the women as warriors is quite interesting. The Indo-European Danaans (related to the Goddess Danu) are known to have traveled far and wide, even colonizing Ireland. Bernal argues that "there is no doubt that, according to the tradition, Danaos came from Egypt and that the cults attributed to him and his daughters were Egyptian."[102] Miriam Robbins Dexter's interpretations suggest that, because of a dynastic fight between Egypt and Libya, the Libyan branch (symbolized by Danaos and his fifty daughters) migrated to Argolis, and there the Danaïds (who are linguistically connected to the water element) "invented the art of sinking wells."[103]

According to Barbara Walker (and others), north African Berbers still call themselves "Amazigh."[104] And what about the many descriptive reports of African Amazons, from the famous Dahomey Amazons of the West African nation of Benin to the thousands of women soldiers sighted in the 1500s by Portuguese explorers? Eyewitness reports of the "Amazons of Black Sparta," as one recent book calls the Dahomey women,[105] begin in the seventeenth century C.E. and continue until the present day.

A Dutch officer writing in the 1640s gave this personal report of a powerful African warrior queen, Nzinga of Matamba (Angola). Referring to her as "a very stouthearted virago," he wrote that "she enjoyed fighting, and dressed like a man. Before going to war, she danced in animal skins, a broadsword suspended from her neck, an axe stuck in her belt, and a bow and arrows in her hands, as nimble as a young man" (see fig. 4.35). He also said she kept a harem of male concubines who dressed like women, and that he watched with his own eyes while she beheaded an enemy and drank his blood.[106] In an eye-witness account of a Dahomey female "general," she confronts the local male warriors and challenges the "very best of them to a duel with swords to determine which sex was stronger." She is quoted as saying: "In less than two minutes . . . his head will adorn the tip of my sword!" The commentator, embarrassed for his sex, says "not one warrior volunteered."[107]

In some cases the women push the envelope of gender, showing a kind of prescience about the transgender movement today, in which the fixity of gender is challenged directly by men who would be women and women who would be men. "By equalling or surpassing men in the arts of war, (the Dahomey Amazons) felt not that they had proved themselves as females but that they had qualified as males." A woman officer proclaimed: "As the blacksmith takes an iron bar and by fire changes its fashion, so we have changed our nature. We are no longer women, we are men."[108] Stories like this leave no doubt that the female warrior has been a strong part of African history, and most of the scholars believe that history must go back well into ancient times.

I have a slide showing a tribe of twentieth-century Black African Dahomey (Benin) women dancing energetically in a circle with their impressive crescent knives raised high above their heads, and I generally present it in a visual relationship to the Tibetan Buddhist Black Dakini with her crescent knife similarly raised. The Black African Amazons, like the dakinis and yoginis of lands farther east, provide a model of the unbridled freedom of untamed women, women who at times boldly overstep "woman's place" and usurp the power of the opposite sex. The Amazon, after all, is the quintessential male nightmare.

STANDING HER GROUND

With the mass of recorded history, mythology, and artifactual evidence, the existence of Amazon Queens and warrior women can hardly be contested, yet it is consistently denied, ignored, and erased by contemporary academic scholars. Amazon warrior women exemplify female resistance movements everywhere. They evoke the wild women who, like Miranda Shaw's eternally transgressive Indian yoginis, "always speak truthfully and are proud of their strength; women whose minds are powerful and energetic; women who delight in shrewish behavior and speak boastfully; women who are fearless, revel in their own ferocity, and like to eat meat and frequent cemeteries; and women who derive pleasure from the fact that they are untamable."[109] The warrior woman stands her ground in the physical world, like an archer or martial artist. The priestess fights her battle on the invisible plane, using the tools of her trade to support the powerful working of her focused mind. Together, in the tradition of Amazons from every time and place, they fight back in an ongoing refusal to allow the world to be destroyed.

FIVE

Sacred Sexuality and Shape-Shifting

The thread of connection and continuation, the female lineage or chain of matrilineal descent that can be seen in the Double Goddess figures, is reflected in the meaning of the word most often associated with sacred sexuality: *tantra*. According to Tsultrim Allione, a Western Tibetan Buddhist teacher and author of *Women of Wisdom,* tantra *means* thread, literally a "luminous thread."[1] The interconnectedness of all life is central to Buddhist philosophy, as it is to pagans, environmentalists, systems theorists, and all those who worship the Great Mother. Feminist spirituality has always taken this precept to be a crucial one, and the egalitarian concept of full inclusion is one for which we have worked hard and struggled long. Sacred sexuality belongs at the center of the "Old Religion" of pagans, "tantrikas" (tantric adepts), and feminist revisionists, having come down through the ages to the modern day through a continuous (if underground) lineage of ancient shamanistic priestesses.

The study of tantra, especially within Tibetan Buddhist practice, concerns itself primarily with the subtle psychic energies and channels. Using the "subtle body" as the ground, anyone practicing tantra works to heighten awareness of the invisible currents of energy running through everything. This awareness of the unseen, subtle energies all around us leads to being radically awake, which is a central goal of tantra. When we awaken to what is, we come to realize that we have been living in a dream or fantasy, seeing reality in a limited way. We have been seeing what we *want* to see, or what we *fear* to see, rather than what actually *is*. The dullness or lethargy that characterizes our "normal" or ordinary state of consciousness is disrupted through tantric techniques designed to heighten our awareness and move our energies through invisible channels (luminous threads) in the body (and in space). This movement of energy is tantamount to healing and revitalization, and it can lead to improved health, longevity, a more consistently positive attitude, or even a state of bliss and magical powers known as *siddhi* (for which the yoginis in India and Tibet were famous).

Needless to say, one of the deepest and most profound ways of establishing such a double conduit for energy is through the structured ritual practices of a tantric sex exchange. Apropos of our Double Goddess study, the tantric scriptures in India contain material about the superb energy generated by two women practicing tantric sex together.[2] And there have been volumes written on the powers of heterosexual tantric practice. In fact—as tantra has been brought to the West from India and Tibet—it sometimes seems as if the only part of it that interests Westerners is the sexuality, which, ironically, is almost meaningless without the "view." Sexuality is a small part of the whole, as sex (even divine sex) is only one channel or outlet for the energy.

THE SHAPE-SHIFTING SHAMANISTIC FEMALE

Perhaps the esoteric meaning of all Double Goddess figures is related to the recognition of a simple energetic tenet that any woman can function

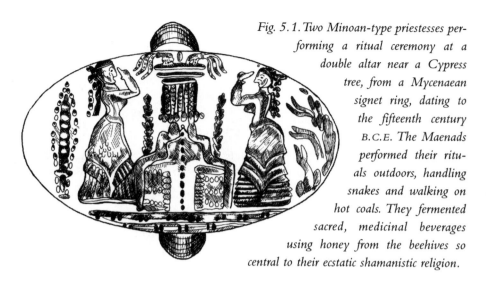

Fig. 5.1. Two Minoan-type priestesses performing a ritual ceremony at a double altar near a Cypress tree, from a Mycenaean signet ring, dating to the fifteenth century B.C.E. The Maenads performed their rituals outdoors, handling snakes and walking on hot coals. They fermented sacred, medicinal beverages using honey from the beehives so central to their ecstatic shamanistic religion.

as a sacred vessel for the divine, high-voltage energies of healing, transformation, and oracular speech. Given this natural capacity, when two women come together and join their two electromagnetic fields, they are capable of especially powerful psychic and ritual work. A seal stone from Crete shows two sacred women working in tandem at a central altar. One can almost see the energy crackling between the pair of priestesses. I have a hunch that because of what I have been calling the natural bipolarity of the woman, when any two women link their energies together on a psychic level, one of them is going to be broadcasting a positive charge and the other will naturally be the negative pole. This shape-shifting ability is female by nature, ruled by the Moon, and allows for a certain kind of fluidity within the usual laws that govern the physical world. In a sense, this

Fig. 5.2. This Double Vessel from Nazca, Peru (400 B.C.E.), is formed in the explicit shape of female breasts, pointing to the ancient and widespread connection between containers and the female body as providers of life and nourishment.

Fig. 5.3. This Double Vessel from Nazca, Peru, is shaped as breasts with the nipples painted in a contrasting color. Double Vessels are still presented to nursing mothers in Slovakia today, suggesting a religious rite around birthing and the miraculous transformation of blood into milk.[3]

is the whole basis of what we call shamanism and why women are generally acknowledged to be "better" (more natural) at it.[4] It is entirely possible that some of the Double Vessels found in all the cultures we have been discussing point to an ancient esoteric understanding about the power that two women can generate together through a linking of their subtle bodies, as is typically done in tantra.

A "Double Bowl Figure" from Zaire shows two women sitting with an object between them, their hands touching at the fingertips, legs intertwined in what certainly, if the two figures were male and female, would be called a tantric posture. Both women wear sacred cowry shells ("yoni" or vulva symbols) as hair ornamentation, with special hairdressings or headdresses and waist beads. It strikes me in looking at this pose that the two women are performing a psychic exercise or technique known as creating a battery for the high-vibrational healing

Fig. 5.4. This beautiful "Double Bowl Figure," perhaps showing priestesses engaged in tantric-type energetic practices, comes from Luba, Zaire. In Indian or Tibetan tantric practices, partners send and receive subtle energies that flow through both bodies in a continuous circle, creating a battery for performing powerful magical healing rites; such rites often include sacred sexual practices.

energies to pass through. In the shamanistic healing work I teach in my courses, we always create such a battery, either by consciously using the right and left hands for the healing work, or better yet, by having two people joining together as these partners do for hands-on healing or energy medicine. This circuit of energy *could* be used between two people in a tantric sexual exchange, but sex is not at all the only channel for expression. It is just as likely that the vibrational connection will create a circuit that will stimulate or allow one or both of the priestesses to become oracular and give prophecies, advice, information, or guidance, or access healing energies for laying on of hands.

The two priestesses are probably performing a psychic technique that might be compared with the use of a modern-day Ouija board: The two partners put their hands on the moving piece, become receptive to a higher power, and allow the potent electromagnetic energies to direct the movements over letters on the board. When Karen Vogel and I were first making the *Motherpeace* cards in the 1970s, we used a Ouija board for awhile. It was quite an interesting exercise in exploring the unknown territories of the invisible psychic world. We began by following the directions and letting the moving piece spell out words on the board, which seemed to be directed by an unseen hand. As any teenager who has tried this form of occult play will tell you, we could *feel* the force of the energy making the thing move across the board. Because we Westerners are schooled in the science of solid state reality, this unseen pressure or force can bring up fear or anxiety for many people. But in tribal cultures, where its presence is taken for granted, studied, and interacted with, people have developed amazing techniques for utilization of the invisible forces and electromagnetic healing powers present in nature.

EMPTINESS AND FEMALE SHAMANISM

The female capacity to become "empty" and channel some other energy is well recognized around the world. In India and Tibet, self-proclaimed *devis* are called to their office through spontaneously being possessed by various Goddesses who act and speak through them. Female mediums are the norm, rather than the exception, in most cultures with any remaining vestiges of shamanism. In the classic text on the subject, *Ecstatic Religion,* I. M. Lewis observes that women in various cultures around the world participate in peripheral "possession cults," which function alongside of the more staid male-dominated "state" or central religions. Women become "ill" with recognizable symptoms of a shamanistic healing crisis, and they are only made well when they own up to their calling and join the active group of older women who shamanize and act as mediums for their communities. In some places there is conflict between the ways of the men and the ways of the women, but the conflict is partly resolved (as Lewis sees it) by the outlets for female expression that are represented by the possession cults.

In other places men and women cooperate in an institutionalized division of (religious) labor, such as in South Korea for example, where men in the family practice the public religion of Confucianism, whereas women practice the older animistic religion of shamanism. People come to the women for shamanistic rites and rituals of healing and prophesy, and continue to participate in the general male-led community ceremonies as well.[5] I also saw this in 1991 when I visited Bali. Brahmin men preside over the official public religion of Hinduism, but I was able to visit a Balian (female shaman) in private in order to receive healing in a more ancient, animistic way. I held a question in my mind while she made offerings and chanted at an altar in a small structure in her backyard (as children were playing nearby), emptying herself to receive. Then she began to channel the voices of her ancestors as they made their presence known through her body and responded to my unvoiced question. (A Brahmin man translated for me during my session with the shaman woman!)

In Tibetan tantra, sexual union is a method by which a dakini blesses a yogin (or presumably another female yogini) with the gift of her own body, as Judith Simmer-Brown explains: "The body of the dakini, whether visionary or human, is a subtle body of vital breath, channels, and essences . . . she blessed him with her empty and radiant body, a direct transmission of her nature."[6] This whole issue of female "emptiness" is paradoxical, since in one way women are valorized as "natural" tantrikas (with capacities superior to those of male adepts) whose presence is essential, and in another sense they are almost universally demonized and held in contempt for the same spacious mediumistic abilities. In contemporary cultural terms, Leonard Cohen expresses this painful and perplexing dichotomy on his album, *The Future,* in a song titled "Light as the Breeze."[7]

He begins by describing the female partner standing before a man naked, bringing him to a state of worship: "So I knelt there at the delta, at the alpha and the omega, at the cradle of the river and the seas. And like a blessing come from heaven for something like a second I was healed and my heart was at ease." But as the song (and their relationship) progresses, he withdraws into coldness and hardens his heart against the same woman. "Then she dances so graceful and your heart's hard and hateful and she's naked but that's just a tease . . ." But eventually he needs her "and it's 'Please baby please baby please.' And she says, 'Drink deeply, pilgrim but don't forget there's still a woman beneath this resplendent chemise.'" He kneels again at the "delta," and the song ends as it began, he "was cured and my heart was at ease."

The narratives of the great Tibetan and Indian "masters" generally contain a segment in which the yogi is awakened or initiated by a yogini or female guru, often disguised as an "ordinary" woman. The dakini's identity is "ambiguous" and she is often not recognized for who she is, even by advanced yogis.[8] In Asia, where tantra originated, the use of a partner's body ("consort") in support of one's meditation, chanting, and visualization practices is believed to facilitate more progress than can be made in a solitary way, and in certain sects of Tibetan Buddhism, it is considered to be absolutely necessary for a "final liberation."

This is complicated by the fact that Tibetan Buddhist tantra has been practiced mostly in monasteries that are exclusively male by monks who have taken celibacy as a necessary precept. As June Campbell has shown, the actual women who have functioned in this system as "secret consorts" are not equal and are not able to have their own agency, being seen as support to the evolution of the male lamas and required to be "secret" from public view.[9] But even when men and women are free to act as equals and practice freely, there is still the understanding that because human sexuality is such a volatile, unpredictable, and often uncontrollable force, sexual yoga is a dangerous, albeit interesting and effective, short-cut to spiritual evolution. Unlike the American "do it in a weekend" workshops on tantra, embarking on the actual sexual practices requires strenuous preparation beforehand.

ROOTS OF TANTRA: PRIESTESSES AND GODDESSES

By the first millennium of this era, women shamans and priestesses had been peripheralized and marginalized away from the urban centers of greater Europe, Africa, and Asia. Legends and traveler's reports often refer to pockets (remnants) of potent female activity—secret islands of women, even a country of women to the north (of India) or the west (of China), and Tibet's famous land of the dakinis (Uddiyana, on the border of what is now Afghanistan and Pakistan). Amazing round stone open-air yogini temples were built in northern India during the centuries (eighth through tenth) that certain famous yoginis were having a lasting impact on the development of Buddhism in Tibet. The best-remembered women of this tradition are Yeshe Tsogyal (eighth century) and Machig Lapdrom (tenth century). Both biographies are characterized by tenacious female autonomy and an ardent desire, like that of the ancient Amazons, to remain unmarried.

Lady Yeshe Tsogyal and the Terma Tradition

There are so far three translations available in English of the story of Yeshe Tsogyal's remarkable life. The first—Tarthang Tulku's *Mother of Knowledge,* published in 1983—presents the narrative of her life with very little commentary. He points out that she was the primary consort of Padmasambhava (the founder of Tibetan Buddhism in the eighth century) and that "it could be said that all of Padmasambhava's teachings came to us through Ye-shes mTsho-rgyal."[10] The second version, *Sky Dancer: The Secret Life and Songs of the Lady Yeshe Tsogyel,* was translated by Keith Dowman in 1984, with wonderful illustrations by Eva van Dam. Dowman's lengthy commentary is eloquent and richly informative. He sees Tsogyal as "the embodiment of the female Buddha."[11] The most recent translation, done by the Padmakara Translation Group in 1999, is called *Lady of the Lotus-Born: The Life and Enlightenment of Yeshe Tsogyal.* The publisher celebrates Tsogyal as "the first Tibetan ever to attain complete enlightenment . . . herself becom(ing) a Guru of great power and wisdom."[12]

Tsogyal was born a princess in Chärchän (Cherchen, Kharchen) which is one of the oases along the Tarim Basin where European mummies were discovered from late in the second millennium B.C.E. One famous "Cherchen Woman" (1000 B.C.E.), who wore a red dress and white deerskin boots, was fifty-five years old and could be an ancestress of Tsogyal—and thus directly related to the roots of Tibetan Buddhism. Her red wool dress contains threads of cashmere obtained from Kashmir in India, showing connections to the yogini tradition there as well.[13] Tantra, which developed in India and spread into Tibet, is related to both places, and the female lineage can be traced from both places. The importance of textiles to these early Tarim Basin immigrants—reported by Elizabeth Wayland Barber in her fascinating book, *The Mummies of Ürümchi*—reminds us that tantra itself means "thread" and links to weaving, that ancient magical art of women around the world.

Tsogyal was born at the time of greatest expansion of the Tibetan empire, when it ruled over all the neighboring realms as far as China, Nepal, and the Silk Road. Very much in the tradition of the yoginis of India and the shaman women of Central Asia, from the moment of her birth (even her conception) it was clear that Tsogyal was not an ordinary woman, but a highly advanced shamanic priestess with magical signs and supernatural powers. She consciously orchestrated her own conception and—as her mother and father "were enjoying the pleasures of love-making"—her mother had a vision. "Coming out of the west she saw a golden bee, its hum sounding like a sweet stream of lute music," perhaps pointing to a connection with the Bee Priestesses ("Melissae") of the Mediterranean region.[14] Nine months later, her mother "gave birth painlessly. The earth shook, thunder rolled, and a rain of flowers fell from the sky. The lake increased in size," and for this she was named Tsogyel (Tsogyal), "Dakini of the Ocean."[15]

Tsogyal is known as the female founder of Tibetan Buddhism and primary consort of Padmasambhava, its male founder who came to Tibet from Oddiyana (the "Land of the Dakinis") with "retinues of dakinis" all around him. They practiced "mystical sexual yoga in the cave called the Assembly Hall of the Dakinis," where she later continued to practice on her own; she quickly reached enlightenment and set about helping others.[16] Besides receiving the entire transmission of teachings from Padmasambhava, the magician-Guru with whom she is in eternal union *(yab-yum)*, the main contribution for which Tsogyal as Guru-Dakini is remembered is that she hid treasures *(terma* texts) for the use of future generations.

In the terma tradition, it is believed that students of Padmasambhava reborn in later centuries would remember their earlier incarnations through the vehicle of revealed treasures, which they spontaneously express in unique ways in each lifetime. The terma treasures are sometimes physical (texts, amulets, relics), but frequently they are treasures of the mind. In a broad understanding of the concept, one might say that the excavation of European mummies in China and Mongolia counts as terma, along with the more technical artifacts unearthed in Tibet over the centuries.

Treasure-finders known as Tertons (sometimes female terma-finders are referred to as Kandroma, which basically means "dakini") receive their termas in "the language of the dakini," which is a secret script that has to be decoded. Terma-finders must have a consort with whom to practice their mystical yoga. "The support of the consort has two purposes . . . to produce and maintain the wisdom of the union of great bliss and emptiness (freedom), by which the adept attains the ultimate state . . . (and) the consort causes him or her to awaken the realization as well as to discover the Termas."[17] The "special consort who has made the appropriate aspirations in the past" is "the key to accomplishment," which is "one of the reasons why all Tertons happen to have consorts."[18]

Wisdom Transmission Tradition of the Dakinis and Yoginis

It is necessary here to insert some biographical information in order to demonstrate that the method by which the lineage of the yoginis and dakinis is passed on is alive and well in our own time. True to the central premises of shamanistic practice, the information and knowledge held by women shamans and yoginis is realized through spontaneous direct experience, inspiration, and telepathic contact. I have written elsewhere[19] that I believe Motherpeace falls into the category of terma, having been inspired by visionary activity and direct transmission of energy, symbolic images, and enigmatic written script. Classically, its discovery was catalyzed by spontaneous and potent tantric consort yoga, which my partner Karen Vogel and I described as mysterious continuous rushes of energy; only later through introduction to yoga did we come to know it as kundalini. A Tibetan expert on Terma, Tulku Thondup Rinpoche, affirms that "it is impossible for Tertons not to have inner experiences such as excitement, delight and bliss at the time of discovery of the Terma."[20]

At the time that these visions and psychic events were happening to me, I had no context for understanding them, except that I knew they were sacred and belonged to the realm of the Great Mother. Tertons and Kandromas (the female version) express their discoveries through the particular vernacular of their time and for the direct benefit of their special constituency of students—in my case the contemporary feminist women of the late twentieth and early twenty-first century. At a breakthrough point in my evolutionary process (1977), I was shown—in a waking state—images on an African tie-dyed wall-hanging that flashed like slides being projected on a screen. The images included Amazons, Goddesses, griffins and gorgons, the Milky Way, and the solar system in motion. A tunnel presented itself, and then a script that I anxiously could not read, which then dissolved and reformed into English words: "Heal All," "Hell No," "Helena," and "I AM All" (the last undulated for a few minutes, as if to emphasize the point). Tulku Thondup Rinpoche describes this phenomenon as part of the unfolding of the Terma: "By concentrating on the symbolic script the Terton perceives in his or her awareness state that the scripts are changing miraculously every moment into different forms."[21] The Motherpeace project that I undertook with Karen Vogel after that came directly out of this visionary experience of direct primordial wisdom.

In 1980 I attended my first Tibetan Buddhist lecture at the Nyingma Institute in Berkeley, where I discovered the chanting practice (mantra) of calling on Guru Padmasambhava that I have used ever since. I had a vision (while performing a yoga posture in front of a mirror) of the "Vajra (Diamond) Yogini," which I made into the Ace of Swords in the Motherpeace, and after that I also chanted the mantra to her. When I first read the biography of Yeshe Tsogyal in the mid-1980s, I used it as a text for the women students learning female shamanism from me. It was around that time that I discovered the second great historic yogini memorialized in Tibetan Buddhist literature, Machig Lapdrom, and her shamanistic rites in honor of the Black Dakini (whose picture I used on my book *Shakti Woman* when it was published in 1991).

Machig Lapdrom and the Feast of Chöd

Tsultrim Allione's *Women of Wisdom* (first published in 1984 and updated in 2000) contains a biographical sketch of this "renowned and beloved" Tibetan woman mystic who was prophesied to be born as the reincarnation of Yeshe Tsogyal.[22] Machig's lifetime (late tenth to early eleventh centuries) corresponds to a period when Buddhism flourished for the second time—the first period being Yeshe Tsogyal's lifetime (eighth century). Although Machig Lapdrom is primarily remembered for her Chöd teachings, Reginald Ray makes it clear that she is the original Tülku (a reincarnated teacher in world service) with "self-recognition" of her status and "explicit memories" of her past lives.[23] In the centuries following her lifetime, the "Tülku tradition" became institutionalized within the male monastic setting. Machig was a "wisdom dakini—a fully realized being in human form," and like Yeshe Tsogyal, she also hid terma.[24]

The Chöd ritual is a visualized "feast" in which the body of the practitioner is offered to all the beings anywhere who might need anything. "One cuts ego at the root by offering one's body, mind, and all one's attachments to the most hungry and fearful beings in samsara."[25] The chant in Tibetan is accompanied by the loud sounds of *damaru* (drum), bell, and thigh-bone trumpets. The ritual practices of Chöd ("cutting through") are "now found in all lineages," but at one time they "were specifically charnel-ground practices."[26] All we have to do to understand the context leading up to Machig Lapdrom's expression is to go back to chapter three, remembering the ancient shaman women and their funerary practices. Allione states that the "training for Chöd took place in colleges founded specifically for this study," which took five years. The students would be sent out toward the end of the training, "in groups and finally alone," to do their practice. "Chödpas were always called in when there were epidemics of infectious diseases, such as cholera. They took care of the corpses, chopping up the bones and conducting the funeral ceremony, apparently impervious to infection."[27]

The Tantric Feast and Ancient Female Sexuality

The "tantric" feast belongs to a "pattern of women's religious practices" according to Miranda Shaw in her illuminating book, *Passionate Enlightenment: Women in Tantric Buddhism*.[28] Tantric feasts are "communal assemblies" ("ganachakra" and "chakrapuja"), what Shaw describes as "an esoteric ritual that unfolds in many stages."[29] Shaw believes that "women gathering in nonhierarchical circles may have been a non-Buddhist practice that Tantric Buddhists adopted, memorialized in their literature, and replicated in their ritual and iconography."[30] I believe the potent visual iconography of the dakinis in Tibetan Buddhist tantric practices also descends from the actual historical reality of the lives of powerful shamans, yoginis, and female gurus of the type that Shaw is describing.

Ritual feasting is depicted from at least as early as the Hittites in central Turkey in the mid-second millennium B.C.E.[31] It almost certainly dates back much earlier to funerary practices from the most ancient times. A late (probably somewhat degenerate) form of the feast belongs to the yogini cult in India, in which yoginis are depicted in the charnel grounds and cemeteries, feasting on human flesh and partaking of the sacred sexual rites—sometimes on top of the corpses. The Great Goddess Kali is similarly depicted straddling her consort Shiva's corpse, with a huge curved knife in her hand or swung rapturously over her head. These corpse rituals most likely stem from earlier communal funerary rites, in which the priestesses naturally learned, through their intimate shamanistic contact with the dead, to work ritually with the nonhuman, nonrational energies and palpable forces connected with the realm of death.

Just as in medieval Western witchcraft reports, there is an odd commingling of sexuality and the more macabre themes of corpses and cannibalism. In the biography of Yeshe Tsogyal, reaching a desperate point in her solitary austerities (practices), she prays for help. It is (rather shockingly) the Great Queen of the Dakinis, Vajrayogini, the embodiment of psychic heat, who responds to her plea with the nourishment of a direct transmission of menstrual blood. "Then a vision came to me. A woman, red-skinned, naked and without the ornaments of bone, appeared and pressed her bhaga to my mouth so that I drank deeply of the blood that flowed from it. My whole being was suffused with bliss. . . ."[32] Tantric scholar David Gordon White clarifies this somewhat by reminding us that "erotic practice involving the use of a female part-ner's sexual fluids as power substances" was specific to tenth-century Indian tantra.[33] White also tells us that "People used to do the corpse ritual . . . and sit on the body . . . and the body would come back to life and talk."[34] Oracular shaman-priestesses would have been the original facilitators of such arcane ritual activity.

At another point, when Tsogyal is meditating by herself in "the Great Trysting Place of the Dakinis, her secret cave," she has a more elaborate vision of Vajrayogini. The "abode of the dakinis" is a charnel ground with "a mass of corpse-flesh" and "bristling skeletons . . . scat-tered fragments of bone . . . human heads, some freshly cut, some dry, some putrescent . . . Within this enclosed space I saw flesh-devouring birds and wild, blood-drinking beasts, and I was surrounded by ogres and ogresses. . . . " It's clearly the description of a sky burial (see chap-ter three). She enters through successive gates and finds inside "many dakinis . . . presenting (offerings) to the principal dakini." The offerings are "pieces of their own flesh . . . as a ganachakra feast." The dakinis offer everything to Vajrayogini, and "when the moment came for them to make the dedication of their offerings," she appeared in front of each one of them and "snapped her fingers, and the dakinis were made whole again just as before. Then they would request teachings from the principal dakini and go and meditate upon them. This was how they practiced—in all, twelve times a day."[35] This regenerative healing power is the essence of the siddhis (powers) said to belong to the yoginis.

Shaw describes "assemblies of yoginis" who met for nocturnal rit-uals in which they practiced sexual rites and sang songs of realization to one another. These independent, powerful women formed the center of a movement that developed into Buddhist tantra. Tantric scriptures present communal feasting "as a ritual that is staged and presided over by women." Certain special yogis may be invited in, but not without knowing the password. "A significant portion of the (tantric scriptures) focuses on how to locate yogini feast assemblies and gain attendance to them." To do this a man must use "the proper secret signs to communicate with yoginis." She states that the literature "typically describes feasts staged solely by women or by equal numbers of men and women," and that "inclusion in a yogini feast is seen as a high honor for a male practitioner."[36] Since sacred sexual rites are considered a mandatory part of such feasts, we can then implicitly understand that some form of lesbian sexuality is taken for granted (especially in the circles made up of exclusively women). "Women gathering in circles to feast, perform rituals, teach, and inspire one another constitutes a practice that also appears in the secular literature of the period."[37]

White discusses early tantrism as "realized through the conduit of a horde of wild goddesses (which the tantrikas identified with their human consorts), generally known as *yoginis*. These 'bliss-starved' goddesses, attracted by offerings of mingled sexual fluids, would converge into the consciousness of the practitioner, to transform him, through their limitless libido, into a god on earth."[38] Later "most of the messy parts of tantric practice . . . were cleaned up, aestheticized, and internalized in different ways." The "consumption of sexual fluids," which had played a central role in the earlier collective rites, became restricted to "secret practice" in an inner circle, while the personal "bliss of sexual orgasm" came into the foreground where it remains today.[39] The irony of this unfortunate transition is taken to its extreme logical conclusion in the promulgation of drugs like Viagra, which do nothing to stimulate meaning or sacredness in the act of sexual encounter, but simply produce a mechanical ability to maintain erection and have orgasm.

I think this shift relates directly to the cultural shift from a female-centered ecstatic sacred sexuality to a male-dominated rational one. As the yoginis lost their ground (during the last millennia B.C.E. and the first millennia of this era) and were replaced by male priests in the facilitation of communal rites and rituals—and nuns were pushed out of the monasteries, which became exclusively male—then the sexual rites changed accordingly. The direct, earth-based, body-based intuitive practices developed and facilitated by the magical shaman women (the Maenads or "wild women") over thousands of years of communal, ecstatic rituals gradually gave way to more formalized, abstract and internalized visualizations and energetic transactions of the men. White calls it the "brahmanization" of tantrism and its "departure from the realm of the concrete into that of the sublime."[40]

From the Kaula sect in India (often critiqued by academics as degenerate or debauched), White gathers linguistic data to support the supposition that sexual rites changed from bodily to internalized visualizations and from female-initiated to "high Hindu tantrism." The "true essence of the Kaula" is a term used to "designate the yogini's sexual emission . . . their 'lineage nectar . . . ' the goddess's menstrual fluid or the commingled sexual fluids of Siva and the Goddess."[41] Menstrual fluid for the orthodox tantrikas is "the most powerful fluid in the universe." The "tantrika's favorite sexual partner, [the Dombi] was most prized for the transformative powers of her menstrual blood."[42] And the Dombis take us right back to the ancient primal funerary practices, as the Doms are the "body-breakers" at the sky burials, and they practice "skull-feeding rituals" in order to pacify the spirits and make them protectors. White says, "Skulls awaken the Goddess, and make her present here. Male gods have stones . . . or lingas . . . but goddesses have skulls."[43]

In Sanskrit literature, a yogi describes a yogini feast assembly of spiritual revelers who, like ancient Greek Maenads, "were intoxicated," having become ecstatic through ingesting their sacred fermented beverage (soma). The wild women "sported with a skeleton, pretending that it was their lover."[44] How is this possible, and what does it have to do with female sexuality? It is almost impossible for a Westerner to imagine having a direct energetic experience of death, since our funeral ceremonies are so terribly sterile and deliberately unexciting. We have long since lost the hands-on experience of preparing the corpse for burial, and we have turned it over to professional technicians who do it in a place far away from the house where the loved ones reside. For a glimpse into the bizarre and (to us) unimaginable possibilities associated with animistic funerary rituals, we might look at a contemporary description of a West African death divination ritual witnessed during the twentieth century, in which corpse-dancing is the oracular vehicle for the community.

Diane Skafte explains, in her wonderful book *When Oracles Speak,* that "'death divination' is performed to learn more about the deceased's spiritual condition before, during and after death." Further rituals might be performed, based on the divination, that will "properly protect the deceased and the community from harm."[45] The material in the story comes from a report made by Bruce Grindal, an anthropologist who was allowed to be present during such a ritual and for whom the ritual was absolutely shocking to the core of his being. The funeral was for the chief's drummer, whose corpse was "propped up in a sitting position against the compound wall; a cloth covered his head."[46] The drums he had played were placed directly above the wall. "A group of funerary singers called the *goka* now approached the corpse. They danced forward, drawing close to its shrouded form as though whispering in its ear. Then with a backward jerk of their heads they retreated again. Back and forth, back and forth, their undulating motions against the firelight cast a spell on everyone present."[47]

Grindal, the anthropologist who was watching, was "transfixed," and "it seemed to him that the corpse jerked and pulsated a little whenever the *goka* drew near."[48] Then Grindal himself experienced an influx of high-voltage energy like a lightning bolt through his body, feeling "a jolt as though my head had been snapped off my spinal column."[49] He saw filaments of "fibrous light" stretching from the "amazingly delicate fingers and mouths" of the ritual singers, and "strands of fibrous light played upon the head, fingers, and toes of the dead man. The corpse, shaken by spasms, then rose to its feet, spinning and dancing in a frenzy."[50] Everything became radiant and pulsating, and eventually the drums themselves "began to glow with a light so strong that it drew the dancers to the rooftop" where the "corpse picked up the drumsticks and began to play."[51] When the ritual ended, the corpse was once again propped up against the wall, and the dancers were "panting and dripping in sweat."[52] (The anthropologist remained in such a state of shock for a few weeks that a shaman was required to heal him.)

CAN CONTEMPORARY WOMEN REDISCOVER THE ANCIENT SEXUAL RITES?

In astrology the sign of Scorpio is (paradoxically it seems) connected with both sex and death. Scorpio rules the eighth house of deeply transformative encounters with another being, or with a transformative process that takes you through a descent, disintegration, and rebirth. The Sumerian Inanna's descent to meet the Dark Goddess, Ereshkigal, is a Scorpio myth. In fact, Ereshkigal is a stand-in for Pluto, the planet that rules Scorpio (and the underworld where the Scorpio adventure takes place). Even with only a popular superficial understanding of astrology, people know that Scorpio is all about sex. But what kind of sex are we talking about here, and how many people do you know who are having it? The modern Western investigation into Scorpionic sexuality has become distorted beyond recognition, and the closest we seem to be able to get to it is through the violence so often associated with sexuality these days, and the power struggles that characterize our intense romantic relationships. Perhaps this is because of our particular history, having descended as a culture from Europe during the brutal medieval period when the Inquisition was torturing women for their sexuality and burning them as "witches" in villages all over the continent. The so-called Enlightenment in Europe happened over the murder of its population of women, because of the distorted view of the clergy and the scientists who shared a belief that female sexuality was the root of all evil.

Everything that has been written or reported about the activities of European pagans and witches could be just as effectively used as a description of the yoginis of India and Tibet, whose activities have been recorded in historical texts. They smeared their bodies with "flying ointment" and flew through the air, but so did Medea and, according to Ovid, the Scythian women as well. They met for "nocturnal gatherings" in wild places, just as the yoginis and Maenads did before them. They performed sacred rituals to the Goddess of the Wild Things, Artemis in ancient Greece and Turkey, Diana in pagan Europe. They had profound knowledge of the medicinal uses of plants, and they brewed sacred fermented beers until the church took over in their place. (Pilsner was originally beer made from the henbane plant "bilsa" or "pilsen," sacred to the Goddess, part of a formula for flying. Today some of the world's best ales are still brewed by the Belgian monks.) The "witches" birthed children and healed the population, until profit-making male-dominated Western medicine was developed over their dead bodies.

Part of the Scorpionic legacy is the notion of the shadow, that dark disowned part of the psyche that gets pushed underground into the unconscious, where it lives without our being aware of it. The massive extermination of the shamanistic peasantry in Europe between the thirteenth and the seventeenth centuries, particularly the women, has left a terrifying shadow in the collective psyche. This shadow material tends to get stirred up when we open ourselves to our sexuality and begin to allow its free and uncensored expression once again. The so-called sexual revolution of the 1960s (paradoxically) led to the pornography industry and its misogynistic reign of terror on women. Lesbians who broke free during the women's movement of the 1970s, and to whom the decision to love another woman was a *political act* as well as a personal choice, are often flabbergasted to see the next generation of lesbian women deliberately practicing the rituals of "sado-masochism," known as "S & M" or "dominance-submission." The shattering of the nuclear family—while powerfully liberating in many ways—has come hand in hand with an "epidemic" of "domestic abuse" (note how the expression leaves out any reference to the abuser).

Tantra has been imported to the West and is available absolutely everywhere for a price, but does it contain anything more than simply another quick fix for trying to get that good orgasm? Sacred women were at the center of the tantric movement at its inception. In fact, it was probably women's spontaneous and natural sexual practices that were basically codified into what we know as tantra. Now women are cultivated in the East as consorts in support of the male initiate's spiritual progress, and in the West as the perfect partner—sexy, provocative, available, and knowledgeable in the techniques that give men pleasure. I don't think we could get much farther from the juicy sexual potency of the ancient wild women and their cults of ecstasy.

If there was one single technique we could discuss as having been used by ancient women in their sacred sexual practices, it would be the cultivation of a state of emptiness that allows for natural and spontaneous experiences to happen through the body of the woman. This is the gift that the luminous dakini (sky-goer) bestows on the initiate, or the human one on her human partner—the generous gift of her body, with its luminous channels of light and threads of healing energy. It is this that leads both people in a sacred sexual encounter to bliss. What we have forgotten in our modern fixation on mechanics is that it doesn't matter where you touch, or which technique you use, if you're not present. What matters is actually being able to show up, with an open heart and warm presence. What is required is a resonance with the pulsating primal energies, the power to surrender control, and the magical shape-shifting ability of the sacred woman to expand outside the boundaries of her physical body and fly (ecstatically) through space.

A Western variant on the Tibetan Buddhist Chöd practice is the group transformational healing ritual I invented during the four years I ran the Motherpeace School in Oakland (1987-1991). In our healing rituals we drum, chant, and lay hands on members of our community suffering from life-threatening physical ailments, and our own immunity is strengthened by our collective practice. Chanting one simple healing song for an hour or more, with drumming and powerful vibrational (hands-on) healing, is effective in more ways than one. Sometimes spontaneous recoveries occur, wherein malignant tumors, multiple sclerosis, lupus, or other life-threatening physical manifestations completely disappear (or go into remission).

During the transformative healing rituals, the group often enters a collective state of altered consciousness in which everyone present can have a direct experience of primal energies, frequently allowing for a deep meditative relaxation, with feelings of serenity, ecstasy, or bliss. Sometimes women in my circles have described this experience as having a kind of "free-floating female eroticism" in it, even though ostensibly it has nothing whatsoever to do with sex. At least once that I know of, a woman dancing near the center of the group had an orgasm during a powerful crescendo of energy from the drumming and chanting. There is something magical about women performing a collective ritual practice together that has not been conceived, directed, or mediated by men and is not guided or controlled from an academic agenda or rational point of view. The possibility of entering purely experiential space emerges from the group presence.

LESBIAN SEXUALITY: WOMEN-LOVING WOMEN

We'll probably never know if any of the Double Goddess images from ancient civilizations were meant by their creators to represent physical love between women. Or, more accurately, we may not ever be able to prove that such a likely contention is true. Certainly some Double Goddesses are portrayed in such intimate ways that contemporary scholars discussing them have become tongue-tied or shy about what they are seeing. Recent academic dogma purports that lesbianism is a strictly modern idea, one that cannot appropriately be applied to any cultures before the twentieth century. Yet the reverse seems true. I would argue that modern views of so-called sexual preference, theories of inversion, and perversion, have been superimposed (blindly) over images from ancient contexts that, when perceived through other theoretical lenses, might easily be interpreted as reflections of love between women.

Some double figures show two separate women in significant intimate contact, embracing or wearing a shawl around their shoulders or a girdle around their hips, which may indicate physical same-sex love (see figs. 0.4 and 1.25) Australian scholar Chris Sitka—who gives workshops on "Lesbians in Pre-History" based on these and other Double Goddess images—strongly promotes this view. She further asserts, from the thousands of years of "passionate female representation," that lesbianism must have been common, acceptable, and perhaps the most revered "sacred path to veneration of the female deity."[53]

If we look at what was happening around the Mediterranean area during the time of the Iron Age Amazons, the possibility of lesbianism can be brought into focus somewhat. In Sparta, for example, the girls ran races in tunics that bared their breasts, taking part in naked ritual processions and dances like the boys. Spartan women married late and were known for quite unusual marriage rituals involving "masculinization" (short haircutting and wearing male clothing on their wedding nights) as well as having more than one husband. Girls' upbringing "paralleled that of boys," including "races and trials of strength," such as "running, wrestling, throwing the discus and javelin." They learned to manage horses and, at the festival of Hyacinthia, "they raced in two-horse chariots."[54] Plutarch refers to the love between young virgins and "noble and good women" of Sparta.[55]

Everyone assumes the Greek Olympics were for men, yet one pair of scholars, describing the ruins at Delphi, discusses the "running track" up the hill, the "best-preserved in Greece" with stone seating for about seven thousand people: "The course is shorter than the men's Olympic *stadion;* only 160m, which was . . . the length of the older

Fig. 5.5. This female athlete comes from Dodona, an important early oracular center in mainland Greece, dating to the fifth century B.C.E. Dodona is where priestesses are reported to have used a horsewhip against thirteen bronze cauldrons in order to produce their oracular results.

Olympic *stade*, for girls' races."[56] In creating the Motherpeace deck in the late 1970s, I created the Five of Wands to show a group of young women or girls pitching a mock battle with batons, after reading somewhere that pre-Olympian girls' games were regularly held in the form of a contest in which the High Priestess was determined for the following year. Certainly the track at Delphi could fit such a description, since we know there was a priestess tradition at that site longer than almost anywhere else in Greece. Since many of the Greek religious sites had running tracks and amphitheaters, it behooves us to change some of our assumptions about early athletics. According to Gimbutas, one of the most ancient Greek religious festivals, held in honor of Hera, was participated in by women only. It was held every fourth year at Olympia, and the main event was a "famous foot race featuring virgins who ran in order of age: the youngest first, and the eldest last. The winning virgin received an olive branch crown with an olive wreath," both sacred to Athena.[57]

On the island of Lesbos lived the great teacher and lover of women, Sappho, whose home provides the linguistic root for lesbianism and whose glyph of two women's symbols is a stylized Double Goddess. Born in 612 B.C.E., her poetry was much admired in the ancient world, as is attested by written references and portraits on coins from the late sixth century B.C.E. to the third century C.E.[58] Lesbos was, at the time, a powerful trading center near Samos, where the great temple to Hera was established in the eighth century B.C.E. Some of the teaching and singing traditions attributed to Sappho may have also been part of the "cult" practices at the temple of Hera. "A long tradition of specialized oral composition on the part of women" is suggested by evidence gathered by Sue Blundell in *Women in Ancient Greece*, who believes that "Sappho belonged to a group of women who were united by bonds of affection and by a love of music and poetry" in which "mutual female passion was accorded what would appear to us to be a surprising degree of official encouragement."[59] Demetra George believes Sappho was an avatar, in the tradition of Buddha, Mohammed, and Jesus.[60]

Most contemporary scholars seem to believe that the word *lesbian* (along with the concept) was first used only in the twentieth century, but Bernadette Brooten credits the earliest use of the word to medieval commentators writing about the work of authors from the early Christian period. Greek authors commonly used the word *tribas* from the word *tribo* ("to rub"), referring to women rubbing their genitals together. Another word used by Plato and others, *hetairistria,* could mean "courtesan" or "companion" (*hetaira*) and was equated by one medieval commentator with *tribades,* "women who, like men, are oriented toward female companions for sex." Another commentator equates *tribades, hetairistriai,* and *Lesbiai,* which Brooten says is "the earliest known attestation of 'Lesbian' (literally, 'a female inhabitant of Lesbos') for a woman erotically oriented toward other women." All of this, she says, demonstrates that "people in the ancient Mediterranean had the concept of an erotic orientation with respect to women."[61] The "male-faced" women of Lesbos, she writes, who seem to "constitute a regionally separate group," refused to take the "passive role" with men.[62] Lucian (second century C.E.) tells of "a woman from the island of Lesbos who refers to her female companion from Corinth as her wife."[63]

My first clue that there were overt lesbians in the late classical period of Greek history came from a statuette from the Roman period displayed in the British Museum, showing two women on a couch in an unexpectedly intimate pose. One woman is actually cupping her bare breast in one hand, as the two women lean into each other's

Fig. 5.6. Sculpted and painted image of two women sharing an intimate moment, suggesting that female same-sex love happened in Roman times. This sculpture can be seen at the British Museum.

faces as though to kiss. Brooten's research makes sense out of this and other provocative poses, such as a plate from Thera (620 B.C.E.) showing two women of equal height in a "typical courting position; that is, one is placing her hand below the chin of the other." A *kylix* (drinking cup) from the late sixth century B.C.E. shows "a nude woman caressing the clitoris of a standing nude woman and stroking the standing woman's inner thigh with her other hand," leading to her "visibly erect nipples, which . . . contribute to the impression of sexual arousal."[64]

Plato makes reference to "female homoeroticism" in the *Symposium,* and Aristophanes says that "*hetairistriai,* women who are attracted to women," have their "origin in primeval beings consisting of two women joined together." He imagines that each human being "seeks a partner of the gender to which she or he was originally attached."[65] Brooten tells a story of two women from Samos (Hera's island, close to Ephesus) who are believed by an ancient commentator to be *tribades.*[66] The famous Latin author, Ovid, equates Sappho's homoeroticism with "the distant Greek past" and the story of two Cretan girls "who loved each other and were engaged to marry."[67] Christine Downing sums up the lesbian-fearing Greek literature by taking it to a slightly larger, more universal level, saying that strong-willed women like Medea "do what they do *for themselves,* not out of conscious love of women. Yet in choosing themselves, in loving themselves, they are loving *woman.*" Female autonomy is hereby equated with lesbianism. "Commitment to self is a commitment to a woman, as their contemporaries seem clearly to have understood."[68]

Brooten—whose whole book is a documentation of these widespread practices—uses medical, astrological, and magical texts from Greece, Rome, and Egypt to prove her point that not only were women making love with one another, but they were often legally married. Even, surprising as it seems, "ancient Judaism was not fundamentally opposed to sexual love between women," although two rabbinical schools disagreed in the fifth century C.E. about whether "a woman who engaged in sexual contact with another woman (a *mesallelet*) was unfit for the priesthood."[69] All this began to change with Christianity and the advent of modern medicine, making lesbianism more and more pathologized, until doctors were performing frequent clitoridectomies on "mannish" women. But Brooten shows that for at least the first five centuries of the current era, there can be found "intriguing hints of a social institution, marriage between women, that challenged (the) understandings" of homoeroticism as "unnatural, masculine, active, sick, and comparable to prostitution."[70]

According to the early medical treatises, women's "two-fold sexuality" (*duplex sexus*) meant "having within oneself the characteristics of both sexes." The disease accusation wasn't really focused on homosexuality or the physiological body, but on women's *active* behavior, which was in every case considered sick. It wasn't so much the sexual activity that was condemned, as women's "active preference for women" and their "active pursuit of women," which was (and still is!) considered "masculine."[71]

For modern women, the Double Goddess figures have direct application as representations of the intense closeness and shared intimacy in any relationship between two women. It may even be that this extreme closeness is threatening to scholars and keeps them from relating in a more positive way to the pervasive presence of all the Double Goddess figures. Is it the incipient lesbianism of the vessels and figurines that scares the scholars? Or is it an even deeper, more unconscious fear of being engulfed by the once-powerful mother, as Downing suggests: "The *pull* to reexperience that bond of fusion, that sense of being totally loved, totally known, totally one with another—and the *fear* of reexperiencing that bond of fusion, of being swallowed up by a relationship, of losing one's own hard-won identity. . . ."[72]

Lesbians who have shied away from the Goddess movement because of its largely unconscious, but profoundly heterosexist bias, can relax into the knowledge that a lineage exists, going back to the beginnings of human civilization, sanctioning female-to-female relationship as the original, matriarchal bond and a model of community leadership.

This model has been mostly ignored by mainstream culture, even though it is a truism at this point in history that lesbians were (and are) the vanguard of the women's movement. Any basic survey of feminist institutions that emerged out of the so-called second wave of the women's movement in America will show the profound impact made by lesbian women. Significantly for our discussion, much of this impact was made through the influence and productivity of *lesbian couples*, in a contemporary version of our ancient Amazon Queens. Who would the remarkable Lily Tomlin be to us without the continuously brilliant material generated by her life partner Jane Wagner? The long-lasting partnership of Del Martin and Phyllis Lyon produced one of the most important women's clinics in the San Francisco Bay Area. Producer Lisa Vogel founded the Michigan Womyn's Music Festival as a young woman and collaborated successfully with her partner Barbara Price for a decade before they split up. Mama Bears Bookstore and feminist gathering place in Oakland was pioneered by Alice Molloy and Carol Wilson, who are only just now closing Mama Bears and heading into their retirement together. Krissy Keefer and Nina Fichter, although not lovers, were creatively partnered for twenty years developing first Wallflower Order and then Dance Brigade, groups of feisty feminist dancers still performing brilliantly under Keefer's direction at Dance Mission in San Francisco. Writer and thealogian Mary Daly conjured her famous *Wickedary* with her longtime friend Jane Caputi.[73] Redwood Records (featuring among others the music of Holly Near) sprang from the lifelong partnership of Joelyn Woorley and Jodi Schumacher. Likewise, drummer Edwina Lee Tyler and her longtime partner Roberta are legendary, as is the singing duo of Casslebury and Dupres.

This model can be seen in the tantric counterparts, Athena and Artemis. Athena, credited with inventing all of civilization's arts, became Goddess of the city-state, crafts, and culture, and Artemis remained Goddess of wild nature. Both remained "virgin"—neither was willing to relate romantically with men—and both were connected with

Amazons. Rarely does a scholar mention the all-too-obvious likelihood that either or both of these Goddess types might have found their sexual fulfillment with other women. Artemis, the shaman-priestess, might naturally discover her romantic partner in Athena, the physical warrior and head of state. Instead, both are treated not as if their Virgin Goddess status referred to the intactness of a woman belonging to herself, but rather as a kind of insular chastity that repudiated sexuality altogether. Artemis is infantilized as asexual and attached to her brother, Apollo; and Athena is seen as just one of the boys, bonded with her father, Zeus, out of whose head she supposedly emerged (fully armed).

According to Kerényi, who (controversially) uses an Indo-European root for Athene, she represented the container that held the sacred fire that had to be rekindled each day for "fire worship," and in this way she is similar to the Roman Vestal Virgins in relation to Vesta who is at times described in starkly lesbian, Amazon terms: "The others married . . . of the three, one resisted, refusing to endure a husband . . . and she loves companions [the Vestal Virgins] in her virginity."[74] Is it going too far then to equate Athena's power of containment with the solid, grounded, protective power of the Amazon warrior, and make her the perfect counterpart to the orgiastic, intuitive, emotive power of Artemis and her expressive wild Shakti-women? Is it going too far, then, to equate Athena's power of containment with the solid, grounded, protective power of the Amazon warrior, and make her the perfect counterpart to the orgiastic, intuitive, emotive power of Artemis and her expressive, wild Shakti-women? Two women holding leadership in the Dianic Wiccan Tradition (modern feminist witchcraft or paganism) don't think so. Ruth Barrett and Falcon River have developed a coherent paradigm around women sharing power in the roles of "ritual priestess" and "guardian priestess." The guardian priestess provides energetic support to the ritual priestess and maintains the container of the ritual circle, as the ritual priestess works her erotic magic at the center.[75]

SHAPE-SHIFTING CONTEMPORARY SHAMAN WOMEN

In light of the link represented by the land bridge that once connected Siberia to North America, it is not surprising that respect for the sufficient-to-herself woman represented by shape-shifting warrior/priestess Goddesses such as Artemis and Athena would be found in the Native American populations. It's not much of a stretch to link Native American practices and beliefs to those of the Siberian and Central Asian peoples we have been investigating, since they are understood to be related (genetically and linguistically). The "archaic" shamanism of the Siberian area has always included "transformed shamans, i.e. those who have apparently changed their sex ... (which is) connected with shamanistic exhibitions of power."[76] Customs among some of the north Asian "reindeer shamanism" peoples of Kamchadal and Kuril still included (in the early twentieth century) rites of cross-dressing,[77] and among the Ainu people of Japan (who are related to the Tungus tribes) "mother-right" prevailed.[78] A remnant of this tradition can be seen even to this day in Ireland where on Candlemas Eve (February 1), "boys dressed as women go from house to house carrying [Brigit's] girdle" to protect against physical ailments.[79]

Native American populations have generally recognized that there are more than two genders. Third and fourth genders encompass the men and women who don't fit easily into "male" and "female" with their attendant roles, and indigenous cultures around the world have long made space for these unconventional types who are often considered sacred, part of a "vision complex" in which dreams and visions lead to the adoption of the unique role.[80] Referred to in various ways as "not-men" and "not-women" (with at least two hundred different American Indian terms used by tribal groups to make reference to them), these "special" people are usually discovered to be different in childhood and their differences "encouraged and nurtured."[81]

Like modern radical feminist women, the "Two-Spirit" person or "berdache" in Native American culture represents a "separate gender within a multiple gender system" and is generally perceived to have "exceptional productivity, talent and originality."[82] Berdaches (male and female) tended to cross-dress and partner with "nonberdache members of the same sex," although these characteristics are variable. They were "accepted and integrated members of their communities," enjoying "special respect and honors," and occasionally, like shamans, "feared because of the supernatural power they were believed to possess."[83] Rather than being perceived as a medical or social problem, they were religious leaders, women chiefs and warriors, medicine people of such high standing that "nothing can be decided without their advice."[84]

Kenneth Luckert traces the "role of the supernatural berdache" back to "ancient preagricultural hunting patterns."[85] Among the Navaho (Diné), the term for berdache, *nádleehé*, means "one who changes continuously," suggesting the fluidity of being able to cross back and forth from one gender to another, and from one plane of consciousness to another, without shame or derision, "fluctuating between outer and inner forms of male and female forms."[86] Like the Double Goddess discussed in earlier chapters, the lunar cycle of feminine yin and feminine yang (the light and the dark, the day and the night, the

upper world and the underworld) is available to a

Fig. 5.7. These Double Goddesses from the ancient Mexican Tlatilco culture, 1100–900 B.C.E., would have once fallen into the catch-all category of "dancing girls" and "pretty ladies." Tlatilco figurines were excavated from agricultural fields, suggesting that they were used in ancient magical rites of blessing the fields with fertility.

Fig. 5.8. This double-faced female figure from Tlatilco, Mexico (1100–900 B.C.E.*), has a third eye weirdly placed in the center of her forehead, perhaps suggesting oracular or psychic powers often connected with women's shamanistic worldwide religion. Note how her hands are placed on her breasts, and that she wears a belt or girdle so often seen on ancient female figures.*

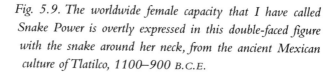

berdache woman who can shape-shift with ease. Not surprisingly, this is close to Giti Thadani's explanation of the Indic concept of the "jami" or twins, two women sharing a yoni or womb space, fluctuating back and forth between the light and the dark,[87] expressed by Double Goddess figures found in Mexico, dating to the first millennium B.C.E. Thadani explicitly discusses the "unconsorted woman," *Bhagini*, symbolizing "the autonomous woman, the *sv-stri* (self+woman)," which like Artemis and Athena, as well as the Native American Berdache, "constellates an independent gender identity and a gynefocal kinship economy,"[88] whose power can be seen in self-contained images like these, also from ancient Mexico.

The Two-Spirit Woman is a known entity with an ancient history among Native populations, including the famous Woman Chief of the Crow Indians, who—besides participating in hunting, war, and tribal leadership—also married four women.[89] Or the warrior woman, Running Eagle (Pi'tamakan) of the Blackfoot Indians, who "wore men's clothes when on a raid and women's clothes in camp," and was eulogized as "Pi'tamakan, virgin, and brave woman chief of our people."[90] Native

Fig. 5.9. The worldwide female capacity that I have called Snake Power is overtly expressed in this double-faced figure with the snake around her neck, from the ancient Mexican culture of Tlatilco, 1100–900 B.C.E.

Fig. 5.10. This double face found with the other figures from Tlatilco, 1100–900 B.C.E., looks as if both mouths are speaking (or more likely singing) about whatever it is she is able to see with her double set of eyes. Perhaps one of her is able to see in this world, and the other looks into the invisible dimension.

American writer Paula Gunn Allen points out that it was the "roles" (rather than the biological sex) in archaic tribal settings that were fixed into clearly marked divisions of labor ("women's work" and "men's work"). Among the Yuma, for example, a girl who "dreamed of weapons became a male for all practical purposes," or a girl "who chose to play with boys or with boys' objects such as a bow and arrow became a male functionary, which was called *hwame*" by the related Mohave people. The *hwame* "took a male name and was in all respects subject to ritual male taboos vis á vis females, such as avoidance of all contact with a menstruating wife . . . (who) was not considered *hwame* but simply a woman."[91]

Contrast this respectful Two-Spirit approach with the current trend in Western psychology to label girls like this as having a "gender identity disorder" and force them into psychiatric treatment while they are still in elementary school. Phyllis Burke's scary point in *Gender Shock: Exploding the Myths of Male and Female* was that this pathologizing of gender fluidity is happening more, rather than less, than it was fifty years ago. She shows how New Age pop psychology icons like John Gray (*Men Are from Mars, Women Are*

Fig. 5.11. This bright and energetic-looking female figure has Double Eyes and a Double Mouth, a strongly marked pubic triangle, and the necklace so often worn as power insignia by Goddesses (or priestesses) in different parts of the ancient world. Michoácan, Mexico, 400–100 B.C.E.

from Venus) and Marianne Williamson (*A Woman's Worth*) invent concepts like negative "role reversal" (Gray) and "Amazon neurosis" (Williamson) as a way of blaming "uppity" women for the failure of contemporary relationships.[92] This wouldn't be so bad if it weren't that these media celebrities have usurped the domain of feminism in the public discourse, while feminist voices have been pushed out of publishing since the broad-scale corporatization that took place in the mid-1990s.

Not only Two-Spirits but Native American queens have been widely documented, married as well as unmarried, as well as women warriors known for "consorting only with women in sexual gratification."[93] In any case, "marriage avoidance is a consistent theme in the lives of many female berdaches,"[94] linking the berdache typologically to Artemis and Athena, and recalling the etymological root of the word Amazon discussed earlier, meaning "no-husband one." It is no accident that early researchers meeting up with Two-Spirit Women in Native cultures referred to them as Amazons.[95]

THE SHAMANISTIC FLUIDITY OF GENDER

Research coming out of women's studies, Native American studies, gender studies, and queer studies academic programs has significantly expanded the previous approaches taken to this kind of material. Obviously, if you are locked into a belief in only two rigid genders, which is conflated with heterosexuality as a divinely ordained state of being, then the gender fluidity implied in these studies will seem far-fetched and unlikely (or perhaps more to the point, unnatural). But for many of us arriving at this important historical moment—the beginning of the twenty-first century—these unorthodoxies are a great relief and resonate vividly with our lived and felt experiences. Similarly, the unearthing of skeletons and mummies of ancient women who obviously lived as warriors, priestesses, lesbians, and cross-dressing shamans is good news and very supportive of our need to invent ourselves with broader models than those offered by conventional mainstream culture.

In anthropological descriptions, women showing gender diversity have been noted as being larger and stronger than their "normal" sisters. Crow Woman Chief was described as "taller and stronger than most women," and others were said to have "often developed great strength."[96] A Bronze Age female mummy from Cherchen, in China, was six feet tall; and an Altai priestess unearthed from a frozen tomb discussed earlier was also taller than other women of her tribe, measuring in at five feet, six inches; but both of them were dressed as women with artifacts to show their roles as typically gendered women or priestesses.

In general in Central Asia, high-status women were often buried by themselves in large kurgans just like their male counterparts, the much-ballyhooed "chieftains" of the Bronze and Iron Ages. Davis-Kimball's survey of Sauromatian and Sarmatian women living along the Volga River—and of the mid-first millennium B.C.E. graves she excavated at Pokrovka (near Kazakhstan)—is illuminating. She shows that Iron Age women (like earlier Bronze Age Double Queens) functioned in specialized roles of warrior and priestess. Warrior women (fifteen percent of the women at Pokrovka) were buried with bronze and iron armaments, like their male counterparts (ninety-four percent of the men); priestesses (seven percent of the women) were buried with their own recognizable accoutrements: portable altars, mirrors, ancient seashells, boar's tusk amulets, a spoon for the sacred fermented beverage, and often a crown, diadem, or headdress.[97]

The majority of women in the burials (seventy-five percent) Davis-Kimball calls "hearth women." They were buried at the center of their mounds seventy-two percent of the time, along with their spindle whorls and the other artifacts related to women's more usual roles. Their central placement in the tombs shows women's generally elevated status in these "matriarchal" tribal societies.[98] On occasion (three percent of the time), a particularly high-status or important woman (perhaps a third gender type) excavated from those burial mounds was buried with "both warrior and priestess artifacts," leading Davis-Kimball to call such a woman a "warrior-priestess."[99]

One such woman—potentially fitting the third gender type—excavated by the Russians earlier in the twentieth century was mistakenly identified as a male warrior, a "young chieftain," because of artifacts found in the grave. Through her insightful scholarly reconstruction, Davis-Kimball has clarified that the so-called "Gold Man of Issyk" was actually a Saka warrior-priestess; she was only five feet, three inches tall. (Saka tribes lived farther east near Mongolia and China, whereas Scythian and Sauro-Sarmatians lived west nearer to the Black Sea.) The fantastic burial contained weapons (short sword and dagger) and precious artifacts, including thousands of gold plaques sewn onto a caftan, jacket, and boots, and a gold-wrapped whip. The whip resembles those buried with Scythian women (see fig. 4.22 in chapter four) and Trojan-Yortan women before them (see fig. 4.21 in chapter four). A belt "accented with thirteen stylized gold deer heads" was made in the "lost-wax" casting method.[100] Thirteen is the female number par excellence, representing the actual number of Full Moons in a year.

But it was the unique headdress "suggestive of the images of shamans," and some jewelry that had "never before been found in an early nomadic male's burial" that caused Davis-Kimball to reexamine the burial from the standpoint of gender. She found that the tomb also contained "such telling artifacts as a gilded bronze mirror, a silver spoon with a bird's-head handle, and a koumiss beater—all of which have cultic significance."[101] She published her radical reframe of the burial in a 1997 *Archaeology* magazine, remarking on the "similarity of the Gold Man's headdress to the traditional hats worn by Kazak brides."[102]

This seems especially important, since I have concluded from my own research that the accoutrements of the priestess were often (perhaps always) transferred over to the bride, as matriarchal cultures gave way to patriarchal ones and women lost their former autonomy. Bridal costumes today in many different countries hold the key to the ancient priestesses' functions. This hidden symbolic language is encoded in embroidery and weaving patterns, rather than in written text, and has therefore been ignored or missed altogether. I like to think that the reason contemporary women—even lesbians—love to put on those white dresses and veils and walk down that aisle is really because we remember in our cells that we were once the queens and priestesses of old.

Breaking Free

Playing around with the fluidity of gender (gender-bending) through costume, behavior, speech, thought, art, music, and writing has become a foreground activity of the younger generation of queers, punks, and cyberpunks, as well as a kind of generalized, even ritualized activity within gay and lesbian communities everywhere. The thrill of breaking free from stereotypical sex roles has been vividly described in a book called *Vested Interests: Cross-Dressing and Cultural Anxiety,* in which author Margorie Garber reveals the "transvestite" as a liminal figure who "already inhabits, indeed incarnates, the margin." Garber posits that the inherently transgressive act of cross-dressing challenges "vested interests," and that the transvestite (male or female) represents "the disruptive element that intervenes, not just a category crisis of male and female, but the crisis of category itself." She speaks of "the extraordinary power of transvestism to disrupt, expose, and challenge," by showing the boundaries or borders to be permeable, allowing "border crossings" from one "apparently distinct" category to another.[103]

To understand the historical implications of these contemporary unconventional vanguard types, one only needs to turn to Biblical injunctions against cross-dressing: "The woman shall not wear that which pertaineth unto a man, neither shall a man put on a woman's garment; for all that do so are abominations unto the Lord thy God,"[104] and then remember that Joan of Arc was burned in large part because of her refusal to stop wearing male garb. The charges brought against her in her trial report that she maintained that her voices (Catherine and Mary) told her "to take and wear a man's clothes," which she did "to such an extent that this woman had declared she would rather die than relinquish these clothes." Joan never tried to pass as a man, but rather "was directed . . . to dress as a man," which was a "source of her subversive strength." One of her biographers describes her in words that could be equally true for a berdache: "She was usurping a man's function but shaking off the trammels of his sex altogether to occupy a different, third order, neither male nor female, like the angels."[105] The tragic story of Brandon Teena, a cross-dressing girl in Nebraska with these tendencies, brutally murdered for her transgressive gender deception, vividly illustrates the current threat and risks of such gender deviance in the modern Western world. Brandon's life was immortalized by Oscar-winning actress Hillary Swank in the movie *Boys Don't Cry*.

"Traversing the boundary of female-to-male" is especially taboo in a male-dominated society in which the male sex is privileged over the female, and the female is reminded at all times to stay in her "proper place." Paula Gunn Allen points out that with European colonization of North American tribes, "Virtually all customary sexual customs among the tribes were changed—including marital, premarital, homosexual, and ritual sexual practices, along with childhood and adult indulgence in open sexuality, common in many tribes."[106] It is this issue that has caused so many writers, beginning with Homer, to distort tales of the Amazons, ostracizing and demonizing them for dressing like men, hunting, fighting, or simply having their own agency.

Garber (like many other gender theorists) maintains that the extreme reactions of contemporary culture to female cross-dressers (the "bull dyke" or "bull dagger") are related to this issue of "usurpation" of the male prerogative and the calling into question of the "social codes" by which such categories were "policed and maintained."[107] The fact that *Vogue* and other women's magazines choose to show models in male "drag" as well as in provocative female-female poses supports Garber's theory that there is a "destabilization" taking place, in which the "figure of the transvestite serves as the hinge of a postmodern culture in the process of political and social rupture."[108]

Transformations

Kim Chernin's *My Life as a Boy* explores her unexpected awakening in her thirties: "No one who knew me back then thought I would turn into a boy," the book opens. "If a woman in her thirties turns into a boy, that may mean she's having trouble getting out of the place she's in. She requires the instinctive, wholly natural ruthlessness of a boy. He will leave home; everyone expects it of him. He won't move in next door to his mother or around the block and raise children, not likely. He won't give it a second thought: he's off into the world, he's a boy, he's going."[109] She perceives this experience as transitional, a liminal (almost supernatural) period during which she deliberately opens herself to possibilities that have not existed for her before.

She accomplishes this shape-shifting through incipient awareness of her own budding lesbianism: "Late in the afternoon, I found myself standing next to a woman who had put her head on my shoulder and was crying silently. I took off my jacket; I put it around her shoulders. I was taller than she was, the sort of person someone would lean up against, the strong one, the one who can support the other. . . . That was, I suppose, the day I first began to be a boy." The rest of the book is a tale of her development, through her realization of the absence of certain traits in herself (which she associates with boys), and the studied cultivation of those very traits, so that she might function in an effective way with women to whom she feels drawn.[110]

Other women, especially artists and not necessarily lesbians, take this "male prerogative" further into consciously rude, antisocial expressions of unexpected and transgressive images and behavior that sound reminiscent of Miranda Shaw's descriptions of the yoginis who couldn't be tamed. "Bad girls like the critical and constructive potential of laughter; they're feeling the intense pleasure of stepping outside the boundaries that, like our mother's and grandmother's girdles, have been cutting off our circulation for too long. . . . Their laughter is raucous, outrageous, and completely out of hand. Bad girls are hysterical! They'd rather stay mad. And bad."[111] Like the "Guerilla Girls" or the "Lesbian

Fig. 5.12. Author photo of postmodern girls at the Michigan Womyn's Music Festival

Avengers," the "Bad Girls" use their artistic expression to make a point, and to protest in a public way the indignity of male dominance and female submission. Isn't this the "warrior" pole of the Amazon duality?

The leading ladies of modern mythologies have been less often the *subject* and more generally the *object* of attention, allowing their male counterparts to perform all the action. Female agency is a quality sorely lacking in Western culture, having been replaced with a tendency on the part of the socialized female population to be there for others: to support, nourish, and enable. Surely that's why *Thelma and Louise* was both extremely popular with women viewers (in the Berkeley theater where I first watched the film, women cheered whenever the two heroines gained the upper hand) and at the same time, very threatening to many men. Interpersonally, the two women differed from each other by having precisely those qualities and skills needed at certain moments by the other, and passionately they joined forces in order to empower themselves and take larger-than-life initiative. In their obviously egalitarian encounter, they "showed up" for each other and stimulated each other to take actions neither of them would have been capable of on her own. Together, they broke loose from their conditioning, went on a rampage normally reserved for men, bonded deeply (leaving the men behind), and triumphantly chose death as an expression of their right to remain free. Exactly this kind of action was taken by priestesses of Athena who—when threatened by patriarchal rape and marriage—chose instead to jump together from the precipice at Cape Sounion.

Similar stories are told about medieval women ("witches") who chose death over the torture offered by the Inquisition.

The Age of Aquarius has to do with innovation, experimentation, and breaking free, so as we move into that period, certain people in our culture are likely to carry the new ideas into embodied existence, giving them shape, making them visible. Celebrities who have come out of the closet, such as Melissa Etheridge, k.d. lang, and Ellen Degeneres, seem to actively embrace this Aquarian destiny. Etheridge, for instance, like an Amazon, sings that she "could hear the thunder" under her feet, and that she sold her soul "for freedom," which she says is "lonely but it's sweet."[112] In February of 1997, she and her partner at the time, Julie Cypher, gave birth to their first child together in a public affirmation of their sexual orientation and "family values." In 1999, they birthed a second child, publicly acknowledging David Crosby as the sperm donor in both cases. Regardless of whatever opinions individuals might hold about marriage, family, and lesbians having babies, their photo together on the cover of *Newsweek* (4 November 1996), with the huge caption, "We're Having a Baby," was a total disruption of the "normal," and a welcome normalization of the extra-ordinary. Like the Tibetan Buddhist dakini, who destabilizes things in order to wake us up to a higher vibration, these "out lesbian" celebrities (with their larger-than-life visibility and counterculture ways) gloriously refuse to be limited to the female sex role stereotype.

The Double Goddess in all her various forms depicts women in relationship to ourselves and one another, with a panoply of potential dynamics from which to choose. It is not so much about difference, but rather a mirroring of the differences within each one of us. At best, our twin selves are met and mirrored back in complexity and an experience of fluidity, a subtle shape-shifting dance, a kind of graceful "taking turns." Each of us is always oscillating between the yin and yang of our own individual experience of radical internal polarity; although we may tend toward one pole or the other, we are actually both, and constantly changing.

CONCLUSION

Acknowledging, Developing, and Sharing Our Power

The Double Goddess provides a much-needed signifier of contemporary female freedom, representing a model of women joining together in an equal encounter from personal passion and for the larger purpose of group leadership. In the 1970s feminists exuberantly conceived of a world created and governed by radical women. Robin Morgan's *Sisterhood Is Powerful* (1970) summarized the early call to female solidarity. Women organized and staffed newly created institutions, including day-care centers, women's health clinics, and battered women's shelters. The creation of "women's culture" went much further, bringing to life women's presses, coffeehouses, bookstores, and music festivals, the best extant example being the Michigan Womyn's Music Festival, which celebrated its twenty-fifth glorious year in the summer of 2000. The corporate megastructure today has absorbed, erased, and broken the back of many of these early women's institutions, but in the shape-shifting tradition of women shamans and warriors throughout the millennia, this only momentarily breaks our stride.

Recognizing that all women everywhere are outsiders in a world system that universalizes as "normal" only the male experience while keeping female reality as "other," modern women like philosopher Mary Daly (surely one of the twentieth century's most courageous radical feminist Amazons) advise simply moving out of the patriarchal, male-dominated "foreground" and into our own female-centered "background," where we can invent, define, and inhabit a world of our own making.[1] Daly's newest work, *Quintessence*, describing her "radical elemental feminism,"[2] partakes of the same coded language that women's textiles and story cloths express, using a special, secret language that men don't perceive and can't decipher.

As illustrated by the examples mentioned above, women are collaborating more these days. Whether we see it in the same-sex (two-mom) couples who are rearing families without men, or women going into business together, or women friends coming together to circle, do ritual, and mutually support one another in carrying out the tasks of our difficult modern lives—it's all a manifestation of women sharing power. The obvious egalitarianism and psychic intimacy of the Double Goddess is empowering, whether in the apparent soul sisters who emerge out of one shared girdle or the enthroned and regal queens who sit in their power side by side and could be running a corporation. Images of strong women engaged with each other in substantive, meaningful interactions are very helpful, showing us the possibility of making intimate exchanges of all kinds, teaching us how to come together in love and trust with another woman. It's crucial that we expand our horizons and learn new skills from each other instead of relying solely on male authorities for support and direction.

Original human social organization was not arranged in nuclear families, and fatherhood was in no way institutionalized. Beyond simple biology, fatherhood was hardly recognized—certainly not deified—until the coming of the patriarchal Indo-European Zeus, a father god, in the late Bronze Age, or the similar arrival of Yahweh in the Middle East at about the same time. Earlier male role models for individual children would have naturally been a woman's brother, as is true in any matrilineal culture. We see this clearly in the Na of China and their "society without husbands or fathers."[3] The invention of the male "God-the-father" concept, along with its concomitant "divine king-ship," mirrors the temporal and religious usurpation of women's roles in daily life as the ruling queens (by "mother right") that they had been before that time.

Like legendary Amazons, some contemporary women find our-selves preferring our own company, fighting back against injustice, and creating innovative new social forms to replace the outdated ones that we can no longer tolerate. Visionaries and pioneers many of us, we're out on the edge scouting new trails and inventing paradigms of trans-formation and change, seeking solutions to the virulent, nature-killing problems of patriarchy. Whores, dykes, ball-busters, hags, and prudes, or even "not-women"—whatever names our culture chooses to call us, we represent the Maenads, Amazons, and Two-Spirit Women of our time, united in an all-out refusal to toe the line. Instinctually moving from some cellular memory of a time when autonomy and self-government were ours to wield, we keep breaking the rules of male domination.

FIGHTING BACK

When contemporary women wear the Labyris, we join in solidarity with the heretical resistance practiced by women down through the ages, and we reawaken the ancient lineage of female empowerment that Amazons and yoginis represent. How fitting that the paperback version of Mary Daly's *Quintessence* should picture the author on the cover holding her impressive Double Axe. Herself a well-known and proudly self-proclaimed heretic—author of *Gyn/Ecology* and *Beyond God the Father*—Daly urges contemporary women to "think our own thoughts" and "sin big,"[4] refusing to be silenced by the continuous, forceful threats

Fig. 6.1. Mary Daly with Double Axe. This image of Mary Daly comes from the cover of her most recent book, Quintessence, *in which she brings her awesome thealogy of radical elemental feminist resistance to new heights of Amazon brilliance. A self-proclaimed Heretic, Contrary-Wise Crone, and proud exponent of "Wild Elemental Genius," Daly models for generations of women how to "Act out of Original Integrity and to Spring more Wildly in Be-ing."*[5]

of patriarchy that have recently deposed her from what should have been the lifelong security of her tenured position at Boston College.

Rather than asking if it is "appropriate" for women to use the Double Axe symbol or revere Amazon warriors as positive role models, I find myself asking, "In a time of such horrific violence against women, why don't more women fight back?" It is astonishing, really, how little aggression contemporary women enact against their dominators, attackers, rapists, and killers. Our so-called natural pacifism (an elevated concept with lofty spiritual overtones) can sometimes be self-defeating masochism that does not bode well for the survival of our species. As the UCLA study mentioned in the Introduction has proven, the fight-or-flight response that characterizes men's response to danger does not apply to women, whose hormonal responses have evolved in such different ways. Female systems generate, instead of testosterone, a chemical called oxytocin, which stimulates women to reach out, gather in the children, and collaborate in creating strategies for defense and protection.

Women's lives in our distorted contemporary society unfortunately work against this biological strategy. Modern Western women—isolated in nuclear families, imprisoned alone in identical houses without benefit of sisterhood or extended family—apparently experience a crippling defenselessness in the face of collective dangers. When you add to this that contemporary women have cause to fear those men who are closest to them, the potentially abusive husbands and boyfriends and fathers who live in their own homes, then you begin to see the enormity of the problem that confronts our species at the moment. The self-destructive female passivity that prevents women from defending ourselves and our children against what the media refer to as "an epidemic" of domestic violence must surely function as positive reinforcement for that "virus" to continue to replicate itself in the next generation.

What does it mean to fight back? Does the Double Axe (and its concomitant figure-of-8 Shield Goddess) represent a War Goddess in the sense of women using arms and going into battle? Perhaps. Is that a good or "appropriate" icon for women of the twenty-first century to be using? I have to admit personally that Demi Moore in *G.I. Jane* was a thrilling departure for me from the normal feminine stereotypes we are spoon-fed by the mass media. Naturally there is endless discussion of this dilemma in the women's spirituality movement, which is made up largely of pacifist-type women, including myself, who repudiate war and violence of any kind. For twenty-odd years we have attempted to reconstruct a working model of the nurturing, egalitarian, peaceful Goddess-worshipping cultures that predated the onslaught of patriarchy some five thousand years ago. However, what is frequently missing from our reconstruction is an understanding of the extremely potent shamanistic warfare and defense that can be (and most certainly was) performed through magical and supernatural agencies. (If we still had the ability to walk on water, fly through the air, or go through solid walls unimpeded, I hardly think modern women would have to lie awake at night in fear of random or deliberate male violence.)

Many contemporary women relate positively to Buddhism, with its powerful mantras and meditation and visualization practices, as well as intellectual and conceptual frameworks that support our leaning into the invisible world of spirit for guidance and grounding in tranquility. But one must distinguish between the two kinds of Buddhism: the original version supposedly taught by the Buddha that requires us to extinguish all emotional expression and root out desire; and the tantric branch in Tibet that has retained magic, incantation, dance, divination, weather-working, and even the active use of sacred sexuality in its practices. It is the shamanistic and mediumistic forms of Buddhism that relate to Amazons and the Double Axe.

The shamanistic practices of Tibetan Buddhism, as I have shown in this book, are iconographically and experientially related to the earlier women-centered religion of Crete and the Aegean area, and may even be *literally* connected to those cultures. My research shows meandering, possibly unbroken, links between the Cretan and Thracian Maenads and some of the Europoid mummies of China, whose ancient extinct Tocharian script is related to the originators of Tibetan Buddhism, the Kushana dynasty. This means that the Tibetan Buddhist dakinis, central to my daily chanting, meditation, and visualization practices, are not only similar to the ecstatic priestesses and yoginis from Crete and Central Asia, but might actually be descended (in part) from those Caspian female ancestors—literally cut from the same cloth, as can be seen in the connections documented by textile expert Elizabeth Wayland Barber.

The emergence of the Amazon into the collective psyche at this time cannot be accidental. Art forms such as the popular television show, *Xena,* as well as the unearthing of "real life" skeletons of women warriors and priestesses buried in southern Russia, China, and Siberia, and the dissemination of Tibetan Buddhist practices into the West, combine in a dramatic and urgent wake-up call to humans at this desperate moment on the planet. As corporate and military technologies race blindly toward obliteration of the "natural" world, disrupted global weather patterns mirror back to us the devastation we have set in motion by our mechanistic programs. We may find that there is a calling for weather-working yoginis yet in our own lifetimes.

At the same time, a more hopeful sign might be taken from a fascinating newspaper account from the late 1990s that described scientists having set up an official "team" at a site high in the mountains of Colorado to study phenomena they have named Blue Jets and Sprites. Eyewitness reports of giant eight-story-high dancing "light shows" are frequently sighted by airplane crews flying at thirty-three thousand feet. They sound amazingly like the sky-dancing dakinis described in Tibetan Buddhist texts. Could it be we have supernatural helpers, whose ongoing presence in our world has been variously described over the millennia as "giantesses," "ogresses," "fairies," and "sky-walking women"? Early on the morning of February 1, 2003, the space shuttle Columbia disintegrated on its reentry into the earth's atmosphere after the crew had observed such phenomena from space. The scientists onboard reported, on January 31, the day before the shuttle exploded, that "they had clear images of cloud-to-space lightning, called sprites, and the first scientific pictures recorded from space that show an elf, a luminous doughnut-shape electrical glow above a thunderstorm..."[6] A week later, on Friday, February 7, the *San Francisco Chronicle* ran a huge front page headline with full-color photos alleging that a blue jet might be responsible for bringing down the Columbia. The paper described a "faint thunderclap in the upper atmosphere at the same time a photograph taken by a San Francisco astronomer appears to show a purplish bolt of lightning striking the shuttle."[7] The photos were turned over to NASA and nobody has heard anything about sprites or blue jets since then. But the fact that this event took place on Candlemas—the Goddess's own special crossquarter holiday, celebrated by witches and pagans everywhere—means to me that the supernatural display can be attributed to forces and influences larger than those defined by Western science.

Monica Sjöö, coauthor with Barbara Mor of *The Great Cosmic Mother,* asks in an original poem written in the late 1990s: "Are there Great Female Beings out there waiting for us to be free?"[8] I think so, and I won't be surprised to see them toting Double Axes or crescent knives in a profound call to women of the world to empower ourselves to save what we love, as the warrior women and priestesses from times past have likewise always had to do.

SUFFICIENT-TO-HERSELF

The Double Goddess, as we have seen in earlier chapters, is a potent symbol of the woman in relation to her Self, living *for* herself. In this model, she is intact, inviolable, and autonomous, like Artemis and Athena of old. As a glyph of ego integration or fusion, the Double Goddess image shows a woman who is both lunar and solar, who owns and expresses her outer and inner experience, and moves through the world with dignity and a sense of *agency* in response to her own subjective agendas. I have always felt that at its core, feminism is no more than that refreshing ability of women to be agents of our own reality. Certainly the Amazons and priestesses we have been investigating retained that capability, even in the face of the external collapse of women's culture.

The Double Goddess is an archetype from the past that offers modern women entering the Age of Aquarius a way of conceptualizing the female role as something other than being subsidiary to (and defined by) the male. The inner dynamism clearly portrayed in the lunar yin and yang (see fig. 1.3 in chapter one) of the two women depicted in Double Goddess figures encourages us to rethink our biological situation for what it's worth, so that we might not be so quick to knuckle under to accusations of essentialism. Essentialism, as I understand it, is what academic feminists have misunderstood the women's spirituality movement to mean when we equate power with biological capacities, or being female with lunar cycles, or imply that there is something "essential" and unconstructed about being a woman that makes us positively different from men.

In the broadest sense, of course, we are all the same in our basic nature; yet in the concrete, everyday world, the documented physical and biological differences between man and woman really do amount to something. Buddhists discuss this apparent dualism by using the words *absolute* and *relative* to describe the two states of existence. In the absolute sense, we all have exactly the same pure nature. In the relative sense, we are each unique and limited by the exigencies of our physical form and species.

Our twinlike capacities provide the basis in women for a remarkably broad and varied repertoire of emotional and sexual experience, which serves us well in our relationships with one another, as well as with the men and children in our lives. The evolutionary mechanism contained in the menstrual cycle is obviously still at work even today, providing in women a model of successful biological adaptation to our environment (whether we know it or not).

The Mountain Goddess from Çatalhöyük with her Twin Priestesses (see fig. 1.6 in chapter one) is a reminder of Artemis and her untamed yoginis, who drew their strength from a birthright of being female and free. The Double Goddess is a reminder to all of us women to tap into the powerful underground stream of female energy that flows to where we are, from the most ancient times up to the present moment, and celebrate the ceaseless, constantly oscillating current of yin and yang, dark and light, within each woman born. We all belong by birth to the cult of the Double Goddess, whose powerful image provokes us toward autonomy and female bonding, without reference to any man.

Time Line

7th Millennium B.C.E.

Catastrophic Black Sea Flood. (Ryan & Pitman, *Noah's Flood*)

Çatalhöyük (originates 6700 B.C.E.): agriculture, animal domestication, enthroned Mother Goddess found in grain bin, Cow Goddess, Vulture Goddess, many Double Goddesses (murals, figurines), women in yoga postures, giving birth, women shown with leopards, older women buried with obsidian mirrors and boar's tusks

Middle East: Neolithic Jericho (skulls decorated with cowry shells), Ain Ghazal near the Dead Sea—earliest sculpted Double Goddesses (plaster, life-size, trance eyes)

Lepinski Vir (Europe on the Danube): triangular "shrine" huts, funerary ritual place (rites of "excarnation"), fish goddess

6th Millennium B.C.E.

6000 B.C.E. Snake Goddess figurines in Aegean region in meditation (yoga) postures, agriculture (Neolithic) begins in Crete, Naxos, and some other Greek islands

Neolithic Sesklo culture in Thessaly (northern Greece) profoundly female-centered, Nea Nikomedeia ("new victory to/of the wise woman") Double Goddess

Neolithic Hacilar near Çatalhöyük, polychrome pottery, Double Goddess, women with leopards

Neolithic Ubaid culture in Iraq: Tigris/Euphrates River Delta (snake-faced madonnas, polychrome pottery, irrigation)

Neolithic Vinča: Copper metallurgy, sacred script, female figurines, Double Goddess

5th Millennium B.C.E.

5000 B.C.E. Greece: Dimini culture in Thessaly, continuation of Sesklo (6th millennium), Goddesses, temple buildings, possibly a theacracy of priestesses

5000 B.C.E. China: Yangshao Culture ("proto-Chinese") neolithic, matriarchal Banpo

4700 B.C.E. China: Neolithic "female spirit temple" (shamanistic), the Wu (women shamans)

4500 B.C.E. Malta: Gigantija double temple, Double Goddess, Hypogeum (burials 1500 years), Yogini figures, priestess figures

Africa: Rock art (shamanistic females)

Europe/Balkans: Vinča culture (continues) with sacred script, female figurines, temples, two-headed Double Goddesses (ends abruptly in 4500 B.C.E.)

Black Sea area: Karanovo culture (similar to Vinča), female figurines, female (breasted) centaurs

Varna on the Black Seacoast: earliest goldsmithing, more gold than anywhere, priestesses, Goddess images, female "symbolic" (mask) burials, hieroglyphic tablets

Black Sea-Caucasus Region: Horse domesticated (4500 B.C.E.), long-haired sheep domesticated and woven wool twill invented, eventually dispersed from this area to places east and west

Palestine: Double Goddess ossuary lid in Pe'qin cave from mid-5th millennium B.C.E.

4th Millennium B.C.E.

Egypt: predynastic Vulture Goddess (bird woman figurines), Cow Goddess, neolithic settlements along the Nile, gold-mining, beer-brewing, queens in tombs

Malta: continues to develop, more complex temples, Hypogeum funerary rituals the whole millennium (the remains of 7000 people housed there)

Sicily & Sardinia: Hypogea (underground tombs) like Malta

Europe: long-barrow tombs, the entrance to the Goddess's underworld

Middle East: Uruk replaces Ubaid in Iraq, end of polychrome pottery, beginning of mass production, capitalism; proto-Elamite script (disappears eventually)

Tell Brak (Syria/Iraq): thousands of Eye Goddesses found in the layers might be home of Hurrians (non-Indo-European, non-Semitic mystery people)

China Liangzhu culture: advanced silk industry by 3200 B.C.E.

Indus Valley cultures: 3500 B.C.E.

3rd Millenium B.C.E.

Egypt: Old Kingdom (1st four dynasties) included powerful queens like Neit-hotep. Two Ladies; Isis-Nepthys; Vulture-Cobra; the "Great Ones"; royal woman depicted wearing leopard-skin garment (Egyptian "Maenad")

Greek Islands: (cemeteries, platforms) Cycladic figurines made of marble, known as "stiff nudes," vertical Double Goddesses, women buried with more goods than men, saffron trade

Lerna in the Greek Peloponnese, great House of Tiles (temple), seal stones, destroyed toward end of millennium

Anatolia (Turkey): Alaca Höyük in Cappadoccia, early Troy on west coast (both with gold, high status female burials and/or artifacts); Mellaart's Yortan figures (Double Amazon Queens); Double Goddess "disc" figurines, sites destroyed at end of millennium

Caucasus: Maikop culture (gold, bronze cauldrons), entry point to eastern trade routes

Indus Valley Civilization in India (Harappa, Mohenjo Daro) connected across trade routes to Central Asian sites and points west, as well as China and Africa

Sumer: 1st dynasties, Inanna temple built (would be active for 3000 years) High Priestess Enheduanna writes first recorded poetry, hymns to Inanna (2600 B.C.E.), first epic writing includes Inanna-Ereshkigal (Double Goddess)

Tell Brak (Syria/Iraq border): Final Eye Goddess temple of Inanna-Ishtar 3000 B.C.E.

BMAC cultures along Silk Road (2300–1800 B.C.E.) migrations of Goddess-worshipers? Seal stone with Double Axe sign discovered recently at Anau (2300 B.C.E.)

2nd Millenium B.C.E.

2000 B.C.E. Crete: New admixture, burials; mountain shrines "spontaneously" appear; "palace" culture begins, female-centered religion, the Double Axe, griffins, Maenads, murals

Cyprus: Double Goddesses in plank style inscribed with "language of the Goddess"

2000–1700 B.C.E. Thera: Female-centered religious ceremonial center established on Thera (Santorini) with extraordinary murals, destroyed by volcanic explosion that left the island a crescent shape and preserved the site; largest image of Nature Goddess in Aegean

1800–1700 B.C.E. (approx.) Crete: earthquake devastates palaces, Snake Goddesses buried under floor stone near throne room at Knossos (until 20th century excavation)

1800–1700 B.C.E. (approx.) Hamurabi destroys Mari in Iraq, misogynistic law codes

1400 B.C.E. Crete: dominated by Mycenaeans (Minos?), "weaving factory" at Knossos created with slave women brought as booty; Hagia Triada sarcophagus with Double Amazon Queens in chariots, high priestess buried at Archanes cemetery in Crete (with horse)

2000 B.C.E. Tarim Basin (north of Tibet): European burials (migrations) begin and continue through Iron Age, woven clothing matches Hallstatt in Europe/Scotland tartan plaid

2000 B.C.E. Anatolia: Amazon Queens said to have founded cities on west coast of Turkey, such as Ephesia (founded Ephesus), Myrina on Lemnos, perhaps Troy

1700 B.C.E. Hittite civilization in Turkey (amalgam with indigenous Hatti): King marries Hurrian Queen and keeps Goddess religion, sphinxes, lion gate, Double Eagles

1700 B.C.E. Mycenaean "royal shaft graves" appear in Greece, filled with gold artifacts, lots of awesome female finds, gold Amazon girdles, "forebears" of later Mycenaeans

Entire 2nd millenium Caucasus, Colchida (Colchis) and around the Black Sea: the North Pontic culture (proto-Cimmerians) thriving, Medea's area, many languages spoken (Indo-European as well as non-Indo-European), metallurgy highly evolved, Indo-Europeans may have originated and spread to all parts of the world from here, showing up in the west (Anatolia, Crete and the Aegean), as well as east (Tarim Basin)

China: Shang Dynasty (oracle bones), may be partially product of western migrations

Mid-2nd Millenium Egypt: Hyksos establish dynasty at Avaris with Cretan murals of bull-leapers, etc., Snake Goddess found in midwife's "bundle" that closely resembles Snake Goddesses in Crete; 18th Dynasty in Egypt very artistic, refreshing, resonant with Crete

Greece: Mycenaean artifacts at lowest level of Eleusis, beginning of Demeter-Persephone (Double Goddess) mystery religion that would last 3000 years; Trojan War (1250 B.C.E.)

Thrace: Late Bronze Age Mycenean artifacts show up in fantastic "hoards" buried in Bulgaria and other places in Europe, probably left by refugees, Double Axe with animals of the Goddess

Central Europe: Phenomenal hammered-gold conical hats buried upright under the earth, hoards of gold jewelry, including large "torc" necklaces, and huge boar's tusks encased in decorative metal (buried with women)

Late Bronze Age: 1400–1200 B.C.E.

Mycenaean civilization flourishes on Crete and mainland Peloponnese (Argolid), famous Lion Gate at Mycenae (double lionesses with goddess pillar and double altar), cult rooms filled with female imagery, murals, figurines, etc. War Goddess plaque, warrior woman wearing boar's tusk helmet (Athena), Goddess with the Sheaves, processions of women, priestesses in action

Midea: (named for Medea?) Site near Mycenae, Tiryns (Double Queens in chariot), Hera's temple in Argos, Hera's temple on the peninsula of Perachora (Hera of the Harbor), an oracle site connected with Medea's children; Medea (and other royal women like Helen) were brought home as trophies; Medea instigates the worship of Hera in the Peloponnese. Was Hera, the Queen of Heaven, an Amazon Goddess before she was forced to be the wife of Zeus? (lots of horse offerings and griffins at the Hera temples)

Keos: More than 50 female terracotta "Maenad" figures (some lifesize) made for dancing ritual performance at largest temple in Bronze Age Aegean

1250–1200 B.C.E. Total devastation in Aegean and Mediterranean areas, empires crushed (Hittites, Egyptians, Mycenaeans, Trojans, Canaanites, etc.), terrible earthquakes, bringing in Dark Age

Delphic Oracle brought from Crete around 1200 B.C.E. (shrine to Ge the Earth Goddess)

Iron Age (1st millennium B.C.E.):

10th–8th century B.C.E. Koban culture in Caucasus (near Black Sea); Medea's region

8th century B.C.E. Cimmerians in Black Sea area

8th Century B.C.E. Homer (*Iliad, Odyssey*), Hesiod (first mention of Medea), Temple to Apollo built at Delphi (Apollo kills the Python)

6th century B.C.E. Sappho of Lesbos has a school for young women, writes love poetry to male and female lovers

8th century B.C.E.: Cimmerians (whose ancestor may have been Medea of Colchis) chased out of Black Sea area and into Anatolia by Scythians who come from farther East and eventually settle north of the Black Sea

8th century B.C.E.: Grand Hera temples built in Argos, Perachora, Olympia, the island of Samos—international places of meeting, commerce, and religious activity

8th century B.C.E.: Etruscan civilization emerges in Tuscany, free and independent women, burials of priestesses, images of Amazons, griffins, dakinis

6th century B.C.E.: Sauromatians live between the Don and Volga Rivers in southern Russia, female government; the western ones (near the Sea of Azov) may be Amazons who had to flee from Cappadoccia (Turkey) in earlier centuries—chased out by the Greeks (?) living for a while on the Black Sea, and eventually settled near Scythian territory; warrior women and priestesses excavated (Dual Queenship)

6th century B.C.E.: Pazyryk tombs in Siberia, High Priestess buried in the Altai mountains, Issyk (Saka) "Gold Man" (who is really a woman with armaments), the 3 "Witches of Subeshi" (Europoid priestess mummies wearing high pointy hats buried in China)

5th century B.C.E.: Herodotus (the first history), Euripides (*Medea, Trojan Women*), Greek colonies around Black Sea, Greek vases depicting Amazons found in Amazon graves from this period

5th century B.C.E.: Parthenon built on Acropolis to house huge statue of Athena, divine "Head of State"; women in Athens basically lose all their rights; Temple of Artemis of Ephesus built (one of the 7 wonders of the world); gorgons appear in Greece, Italy, Sicily, Turkey, and all across the steppes. Greeks obsessed with Amazons—more images of Amazons created in classical Greece than any other theme

Notes

Introduction

1. Adrienne L. Zihlman, *The Human Evolution Coloring Book* (New York: HarperPerennial, 1982), 62.

2. Judy Grahne, *Blood, Bread, and Roses: How Menstruation Created the World* (Boston: Beacon Press, 1994).

3. Giti Thadani, *Sakhiyani: Lesbian Desire in Ancient and Modern India* (London: Cassell, 1996), 20.

4. Ibid., 21.

5. Ibid., 22.

6. Ibid., 24.

7. S. E. Taylor, L. C. Klein, B. P. Lewis, T. L. Gruenewald, R. Gurung, and J. A. Updegraff, "Female Responses to Stress: Tend and Befriend, Not Fight or Flight," *Psychological Review,* 107 (3), 41–42.

Chapter One

1. Andrew Weil, *Spontaneous Healing* (New York: Alfred A. Knopf, 1995), 204.

2. Edwin Bernbaum, *Sacred Mountains of the World* (Berkeley, Calif.: University of California Press, 1997), 6–15.

3. Marija Gimbutas, *The Language of the Goddess* (San Francisco: Harper and Row, 1989), 40.

4. Ibid.

5. Marija Gimbutas, *The Civilization of the Goddess* (San Francisco: HarperSanFrancisco, 1991), 343.

6. James Mellaart, Udo Hirsch, and Belkis Balpinar, *The Goddess from Anatolia,* vols. 1–4 (Adenau, West Germany: Eskenazi, 1989).

7. Vicki Noble, *Shakti Woman: Feeling Our Fire, Healing Our World (The New Female Shamanism)* (San Francisco: HarperSanFrancisco, 1991), 17.

8. Private communication from Janet Balaskas, author of *Active Birth: The New Approach to Giving Birth Naturally* (rev. ed.) (Harvard, Mass.: The Harvard Common Press, 1992).

9. Joan Harrod in Marler, ed., *From the Realm of the Ancestors: An Anthology in Honor of Marija Gimbutas* (Manchester, Conn.: Knowledge, Ideas and Trends, Inc., 1997), 492.

10. Starhawk, *The Spiral Dance* (San Francisco: HarperSanFrancisco, 1999).

11. Christine Downing, *Myths and Mysteries of Same-Sex Love* (New York: Continuum, 1989), 202.

12. Patricia Monaghan, *The Book of Goddesses and Heroines* (revised and enlarged) (St. Paul, Minn.: Llewellyn Publications, 1990), 24.

13. Diane Wolkstein and Samuel Noah Kramer, *INANNA: Queen of Heaven and Earth: Her Stories and Hymns from Sumer* (New York: Harper & Row, 1983), 52.

14. Erich Neumann, *The Great Mother: An Analysis of the Archetype,* Bollingen Series XLVII (Princeton, N.J.: Princeton University Press, 1963), 83.

15. Marija Gimbutas, *The Living Goddesses,* ed. and supplemented by Miriam Robbins Dexter, (Berkeley, Calif.: University of California Press, 1999), 161.

16. Frédérique Marglin, *Wives of the God-Kings: The Rituals of the Devadasis of Puri* (New York: Oxford University Press, 1985), 240.

17. Miranda Shaw, *Passionate Enlightenment: Women in Tantric Buddhism* (Princeton, N.J.: Princeton University Press, 1994).

18. Sylvia Brinton Perera, *Descent to the Goddess: A Way of Initiation for Women* (Toronto, Canada: Inner City Books, 1981), 39.

19. Marija Gimbutas, *The Goddesses and Gods of Old Europe, 6500–3500 BC, Myths and Cult Images* (Berkeley, Calif.: University of California Press, 1982), 135.

20. Ibid., 112.

21. Neumann, *The Great Mother: An Analysis of the Archetype,* 307.

22. Carol A. Grissom, "Neolithic Statutes from Ain Ghazal: Construction and Form," *American Journal of Archaeology* 104 (2000): 25–45.

23. Jonathan Tubb, *Bible Lands: Eyewitness Guide* (London: Dorling Kindersley in association with the British Museum, 1991), 9.

24. Gimbutas, *Goddesses and Gods of Old Europe, 6500–3500 BC, Myths and Cult Inages,* 136.

25. Gimbutas, *The Language of the Goddess,* 3.

26. Ibid., 12.

27. Gimbutas, *Goddesses and Gods of Old Europe, 6500–3500 BC, Myths and Cult Images,* 113.

28. Ibid., 116.

29. Gimbutas, *The Living Goddesses,* 76.

30. Gimbutas, *Goddesses and Gods of Old Europe, 6500–3500 BC, Myths and Cult Images,* 122.

31. Ibid., 126.

32. Gerald Sinclair Hood Cadogan, ed., *The End of the Early Bronze Age in the Aegean* (Leiden, Netherlands: E.J. Brill, 1986), 52.

33. Gimbutas, *The Civilization of the Goddess,* 363.

34. John Opsopaus, "Pauca Anecdota Neapolitana," (Biblioteca Arcana: www.cs.utk.edu/~mclennan/OM/BA/JO-AN.html), 31.

35. Dr. Günsel Renda, curator, *Nine Thousand Years of the Anatolian Woman,* Exhibition Catalogue (Istanbul, Turkey: Ministry of Culture General Directorate of Monuments and Museums, 1993), 90.

36. Thadani, *Sakhiyani: Lesbian Desire in Ancient and Modern India,* 20.

37. Elizabeth Wayland Barber, *Women's Work: The First 20,000 Years* (New York: W.W. Norton, 1994), 44.

38. Ibid., 60.

39. Mellaart, Hirsch, and Balpinar, "Anatolian Kilims Past and Present," *The Goddess from Anatolia,* vol. 4, 64.

40. Ibid., 48.

41. Ibid., 39.

42. Gimbutas, *The Language of the Goddess,* 165.

43. Ibid., 273.

44. June Campbell, *Traveller in Space: In Search of Female Identity in Tibetan Buddhism* (New York: George Braziller, 1996), 7.

45. Ibid., 64.

46. Mellaart, Hirsch, and Balpinar, *The Goddess from Anatolia,* vol. 2, 10.

47. Marija Gimbutas, *The Goddesses and Gods of Old Europe, 6500–3500 B.C., Myths, Legends and Cult Images* (Berkeley, Calif.: University of California Press, 1982), 186.

48. Ibid., 187.

49. Gimbutas, *The Language of the Goddess,* 275.

50. Ibid., 242.

51. Jeannine Davis-Kimball, "Amazons, Priestesses and Other Women of Status: Females in Eurasian Nomadic Societies," *Silk Road Art and*

Archaeology (Kamakura, Japan: *Journal of the Institute of Silk Road Studies,* 1997/98), 22.

52. Jeannine Davis-Kimball, with Mona Behan, *Warrior Women: An Archaeologist's Search for History's Hidden Heroines* (New York: Warner Books, 2002), 166.

53. Vicki Noble, "Medea and the Shaman Women of the Silk Road," paper presented at conference in Bogliasco, Italy, 2002, publication forthcoming.

54. Gimbutas, *The Living Goddess,* 129.

55. Ibid., 121.

56. Ibid., 134.

57. Ibid., 149.

58. Martin P. Nilsson, *The Minoan-Mycenaean Religion and its Survival in Greek Religion,* 2nd rev. ed., (Lund, Sweden: Gleerup, 1950), 79.

59. Gimbutas, *The Goddesses and Gods of Old Europe,* 186.

60. Gimbutas, *The Language of the Goddess,* 271.

61. Gimbutas, *The Living Goddess,* 152.

62. Nilsson, *The Minoan-Mycenaean Religion and its Survival in Greek Religion,* 79.

63. Pat Cameron, *Blue Guide Crete* (New York: W.W. Norton, 1988), 113.

64. Bogdan Rutkowski, *The Cult Places of the Aegean,* (New Haven, Conn.: Yale University Press, 1986), 59.

65. Ibid., 58.

66. Ibid., 43.

67. Ibid., 88.

68. Ibid., 79.

69. Ibid.

70. Ibid., 84.

71. Gimbutas, *The Language of the Goddess,* 268.

72. Veronica Tatton-Brown, *Ancient Cyprus,* (London: British Museum Press, 1997), 56.

73. Donald A. MacKenzie, *Myths of Crete and Pre-Hellenic Europe* (London: The Gresham Publishing Company Ltd., n.d.), 311.

74. Martin Bernal, *Black Athena: The Afroasiatic Roots of Classical Civilization, Vol. I: The Fabrication of Ancient Greece 1785–1985* (Piscataway, N. J.: Rutgers University Press, 1987), 76.

75. Martin Bernal, *Black Athena: The Afroasiatic Roots of Classical Civilization, Vol. II: The Archaeological and Documentary Evidence* (Piscataway, N. J.: Rutgers University Press, 1991), 169.

76. Ibid., 170.

77. John Noble Wilford, *New York Times,* 13 May 2001, section 1, p. 1 (Late Edition).

78. Elizabeth English, *Vajrayogini: Her Visualizations, Rituals, and Forms (A Study of the Cult of Vajrayogini in India)*, Boston: Wisdom Publications, 2002.

Chapter Two

1. Gimbutas, *The Living Goddess*, 113.
2. Ibid., 114.
3. Ibid., 116.
4. Vicki Noble, *Motherpeace: A Way to the Goddess through Myth, Art, and Tarot* (San Francisco: Harper & Row, c1983), and *Shakti Woman : Feeling Our Fire, Healing Our World (The New Female Shamanism)*.
5. Monica Sjöö and Barbara Mor, *The Great Cosmic Mother: Rediscovering the Religion of the Earth* (San Francisco: Harper and Row, 1987), 173.
6. Cai Hua, *A Society Without Fathers or Husbands: The Na of China* (New York: Zone Books, 2001), 20.
7. Ibid.
8. Ibid., 20–21.
9. Alexander Marshack, *The Roots of Civilization* (New York: Moyer Bell Ltd., 1991), 338.
10. M.A. Czaplicka, *Aboriginal Siberia: A Study in Social Anthropology* (London: Oxford University Press, 1914), 244.
11. Mellaart, Hirsch, and Balpinar, *The Goddess from Anatolia*, vol. 1, 84–85.
12. Mary B. Kelly, *Goddess Embroideries of the Balkan Lands and the Greek Islands* (New York: Studio Books, 1999), 89.
13. Ibid., 34.
14. Ibid., 65.
15. Mellaart, Hirsch, and Balpinar, *The Goddess from Anatolia*, vol. 1, 87.
16. Max Allen, *The Birth Symbol in Traditional Women's Art from Eurasia and the Western Pacific* (Toronto: The Museum for Textiles, 1981), 27.
17. Mary Daly, *Quintessence: The Archaic Future (A Radical Elemental Feminist Manifesto)* (Boston, Mass.: Beacon Press, 1998).
18. Mellaart, Hirsch, and Balpinar, *The Goddess from Anatolia*, vol. 2, 21.
19. Gimbutas, *The Living Goddess*, 84.
20. Downing, *Myths and Mysteries of Same-Sex Love*, 209.
21. Veronica Veen, *The Goddess of Malta: The Lady of the Waters and the Earth* (Netherlands: Inanna-Fia Publications, 1992), 58.
22. William Ryan and Walter Pitman, *Noah's Flood: The New Scientific Discoveries about the Event that Changed History* (New York: Simon & Schuster, 1989), 187.
23. Christina Biaggi, *Habitations of the Great Goddess* (Manchester, Conn.: Knowledge, Trends and Ideas, 1994), 30.

24. Reynold Higgins, *Minoan and Mycenaean Art* (London: Thames & Hudson, 1997), 130.

25. Gimbutas, *The Living Goddess,* 152.

26. Christos Doumas, *The Wall-Paintings of Thera* (Athens, Greece: The Thera Foundation, 1992), 30.

27. Amélie Kuhrt, *The Ancient Near East,* vol. 1 (New York : Routledge, c. 1995), 102.

28. Doumas, *The Wall-Paintings of Thera,* 132.

29. Ibid., 131.

30. Robert Briffault, *The Mothers: A Study of the Origins of Sentiments and Institutions,* vol. III (New York: The Macmillan Company, 1927), 34.

31. Ibid., 34.

32. Ibid., 36.

33. Ibid., 37.

34. Ibid., 42.

35. Ibid., 38.

36. Anne K. Capel and Glenn E. Markoe, eds., *Mistress of the House, Mistress of Heaven: Women in Ancient Egypt,* (New York: Hudson Hills Press, 1997), 132.

37. Capel and Markoe, *Mistress of the House, Mistress of Heaven: Women in Ancient Egypt,* 42.

38. Bernal, *Black Athena: The Afroasiatic Roots of Classical Civilization, Vol. I: The Fabrication of Ancient Greece 1785–1985,* 65.

39. Barbara Walker, *The Woman's Encyclopedia of Myths and Secrets* (San Francisco: Harper & Row, 1983), 22.

40. Capel and Markoe, *Mistress of the House, Mistress of Heaven: Women in Ancient Egypt,* 130.

41. Sue Blundell, *Women in Ancient Greece* (London: British Museum Press, 1995), 34.

42. Homer. *The Iliad,* 1:551, 87.

Chapter Three

1. Czaplicka, *Aboriginal Siberia: A Study in Social Anthropology,* 244.

2. Ibid., 171.

3. Ibid., 198.

4. Ibid., 244.

5. Ibid., 245.

6. Josine H. Blok, *The Early Amazons: Modern and Ancient Perspectives on a Persistent Myth* (Leiden, Netherlands: E.J. Brill, 1995), 103.

7. John Vincent Bellezza, *Divine Dyads: Ancient Civilization in Tibet* (Dharamsala, India: Library of Tibetan Works & Archives, 1997), 308.

8. Bedrich Hrozny, *Ancient History of Western Asia, India and Crete,* (Prague, Czechoslovakia: Artia, 1953), 220.

9. Shaw, *Passionate Enlightenment: Women in Tantric Buddhism,* 83.

10. Joseph Needham, *Science & Civilization in China,* Vol. 2 (Cambridge, England: Cambridge University Press, 1969), 134.

11. Ibid., 137.

12. Vidya Dehejia, *Yogini Cult and Temples: A Tantric Tradition* (New Delhi, India: National Museum, 1986), 8.

13. Bellezza, *Divine Dyads: Ancient Civilization in Tibet,* 226–7.

14. Dehejia, *Yogini Cult and Temples,* 68.

15. Shaw, *Passionate Enlightenment,* 79.

16. Dehejia, *Yogini Cult and Temples,* 13.

17. David Gordon White, *The Alchemical Body: Siddha Traditions in Medieval India* (Chicago: University of Chicago Press, 1996), 139.

18. Gimbutas, *The Civilization of the Goddess,* 283.

19. Bellezza, *Divine Dyads: Ancient Civilizations in Tibet,* 211.

20. Ibid., 185.

21. Stephen Batchelor, *The Tibet Guide* (London: Wisdom Publications, 1987), 65.

22. Gimbutas, *The Living Goddess,* 56.

23. Ibid., 61.

24. Ibid., 106.

25. Dianne Skafte, *When Oracles Speak: Understanding the Signs & Symbols All Around Us* (Wheaton, Ill.: Quest Books, 2000), 58.

26. Gimbutas, *The Civilization of the Goddess,* 297.

27. Skafte, *When Oracles Speak,* 57.

28. Oliver Dickinson, *The Aegean Bronze Age* (Cambridge, England: Cambridge University Press, 1994), 284.

29. Andonis Vasilakis, *Minoan Crete: From Myth to History* (Athens, Greece: Adams Editions, 1999), 43.

30. Stephen Harrod Buhner, *Sacred and Herbal Healing Beers: The Secrets of Ancient Fermentation* (Boulder, Colo.: Brewers Publications, 1998), 147.

31. P. P. Kahane, *20,000 Years of World Painting,* ed. Hans L. C. Jaffé, (New York, H. N. Abrams [1967]), 51.

32. Karl Kerényi, *Dionysos: Archetypal Image of Indestructible Life,* trans. Ralph Manheim (Princeton, N.J.: Princeton University Press, 1976), 49.

33. Laslow Torday, *Mounted Archers: The Beginnings of Central Asian History* (Durham, England: The Durham Academic Press, 1997), 66.

34. David Spess, *Soma: The Divine Hallucinogen* (Rochester, Vt.: Park Street Press, 2000), 4.

35. Ibid., 111.

36. *Hymns of the Rigveda,* trans. T.H. Griffith, ed. J.L. Shastri (Delhi, India: Motilal Banarsidass, [1973]), Book I, Hymn II, footnote 1.

37. Dehejia, *Yogini Cult and Temples: A Tantric Tradition,* 57.

38. Spess, *Soma: The Divine Hallucinogen,* 17.

39. Elizabeth Wayland Barber, *The Mummies of Ürümchi* (New York: W.W. Norton and Co., 1999), 163.

40. Ibid., 165.

41. Thomas D. Seeley, "Born to Dance: Choreography in a Beehive," *Natural History,* 108 (1999): 54.

42. Layne Redmond, *When the Drummers Were Women: A Spiritual History of Rhythm* (New York: Three Rivers Press, 1997), 65.

43. Gimbutas, *The Living Goddess,* 69.

44. Davis-Kimball, "Amazons, Priestesses and Other Women of Status: Females in Eurasian Nomadic Societies," 42.

45. James J. Clauss and Sarah Iles Johnston, eds. *Medea: Essays on Medea in Myth, Literature, Philosophy, and Art* (Princeton, N.J.: Princeton University Press, 1997), 206.

46. Jacob Rabinowitz, *The Rotting Goddess: The Origin of the Witch in Classical Antiquity* (New York: Automedia, 1998), 141.

47. Clauss and Johnston, *Medea: Essays on Medea in Myth, Literature, Philosophy, and Art,* 235.

48. Miriam Dexter, "Medea and Her Circumpontic Sisters," paper presented at the Bogliasco Conference, Italy, 2002, publication forthcoming.

49. Spess, *Soma: The Divine Hallucinogen,* 157.

50. Miriam Dexter, personal communication, Feb. 2002.

51. Rutkowski, *The Cult Places of the Aegean,* 193.

52. Gimbutas, *The Civilization of the Goddess,* 317.

53. Ibid., 326.

54. Gimbutas, *The Living Goddess,* 117.

55. Deborah E. Klimburg-Salter, ed., *The Silk Route and the Diamond Path: Esoteric Buddhist Art on the Trans-Himalayan Trade Routes* (Los Angeles: UCLA Art Council, 1982), 29.

56. Vivian Davies and Renée Friedman, *Egypt* (London: British Museum Press, 1998), 109.

57. Gimbutas, *The Civilizations of the Goddess,* 118.

58. Ivan Marazov, ed., *Ancient Gold: The Wealth of the Thracians (Treasures from the Republic of Bulgaria)* (New York: Harry N. Abrams, Inc. in cooperation with The Ministry of Culture of the Republic of Bulgaria, 1997), 35.

59. Yordanka Yurukova, curator, *Glorie di Tracia: L'oro Più Antico I Tesori I Miti* [The Glories of Thrace: The Most Ancient Gold, the Treasures, the Myths] (Florence, Italy: Ermes, 1997), 49.

60. Ibid., 58.

61. Gimbutas, *The Civilization of the Goddess*, 118.

62. Yurukova, *Glorie di Tracia: L'oro Più Antico I Tesori I Miti* [The Glories of Thrace: The Most Ancient Gold, the Treasures, the Myths], 49.

63. Ibid., 51.

64. Ibid., 55.

65. Marazov, ed., *Ancient Gold: The Wealth of the Thracians (Treasures from the Republic of Bulgaria)*, 14.

66. Gimbutas, *The Civilization of the Goddess*, 242.

67. Ibid., 243.

68. Yurukova, *Glorie di Tracia: L'oro Più Antico I Tesori I Miti* [The Glories of Thrace: The Most Ancient Gold, the Treasures, the Myths], 217.

69. Marazov, ed., *Ancient Gold: The Wealth of the Thracians (Treasures from the Republic of Bulgaria)*, 213.

70. Joan Aruz, Ann Farkas, Andrei Alekseev and Elena Korolkova, *The Golden Deer of Eurasia: Scythian and Sarmatian Treasures from the Russian Steppes* (New York: Metropolitan Museum of Art, 2000), 10.

71. Mellaart, Hirsch, and Balpinar, *The Goddess from Anatolia*, vol. 2, 156.

72. Jürgen Thimme, ed., *Art and Culture of the Cyclades in the 3rd Millennium BC* (Chicago: Chicago University Press, 1977), 158.

73. Bellezza, *Divine Dyads: Ancient Civilization in Tibet*, 65.

74. O. G. S. Crawford, *The Eye Goddess* (Oak Park, Ill.: Delphi Press, 1991).

75. Kuhrt, *The Ancient Near East*, vols. 1–2.

76. M. E. I. Mallowan, *Early Mesopotamia and Iran*, (New York, McGraw-Hill [1965]), 46.

77. Ibid., 42.

78. Kuhrt, *Ancient Near East*, vol. 1, 298.

79. Ibid., 301.

80. Ilmo Robert Von Rudloff, *Hekate in Ancient Greek Religion* (Victoria, B.C., Canada: Horned Owl Publishing, 1999), 45–46.

81. Pat Getz-Preziosi, *Early Cycladic Art in North American Collections* (Richmond, Va.: Virginia Museum of Fine Arts, 1987), 29.

82. Thimme, *Art and Culture of the Cyclades in the 3rd Millennium BC* 157.

83. Gimbutas, *The Living Goddess*, 21.

84. Getz-Preziosi, *Early Cycladic Art in North American Collections*, 15.

85. Mellaart, Hirsch, and Balpinar, *The Goddess from Anatolia*, vol. 3, 55.

86. Kelly, *Goddess Embroideries of the Balkan Lands and the Greek Islands*, 35.

87. Thimme, *Art and Culture of the Cyclades in the 3rd Millennium BC*, 457.

88. Susan Whitfield, *Life Along the Silk Road* (Berkeley, Calif.: University of California Press, 1999), 21.

89. Torday, *Mounted Archers: The Beginning of Central Asian History,* 409.

90. Peter Warren in Doumas, *The Wall-Paintings of Thera,* 13.

91. Ibid., 159.

92. Davies and Friedman, *Egypt,* 171.

93. Ibid., 173.

94. Gimbutas, *The Living Goddess,* 121.

95. R.L.N. Barber, *The Cyclades in the Bronze Age* (London: Duckworth, 1987), 188.

96. Kerényi, *Dionysos: Archetypal Image of Indestructible Life,* 34.

97. Miriam E. Caskey, *Keos II: The Temple at Ayia Irini; Part I: The Statues* (Cincinnati, Ohio: University of Cincinnati, 1985), 39.

98. Ibid., 39.

99. Ibid., 41.

100. Ibid., 41–42.

101. Betty De Shong Meador, INANNA Lady of the Largest Heart: Poems of the Sumerian High Priestess Enheduanna (Austin, Tex.: University of Texas Press, 2000), 8.

102. Ibid., 13.

103. Ibid., 14.

104. Ibid., 43.

105. Ibid., 66.

106. Jeannine Davis-Kimball, Vladimir A. Bashilov and Leonid T. Yablonsky, eds., *Nomads of the Eurasian Steppes in the Early Iron Age* (Berkeley, Calif.: Zinat Press, 1995), 11.

107. Davis-Kimball, with Behan, *Warrior Women: An Archaeologist's Search for History's Hidden Heroines,* 87–88.

108. Davis-Kimball, "Amazons, Priestesses, and other Women of Status: Females in Eurasian Nomadic Societies," 31.

109. Davis-Kimball, with Behan, *Warrior Women: An Archaeologist's Search for History's Hidden Heroines,* 58.

110. Council of Europe, *Gods and Heroes of Bronze Age Europe: The Roots of Odysseus* (Strasbourg, France: Council of Europe, 2000), 80.

111. Ibid., 85.

112. Robert Graves, *The Greek Myths* (New York: Penguin Books, 1960), 114.

113. Davis-Kimball, "Amazons, Priestesses, and other Women of Status," 32.

114. Herodotus, *The History,* 5:6, trans. David Greene (Chicago: Chicago University Press, 1987).

115. Marina Kilunovskaya and Vladimir Semenov, *The Land in the Heart of Asia* (St. Petersburg, Russia: Ego Publishers, 1995), 15.

116. Czaplicka, *Aboriginal Siberia: A Study in Social Anthropology,* 137.

117. Hrozny, *Ancient History of Western Asia, India and Crete,* 64.
118. Kilunovskaya and Semenov, *The Land in the Heart of Asia,* 74.
119. Metropolitan Museum of Art and Los Angeles County Museum of Art, *From the Lands of the Scythians: Ancient Treasures from the Museums of the U.S.S.R. 3000 B.C.–100 B.C.* (New York: Metropolitan Museum of Art, 1975), color plate 27.
120. Davis-Kimball, with Behan, *Warrior Women: An Archaeologist's Search for History's Hidden Heroines,* 70.
121. Bellezza, *Divine Dyads: Ancient Civilization in Tibet,* 434.
122. Tracey Cullen, ed., "Aegean Prehistory: A Review" (Boston, Mass.: *American Journal of Archaeology,* Supplement I, Archaeological Institute of America, 2001), 187.
123. George Spiridakis, (our guide in Crete), personal communication.
124. Dehejia, *Yogini Cult and Temples: A Tantric Tradition,* 67.
125. Bellezza, *Divine Dyads: Ancient Civilizations in Tibet,* 210.
126. Klimburg-Salter, *The Silk Route and the Diamond Path: Esoteric Buddhist Art on the Trans-Himalayan Trade Routes,* 236.
127. Ibid., 238.
128. Andre Gunder Frank, *The Centrality of Central Asia* (Amsterdam, Netherlands: VU University Press, 1992), 1.
129. Campbell, *Traveller in Space: In Search of Female Identity in Tibetan Buddhism,* 37.
130. Shaw, *Passionate Enlightenment; Women in Tantric Buddhism,* 90.
131. Noble, *Shakti Woman: Feeling Our Fire, Healing Our World (The New Female Shamanism),* 28.

Chapter Four

1. Florence Mary Bennett, *Religious Cults Associated with the Amazons* (New York: Columbia University Press, 1912), 32.
2. Ibid.
3. Ibid., 76.
4. Davis-Kimball, with Behan, *Warrior Women: An Archaeologist's Search for History's Hidden Heroines,* 118.
5. Emanuel Kantor, *The Amazons: A Marxian Study* (Chicago: Charles Kerr and Co., 1926), 179.
6. Bennett, *Religious Cults Associated with the Amazons,* 3.
7. Ibid., 6.
8. Monaghan, *The Book of Goddesses and Heroines,* 205.
9. Guy Cadogan Rothery, *The Amazons* (London: Francis Griffiths, 1910), 49.
10. Elizabeth Wayland Barber, *Women's Work: The First 20,000 Years (Women, Cloth, and Society in Early Times)* (New York: W.W. Norton and Co., 1994), 216.

11. Marija Gimbutas, *The Kurgan Culture and the Indo-Europeanization of Europe, Selected Articles from 1952 to 1993,* Miriam Robbins Dexter and Karlene Jones–Bley, eds. (*Journal of Indo-European Studies,* Monograph No. 18., Washington, D.C.: Institute for the Study of Man, 1997), 157.

12. Cullen, "Aegean Prehistory: A Review," 85.

13. Stanley B. Alpern, *Amazons of Black Sparta: The Women Warriors of Dahomey* (New York: New York University Press, 1998), 5.

14. Gimbutas, *The Kurgan Culture and the Indo-Europeanization of Europe, Selected Articles from 1952 to 1993,* 154.

15. Mellaart, Hirsch, and Balpinar, *The Goddess from Anatolia,* vol. 2, 125.

16. Aruz , Farkas, Alekseev and Korolkova, *The Golden Deer of Eurasia: Scythian and Sarmatian Treasures from the Russian Steppes,* 19.

17. Downing, *Myths and Mysteries of Same-Sex Love,* 203.

18. Monaghan, *The Book of Goddesses and Heroines,* 89.

19. Miriam Robbins Dexter, "Reflections on the Goddess Donu," *The Mankind Quarterly,* XXXI, Nos. 1 & 2 (Fall/Winter 1990), 56.

20. Kantor, *The Amazons: A Marxian Study,* 145.

21. Ibid., 73.

22. Ibid., 18.

23. Ibid., 20.

24. Geoffrey Samuel, *Civilized Shamans: Buddhism in Tibetan Societies* (Washington, D.C.: Smithsonian Institution, 1993), 152.

25. "Mahapajapati Gotami: Mother of the Buddha," *Tricycle* (Fall 1998), 23.

26. Kurt Bittel, *Hattusha: The Capital of the Hittites* (New York: Oxford University Press, 1970), 134.

27. Ibid., 6.

28. E.C. Krupp, "Sacred Sex in the Hittite Temple of Yazilikaya," *Odyssey,* (Peterborough, N.H.: Cobblestone Publisher, March/April 2000), 42.

29. Dr. Ekrem Akurgal, *Ancient Civilizations and Ruins of Turkey* (Istanbul, Turkey: Net Turistik Yayinlar A.S., 1993), 313.

30. Kuhrt, *The Ancient Near East,* vol. 1, 287.

31. Ibid., 298.

32. Ibid., 299.

33. Ibid., 299.

34. Ibid., 279.

35. J.G. Macqueen, *The Hittites and their Contemporaries in Asia Minor* (London: Thames & Hudson, 1996), 76.

36. Kuhrt, *The Ancient Near East,* vol. 1, 241.

37. Macqueen, *The Hittites and their Contemporaries in Asia Minor,* 101.

38. Kenneth Pearson and Patricia Connor, "The Strange Case of James Mellaart or The Tale of the Missing Dorak Treasure," *Horizon,* vol. 9, no. 3 (Harare, Zimbabwe: Column Width (Pvt.) Ltd., Summer 1967), 14.

39. Pearson and Conner, "The Strange Case of James Mellaart or The Tale of the Missing Dorak Treasure," 6.

40. Turhan Kâmil, *Yortan Cemetery in the Early Bronze Age of Western Anatolia* (Oxford, England: BAR International Series 145, 1982), 22.

41. Ellen Reeder, *Scythian Gold: Treasures From Ancient Ukraine* (New York: Harry Abrams, Inc., 1999), 117.

42. Jessica Amanda Salmonson, *The Encyclopedia of Amazons: Women Warriors from Antiquity to the Modern Era* (New York: Doubleday/Anchor Books, 1991), 210.

43. Ibid., 15.

44. Kantor, *The Amazons: A Marxian Study,* 46.

45. Salmonson, *The Encyclopedia of Amazons: Women Warriors from Antiquity to the Modern Era,* xii.

46. Herodotus, *The History,* 1:205–6.

47. Ibid., 1.212–14.

48. Bennett, *Religious Cults of the Amazon,* 7.

49. Gimbutas, *The Language of the Goddess,* 171.

50. Blok, *The Early Amazons: Modern and Ancient Perspectives on a Persistent Myth.*

51. Litsa Kontorli-Papadopoulou, *Aegean Frescoes of Religious Character* (Göteborg, Sweden: Paul Aströms Förlag, 1996), 105.

52. Ibid., 99.

53. Higgins, *Minoan and Mycenaean Art,* 6.

54. Kontorli-Papadopoulou, *Aegean Frescoes of Religious Character,* 121.

55. Kontorli-Papadopoulou, *Aegean Frescoes of Religious Character,* 103.

56. Athens Ministry of Culture, *The Mycenaean World: Five Centuries of Early Greek Culture (1600–1100 B.C.)* (Athens, Greece: National Hellenic Committee, 1988), 189.

57. Kontorli-Papadopoulou, *Aegean Frescoes of Religious Character,* 81.

58. Monaghan, *The Book of Goddesses and Heroines,* 19.

59. Kuhrt, *The Ancient Near East,* vol. 2, 393.

60. Czaplicka, *Aboriginal Siberia: A Study in Social Anthropology,* 244.

61. Akurgal, *Ancient Civilizations and Ruins of Turkey,* 167.

62. Ibid., 225.

63. Gimbutas, *Goddesses and Gods of Old Europe: 6500–3500 BC, Myths and Cult Images,* 148.

64. MacKenzie, *Myths of Crete and Pre-Hellenic Europe,* 160.

65. Miriam Robbins Dexter, *Whence the Goddess: A Source Book* (New York: Pergamon Press, 1990), 119.

66. Rothery, *The Amazons,* 44.

67. Marazov, *Ancient Gold: The Wealth of the Thracians (Treasures from the Republic of Bulgaria),* 39.

68. Ibid., 34.

69. Ibid., 209.

70. Ibid., 43.

71. Ibid., 42.

72. Ibid., 193.

73. Ibid., 90.

74. Ibid., 45.

75. Ibid., 50.

76. Ibid., 49.

77. Ibid., 158.

78. Ivan Marazov, private communication, June 2002.

79. Marazov, *Ancient Gold: The Wealth of the Thracians (Treasures from the Republic of Bulgaria,* 73.

80. Ibid., 72.

81. Ibid., 64.

82. Ibid., 66.

83. Council of Europe, *Gods and Heroes of Bronze Age Europe: The Roots of Odysseus,* 172.

84. Ibid., 180.

85. Ibid., 181.

86. Davis-Kimball, "Amazons, Priestesses and Other Women of Status: Females in Eurasian Nomadic Societies," 35.

87. Tim Newark, *Women Warriors: An Illustrated Military History of Female Warriors* (London: Blandford, 1989), 19.

88. T.V. Miroshina, "The Amazons and the Sauromatians," in *Eurasian Cultural Artifacts of the Scythian/Sarmatian Epoch* (Moscow: Royal Academy of Sciences, Institute of Archaeology, 1995), 17.

89. Apollodorus, *The Library,* with English translation by Sir James George Frazer (Cambridge: Harvard University Press and London: William Heinemann, Ltd., 1961 [c. 1921]).

90. J.P. Mallory and Victor H. Mair, *The Tarim Mummies: Ancient China and the Mystery of the Earliest Peoples from the West* (London: Thames & Hudson, 2000), 196.

91. Ibid., 220.

92. Ibid., Plates VII and VIII.

93. Elizabeth Wayland Barber, *The Mummies of Ürümchi* (New York: W.W. Norton and Co., 1999), Plates 2b & 3a.

94. Mallory and Mair, *The Tarim Mummies: Ancient China and the Mystery of the Earliest Peoples from the West*, 193.

95. Elizabeth Wayland Barber, *The Mummies of Ürümchi*, 40.

96. Ibid., 141.

97. Ibid., 127–128.

98. Ibid., 74.

99. Abby Wettan Kleinbaum, *The War Against the Amazons* (New York: McGraw-Hill Book Company, 1983), 189.

100. Alpern, *Amazons of Black Sparta*, 5.

101. Bernal, *Black Athena: The Afroasiatic Roots of Classical Civilization, Vol. I: The Fabrication of Ancient Greece 1785-1985*, 86.

102. Bernal, *Black Athena: The Afroasiatic Roots of Classical Civilization, Vol. II: The Archaeological and Documentary Evidence*, 422.

103. Dexter, "Reflections on the Goddess Donu," 52.

104. Walker, *The Women's Encyclopedia of Myths and Secrets*, 24.

105. Alpern, *Amazons of Black Sparta*.

106. Ibid., 2.

107. Ibid., 161.

108. Ibid., 117.

109. Shaw, *Passionate Enlightenment: Women in Tantric Buddhism*, 54.

Chapter Five

1. Tsultrim Allione, personal communication, October 2002.

2. Nik Douglas and Penny Slinger, *Sexual Secrets: The Alchemy of Ecstasy* (Rochester, Vt.: Destiny Books, 2000), 259.

3. Personal communication from Helene B. Cincebeaux of the Slovak Heritage and Folklore Society.

4. Czaplicka, *Aboriginal Siberia: A Study in Social Anthropology*.

5. Laurel Kendall, *Shamans, Housewives, and Other Restless Spirits: Women in Korean Ritual Life* (Honolulu, Hawaii: University of Hawaii Press, 1985), 25.

6. Judith Simmer-Brown, *Dakini's Warm Breath: The Feminine Principle in Tibetan Buddhism* (Boston, Mass.: Shambhala, 2001), 249.

7. Leonard Cohen, "Light as a Breeze," *The Future*, a CD (New York: Sony Music Entertainment, Inc., 1992).

8. Simmer-Brown, *Dakini's Warm Breath: The Feminine Principle in Tibetan Buddhism*, 240.

9. Campbell, *Traveller in Space: In Search of Female Identity in Tibetan Buddhism*, 154.

10. Tarthang Tulku, (oral translation of original text by Nam-mkha'I snying-po). *Mother of Knowledge: The Enlightenment of Ye-shes mTsho-rgyal* (Berkeley, Calif.: Dharma Publishing, 1983), xxiii.

11. Keith Dowman, *Sky Dancer: The Secret Life and Songs of the Lady Yeshe Tsogyel* (London: Routledge and Kegan Paul, 1984), xiii.

12. Padmakara Translation Group, *Lady of the Lotus-Born: The Life and Enlightenment of Yeshe Tsogyal* (quote from book jacket, 1999).

13. Elizabeth Wayland Barber, *The Mummies of Ürümchi*, 66.

14. Dowman, *Sky Dancer: The Secret Life and Songs of the Lady Yeshe Tsogyel*, 10.

15. Ibid., 13–14.

16. Ibid., 35.

17. Tulku (Rinpoche) Thondup, *Hidden Teachings of Tibet: An Explanation of the Terma Tradition of Tibetan Buddhism* (Boston: Wisdom Publications, 1997), 82–83.

18. Ibid., 107.

19. Vicki Noble, "Skywalking Woman of the Night," *Mama Bear's News & Notes,* vol. 14, no. 1 (Oakland, Calif.: December–January 1997).

20. Thondup, *Hidden Teachings of Tibet: An Explanation of the Terma Tradition of Tibetan Buddhism,* 140.

21. Ibid., 129.

22. Tsultrim Allione, *Women of Wisdom* (London: Routledge and Kegan Paul, 1984), 165.

23. Reginald Ray, *Secret of the Vajra World: The Tantric Buddhism of Tibet* (Boston: Shambhala, 2001), 367.

24. Reginald Ray, "The Origins of the Tülku Tradition in Tibet," *Indestructible Truth: The Living Spirituality of Tibetan Buddhism* (Boston: Shambhala, 2000), 185.

25. Ibid., 185.

26. Ray, *Secret of the Vajra World: The Tantric Buddhism of Tibet,* 429.

27. Allione, *Women of Wisdom,* 171.

28. Shaw, *Passionate Enlightenment: Women in Tantric Buddhism,* 75.

29. Ibid., 81.

30. Ibid., 84.

31. Akurgal, *Ancient Civilizations and Ruins of Turkey,* plate 17.

32. Padmaka Translation Group, 1999, 75.

33. David Gordon White, ed., *Tantra in Practice* (Princeton, N.J.: Princeton University Press, 2000), 23.

34. Ibid., 76.

35. Padmakara Translation Group (translation of original text by Gyalwa Changchub and Namkhai Nyingpo), *Lady of the Lotus-Born: The Life and Enlightenment of Yeshe Tsogyal* (Boston: Shambhala, 1999), 69.

36. Shaw, *Passionate Enlightenment: Women in Tantric Buddhism,* 82.

37. Ibid., 83.

38. White, *The Alchemical Body: Siddha Traditions in Medieval India,* 4.

39. Ibid., 4.

40. Ibid., 7.

41. Ibid., 138.

42. Ibid., 309.

43. White, *Tantra In Practice,* 77.

44. Shaw, *Passionate Enlightenment: Women in Tantric Buddhism,* 84.

45. Skafte, *When Oracles Speak: Understanding the Signs & Symbols All Around Us,* 146.

46. Ibid.

47. Ibid.

48. Ibid.

49. Ibid., 146–147.

50. Ibid., 147.

51. Ibid.

52. Ibid.

53. Sitka, private communication, November 1998.

54. Blundell, *Women in Ancient Greece,* 151.

55. Bernadette J. Brooten, *Love Between Women: Early Christian Responses to Female Homoeroticism* (Chicago: University of Chicago Press, 1996), 50.

56. A.R. Burn and Mary Burn, *The Living Past of Greece* (London: HarperCollins (IconEditions), 1980), 89.

57. Gimbutas, *The Living Goddess,* 159.

58. Blundell, *Women in Ancient Greece,* 83.

59. Ibid., 84.

60. George, lecture in Greece, 2001.

61. Brooten, *Love Between Women: Early Christian Responses to Female Homoeroticism,* 5.

62. Ibid., 53.

63. Ibid., 107.

64. Ibid., 57.

65. Ibid., 41.

66. Ibid., 42.

67. Ibid., 44.

68. Downing, *Myths and Mysteries of Same-Sex Love,* 185.

69. Brooten, *Love Between Women: Early Christian Responses to Female Homoeroticism,* 67.

70. Ibid., 139.

71. Ibid., 151.

72. Downing, *Myths and Mysteries of Same-Sex Love,* 204.

73. Mary Daly and Jane Caputi, *Websters' First New Intergalactic Wickedary of the English Language* (London: The Women's Press, 1988).

74. Miriam Robbins Dexter, *Whence the Goddess: A Source Book* (New York: Pergamon Press, 1990), 163.

75. Ruth Barrett, *Women's Rites, Women's Mysteries: Creating Ritual in Dianic Wiccan Tradition* (specifically ch. 4, "The Guardian Priestess: A Newly Emerging Dianic Priestess Path,") (1stBooksPublishing.com, 2003).

76. Czaplicka, *Aboriginal Studies,* 86.

77. Ibid., 88.

78. Ibid., 104.

79. Gimbutas, *The Language of the Goddess,* 298.

80. Will Roscoe, *Changing Ones: Third and Fourth Genders in Native North America* (New York: St. Martin's Press, 1998), 125.

81. Lester B. Brown, ed., *Two-Spirit People: American Indian Lesbian Women and Gay Men* (New York: Harrington Park Press, Hawthorne Press, Inc., 1997), 9.

82. Will Roscoe, *Third Sex, Third Gender: Beyond Sexual Dimorphism in Culture and History,* ed., Gilbert Herdt (New York: Zone Books, 1996), 338.

83. Ibid., 335.

84. Ibid., 343.

85. Ibid., 358.

86. Ibid., 356.

87. Thadani, *Sakhiyani: Lesbian Desire in Ancient and Modern India,* 22.

88. Ibid., 62.

89. Roscoe, *Changing Ones: Third and Fourth Genders in Native North America,* 78.

90. Ibid., 81.

91. Paula Gunn Allen, *The Sacred Hoop: Recovering the Feminine in American Indian Traditions* (Boston, Mass.: Beacon Press, 1986), 197.

92. Phyllis Burke, *Gender Shock: Exploding the Myths of Male & Female* (New York: Anchor Books, Doubleday, 1996), xxi.

93. Roscoe, *Changing Ones: Third and Fourth Genders in Native North America,* 74.

94. Ibid., 73.

95. Sue-Ellen Jacobs, Wesley Thomas, and Sabine Long, *Two-Spirit People: Native American Gender Identity, Sexuality, and Spirituality* (Chicago: University of Illinois Press, 1997), 129.

96. Ibid., 128.

97. Davis-Kimball, with Behan, *Warrior Women: An Archaeologist's Search for History's Hidden Heroines,* 47.

98. Ibid., 49.

99. Ibid., 47.

100. Ibid., 101.

101. Ibid., 105.

102. Ibid., 106.

103. Margorie Garber, *Vested Interests: Cross-Dressing and Cultural Anxiety* (New York: Routledge, 1992), 16–17.

104. Deuturonomy 22:5.

105. Garber, *Vested Interests: Cross-Dressing and Cultural Anxiety,* 216.

106. Allen, *The Sacred Hoop: Recovering the Feminine in American Indian Traditions,* 196.

107. Garber, *Vested Interests: Cross-Dressing and Cultural Anxiety,* 32.

108. Ibid., 150.

109. Kim Chernin, *My Life As A Boy* (Chapel Hill, N.C.: Algonquin Books, 1993), 4.

110. Ibid., 10.

111. Catharine Lumby, *Bad Girls: The Media, Sex and Feminism in the '90s* (St. Leonard's, N.S.W., Australia: Allen and Unwin, 1997), 42.

112. Melissa Etheridge, *Yes I Am* (New York: Island Records, 1993).

Conclusion

1. Mary Daly, *Gyn/Ecology: The Metaethics of Radical Feminism* (Boston: Beacon Press, 1978).

2. Mary Daly, *Quintessence: The Archaic Future (A Radical Feminist Manifesto),* (Boston: Beacon Press, 1978), 96.

3. Hua, *A Society Without Fathers or Husbands: The Na of China* (quote taken from the book's title).

4. Mary Daly, "Mary Daly and Sin Big," *The New Yorker* 72 (February 26–March 4, 1996), 76.

5. Daly, *Quintessence,* 104.

6. Warren E. Leary, *New York Times,* 31 January 2003.

7. Russell Sabin, *San Francisco Chronicle,* 7 February 2003, p. 1.

8. Personal communication to the author from Monica Sjöö of unpublished poem by Monica.

Bibliography

Adler, Margo. *Drawing Down the Moon*. Boston: Beacon Press, 1986.

Akurgal, Dr. Ekrem. *Ancient Civilizations and Ruins of Turkey*. Istanbul, Turkey: Net Turistik Yayinlar A.S., 1993.

Alexiou, Stylianos. *Minoan Civilization*. 4th rev. ed. Heraclion, Greece: V. Kouvidis-V. Manouras Co., n.d.

Alkim, U. Bahadir. *Anatolia I (From the beginnings to the end of the 2nd millennium B.C.)*. Geneva, Switzerland: Nagel Publishers, 1968.

Allen, Max. *The Birth Symbol in Traditional Women's Art from Eurasia and the Western Pacific*. Toronto, Canada: The Museum for Textiles, 1981.

Allen, Paula Gunn. *The Sacred Hoop: Recovering the Feminine in American Indian Traditions*. Boston: Beacon Press, 1986.

Allione, Tsultrim. *Women of Wisdom*. London: Routledge and Kegan Paul, 1984.

Alpern, Stanley B. *Amazons of Black Sparta: The Women Warriors of Dahomey*. New York: New York University Press, 1998.

Aruz, Joan and Ann Farkas, Andrei Alekseev, and Elena Korolkova. *The Golden Deer of Eurasia: Scythian and Sarmatian Treasures from the Russian Steppes*. New York: Metropolitan Museum of Art, 2000.

Ashe, Geoffrey. *Ancient Wisdom*. Tumbridge-Wells, England: Abacus Books, 1979.

Athens Ministry of Culture. *The Mycenaean World: Five Centuries of Early Greek Culture (1600–1100 B.C.)*. Athens, Greece: National Hellenic Committee, 1988.

Athens Ministry of Culture. *Greek Jewelry: 6000 Years of Tradition*. Athens, Greece: Archaeological Receipts Fund, 1997.

Bahn, Paul and Jean Vertut. *Journey Through the Ice Age*. Berkeley, Calif.: University of California Press, 1997.

Balaskas, Janet. *Active Birth: The New Approach to Giving Birth Naturally* (rev. ed.). Boston: The Harvard Common Press, 1992.

Barber, Elizabeth Wayland. *Women's Work: The First 20,000 Years (Women, Cloth, and Society in Early Times)*. New York: W.W. Norton and Co., 1994.

————. *The Mummies of Ürümchi*. New York: W.W. Norton and Co., 1999.

Barber, Robin. *Blue Guide to Greece*. New York: W.W. Norton, 1990.

Barber, R.L.N. *The Cyclades in the Bronze Age*. London: Duckworth, 1987.

Barrett, Ruth. *Women's Rites, Women's Mysteries: Creating Ritual in Dianic Wiccan Tradition*. 1stBooksPublishing.com, 2003.

Batchelor, Stephen. *The Tibet Guide*. London: Wisdom Publications, 1987.

Batey, C.E., ed. *Treasures of the Warrior Tombs*. Glasgow Museums, 1996.

Bellezza, John Vincent. *Divine Dyads: Ancient Civilization in Tibet*. Dharamsala, India: Library of Tibetan Works & Archives, First Edition, 1997.

Bennett, Florence Mary. *Religious Cults Associated with the Amazons*. New York: Columbia University Press, 1912.

Bernal, Martin. *Black Athena: The Afroasiatic Roots of Classical Civilization. Vol. I: The Fabrication of Ancient Greece 1785–1985*. Piscataway, N. J.: Rutgers University Press, 1987.

————. *Black Athena: The Afroasiatic Roots of Classical Civilization. Vol. II: The Archaeological and Documentary Evidence*. Piscataway, N. J.: Rutgers University Press, 1991.

Bernbaum, Edwin. *Sacred Mountains of the World*. Berkeley, Calif.: University of California Press, 1997.

Biaggi, Cristina. *Habitations of the Great Goddess*. Manchester, Conn.: Knowledge, Ideas and Trends, 1994.

Birnbaum, Lucia. *Black Madonnas: Feminism, Religion, and Politics in Italy*. Boston: Northeastern University Press, 1993.

Bittel, Kurt. *Hattusha: The Capital of the Hittites*. New York: Oxford University Press, 1970.

Blacker, Carmen. *The Catalpa Bow: A Study of Shamanistic Practices in Japan*. London: George Allen and Unwin Ltd., 1975.

Blok, Josine H. *The Early Amazons: Modern and Ancient Perspectives on a Persistent Myth*. Leiden, Netherlands: E. J. Brill, 1995.

Blundell, Sue. *Women in Ancient Greece*. London: British Museum Press, 1995.

Bornstein, Kate. *Gender Outlaw: On Men, Women, and the Rest of Us*. New York: Routledge, 1994.

Briffault, Robert. *The Mothers: A Study of the Origins of Sentiments and Institutions* (3 volumes). New York: The Macmillan Company, 1927.

Brooten, Bernadette J. *Love Between Women: Early Christian Responses to Female Homoeroticism*. Chicago: University of Chicago Press, 1996.

Brown, Lester B. (ed.) *Two-Spirit People: American Indian Lesbian Women and Gay Men*. New York: Harrington Park Press, Hawthorne Press, Inc., 1997.

Buhner, Stephen Harrod. *Sacred and Herbal Healing Beers: The Secrets of Ancient Fermentation*. Boulder, Colo.: Brewers Publications, 1998.

Burke, Phyllis. *Gender Shock: Exploding the Myths of Male & Female*. New York: Anchor Books, Doubleday, 1996.

Burn, A.R. and Mary. *The Living Past of Greece*. London: HarperCollins (IconEditions), 1980.

Cadogan, Gerald, ed. *The End of the Early Bronze Age in the Aegean*. Leiden, Netherlands: E. J. Brill, 1986.

Cameron, Pat. *Blue Guide Crete*. New York: W.W. Norton, 1988.

Campbell, June. *Traveller in Space: In Search of Female Identity in Tibetan Buddhism*. New York: George Braziller, 1996.

Capel, Anne K. and Glenn E. Markoe, eds. *Mistress of the House, Mistress of Heaven: Women in Ancient Egypt*. New York: Hudson Hills Press, 1997.

Cartledge, Paul, ed. *The Cambridge Illustrated History of Ancient Greece*. Cambridge, England: Cambridge University Press, 1998.

Caskey, Miriam E. *Keos II: The Temple at Ayia Irini; Part I: The Statues*. Cincinnati, Ohio: University of Cincinnati, 1985.

Chadwick, John. *The Decipherment of Linear B*. (rev. ed.) Cambridge, England: Cambridge University Press, 1995.

Changchub, Gyalwa and Namkhai Nyingpo. *Lady of the Lotus-Born: The Life and Times of Yeshe Tsogyal*. Translated by Padmakara Translation Group. Boston: Shambhala, 1999.

Chernin, Kim. *My Life As A Boy*. Chapel Hill, N.C.: Algonquin Books, 1993.

Cincebeaux, Helene, ed. *Slovakia: Slovak Heritage and Folklore Society International* (a newsletter). Rochester, N.Y.

Clauss, James J. and Sarah Iles Johnston, eds. *Medea: Essays on Medea in Myth, Literature, Philosophy, and Art*. Princeton, N.J.: Princeton University Press, 1997.

Cohen, Beth. *The Distaff Side: Representing the Female in Homer's Odyssey*. New York: Oxford University Press, 1995.

Cohen, Leonard. "Light as a Breeze" from *The Future*, a CD. New York: Sony Music Entertainment, Inc., 1992.

Council of Europe. *Gods and Heroes of Bronze Age Europe: The Roots of Odysseus*. Strasbourg, France: Council of Europe, 2000.

Crawford, O.G.S. *The Eye Goddess*. Oak Park, Ill.: Delphi Press, Inc., 1991.

Cullen, Tracey (ed.). *Aegean Prehistory: A Review (American Journal of Archaeology Supplement I)*. Boston: Archaeological Institute of America, 2001.

Czaplicka, M.A. *Aboriginal Siberia: A Study in Social Anthropology*. London: Oxford University Press, 1914.

Daly, Mary. *Beyond God the Father: Toward a Philosophy of Women's Liberation.* Boston: Beacon Press, 1975.

————. *Gyn/Ecology: The Metaethics of Radical Feminism.* Boston: Beacon Press, 1978.

————. *Quintessence: The Archaic Future (A Radical Elemental Feminist Manifesto).* Boston: Beacon Press, 1998.

Daly, Mary and Jane Caputi. *Webster's First New Intergalactic Wickedary of the English Language.* London: The Women's Press, 1988.

Davies, Vivian and Renée Friedman. *Egypt.* London: British Museum Press, 1998.

Davis-Kimball, Jeannine and Leonid T. Yablonsky. *Excavations at Pokrovka 1990-1992: Kurgans on the Left Bank of the Ilek.* Berkeley, Calif.: Zinat Press, 1995.

Davis-Kimball, Jeannine. "Amazons, Priestesses and Other Women of Status: Females in Eurasian Nomadic Societies," *Silk Road Art and Archaeology 5.* Kamakura, Japan: *Journal of the Institute of Silk Road Studies* (1997/98).

————. (with Mona Behan). *Warrior Women: An Archaeologist's Search for History's Hidden Heroines.* New York: Warner Books, Inc., 2002.

Davis-Kimball, Jeannine, Vladimir A. Bashilov, Leonid T. Yablonsky (eds.). *Nomads of the Eurasian Steppes in the Early Iron Age.* Berkeley, Calif.: Zinat Press, 1995.

Dehejia, Vidya. *Yogini Cult and Temples: A Tantric Tradition.* Janpath, New Delhi, India: National Museum, 1986.

Dexter, Miriam Robbins. *Whence the Goddesses: A Source Book.* New York: Pergamon Press, 1990.

————. "Reflections on the Goddess Donu," *The Mankind Quarterly* 31, nos. 1, 2 (Fall/Winter 1990).

————. "The Frightful Goddess: Birds, Snakes and Witches," *Varia on the Indo-European Past: Papers in Memory of Marija Gimbutas.* Edited by Miriam Robbins Dexter and Edgar C. Polomé. Washington, D.C.: *Journal of Indo-European Studies,* Monograph No. 19, 1997.

————. "Medea and Her Circumpontic Sisters," a paper presented at a Conference about the Black Sea flood in Bogliasco, Italy, 2002. Publication forthcoming.

Demakopoulou, Katie (ed.). *The Mycenaean World: Five Centuries of Early Greek Culture 1600-1100 B.C.* Athens, Greece: Ministry of Culture, National Hellenic Committee, 1988.

Dickinson, Oliver. *The Aegean Bronze Age.* Cambridge, England: Cambridge University Press, 1994.

Diop, Cheikh Anta. *The African Origin of Civilization: Myth or Reality.* Chicago: Lawrence Hill and Co., 1974.

Douglas, Nik and Penny Slinger. *Sexual Secrets: The Alchemy of Ecstasy.* Rochester, Vt.: Destiny Books, 1979, 2000.

Doumas, Christos. *The Wall-Paintings of Thera.* Athens: Kapon Editions, 1992.

Dowman, Keith. *Sky Dancer: The Secret Life and Songs of the Lady Yeshe Tsogyel.* London: Routledge and Kegan Paul, 1984.

Downing, Christine. *Myths and Mysteries of Same-Sex Love.* New York: Continuum, 1989.

Duerr, Hans Peter. *Dreamtime: Concerning the Boundary between Wilderness and Civilization.* Oxford, England: Basil Blackwell, Ltd., 1985.

Fitton, J. Lesley. *Cycladic Art.* London: British Museum Publications, 1989.

———. *The Discovery of the Greek Bronze Age.* Cambridge, Mass.: Harvard University Press, 1996.

Frank, Andre Gunder. *The Centrality of Central Asia.* Comparitive Asian Studies 8, Amsterdam, Netherlands: V. U. University Press for Centre for Asian Studies, 1992.

Garber, Margorie. *Vested Interests: Cross-Dressing and Cultural Anxiety.* New York: Routledge, 1992.

Garstang, John. *The Land of the Hittites: An Account of Recent Explorations and Discoveries in Asia Minor, with Descriptions of the Hittite Monuments.* London: Constable and Co, Ltd., 1910.

Getz–Preziosi, Pat. *The Obsidian Trail: 5000–4000 Years Ago in the Cyclades.* Athens, Greece: Nicholas P. Goulandris Foundation, Museum of Cycladic and Ancient Greek Art, 1987.

———. *Early Cycladic Art in North American Collections.* Richmond, Va.: Virginia Museum of Fine Arts, 1987.

Gimbutas, Marija. *The Kurgan Culture and the Indo-Europeanization of Europe, Selected Articles from 1952 to 1993.* Edited by Miriam Robbins Dexter and Karlene Jones-Bley. *Journal of Indo-European Studies,* Monograph No. 18. Washington, D.C.: Institute for the Study of Man, 1997.

———. *Goddesses and Gods of Old Europe: 6500–3500 B.C., Myths, Legends, and Cult Images.* Berkeley, Calif.: University of California Press, 1982.

———. *The Language of the Goddess.* San Francisco: Harper and Row, 1989.

———. *The Civilization of the Goddess.* San Francisco: HarperSan Francisco, 1991.

———. *The Living Goddesses.* Edited and supplemented by Miriam Robbins Dexter. Berkeley, Calif.: University of California Press, 1999.

Graves, Robert. *The Greek Myths.* New York: Penguin Books, 1960.

Griffith, T. H. (trans.), J. L. Shastri (ed.). *Hymns of the Rig Veda.* Delhi, India: Motilal Banarsidass, 1973.

Grimaldi, David. *Amber: Window to the Past.* New York: Harry Abrams, Inc. with the American Museum of Natural History, 1996.

Grissom, Carol A. "Neolithic Statues from Ain Ghazal: Construction and Form." *American Journal of Archaeology* 104 (2000): 25–45.

Guggenheim Museum. *Africa; The Art of a Continent: 100 Works of Power and Beauty.* New York: Time Warner, 1998.

Haitalis, Dimitris. *Crete: Full Travel Guide.* Athens, Greece: Editions Haitalis, 1996.

Herdt, Gilbert, ed. *Third Sex, Third Gender: Beyond Sexual Dimorphism in Culture and History.* New York: Zone Books, 1996.

Herodotus. *The History.* Translated by David Greene. Chicago: Chicago University Press, 1987.

Higgins, Reynold. *Minoan and Mycenaean Art.* London: Thames and Hudson, 1997.

Höfer, Hans. *Insight Guides: The Nile.* New York: Houghton Mifflin Company, 1993.

Hoffman, Gail. *Imports & Immigrants: Near Eastern Contacts with Iron Age Crete.* Ann Arbor, Mich.: University of Michigan Press, 1997.

Hogarth, James. *Egypt: Nagel's Encyclopedia Guide.* Geneva, Switzerland: Nagel Publishers, 1985.

Hrozny, Bedrich. *Ancient History of Western Asia, India and Crete.* Prague, Czechoslovakia: Artia, 1953.

Hua, Cai. *A Society Without Fathers or Husbands: The Na of China.* New York: Zone Books, 2001.

Hull, Alastair and José Luczyc-Wyhowska. *Kilim: The Complete Guide (History, Pattern, Technique, Identification).* San Francisco: Chronicle Books, 1993.

Jacobs, Sue-Ellen, Wesley Thomas, and Sabine Long. *Two-Spirit People: Native American Gender Identity, Sexuality, and Spirituality.* Chicago: University of Illinois Press, 1997.

Kâmil, Turhan. *Yortan Cemetery in the Early Bronze Age of Western Anatolia.* Oxford, England: BAR International Series 145, 1982.

Kantor, Emanuel. *The Amazons: A Marxian Study.* Chicago: Charles Kerr and Co., 1926.

Kelly, Mary B. *Goddess Embroideries of Eastern Europe.* New York: Studio Books, 1989.

———. *Goddess Embroideries of the Balkan Lands and the Greek Islands.* New York: Studio Books, 1999.

Kendall, Laurel. *Shamans, Housewives, and Other Restless Spirits: Women in Korean Ritual Life.* Honolulu, Hawaii: University of Hawaii Press, 1985.

Kerényi, Karl. *Athene: Virgin and Mother in Greek Religion.* Zurich, Switzerland: Spring Publications, 1978.

———. *Dionysos: Archetypal Image of Indestructible Life* Translated from German by Ralph Manheim. Princeton, N.J.: Princeton University Press, 1976.

———. *Eleusis: Archetypal Image of Mother and Daughter.* Bollingen Series LXV, no. 4. Princeton, N.J.: Princeton University Press, 1967.

Keuls, Eva. *The Reign of the Phallus: Sexual Politics in Ancient Athens.* Berkeley, Calif.: University of California Press, 1985.

Kharitidi, Olga. *Entering the Circle: Ancient Secrets of Siberian Wisdom Discovered by a Russian Psychiatrist.* San Francisco: HarperSan Francisco, 1996.

Kilunovskaya, Marina and Vladimir Semenov. *The Land in the Heart of Asia.* St. Petersburg, Russia: Ego Publishers, 1995.

Kleinbaum, Abby Wettan. *The War Against the Amazons.* New York: McGraw–Hill Book Company, 1983.

Klimburg-Salter, Deborah E. (ed.). *The Silk Route and the Diamond Path: Esoteric Buddhist Art on the Trans-Himalayan Trade Routes.* Los Angeles: UCLA Art Council, 1982.

Kontorli-Papadopoulou, Litsa. *Aegean Frescoes of Religious Character.* Göteborg, Sweden: Paul Aströms Förlag, 1996.

Krupp, E.C. "Sacred Sex in the Hittite Temple of Yazilikaya," *Odyssey,* (March/April 2000).

Kuhrt, Amélie. *The Ancient Near East (c. 3000-330 BC).* 2 vols. London: Routledge, 1995.

Lewis, I.M. *Ecstatic Religion: A Study of Shamanism and Spirit Possession.* London: Routledge, 1971, 1989.

MacKenzie, Donald A. *Myths of Crete and Pre-Hellenic Europe.* London: The Gresham Publishing Company Ltd., n.d.

Macqueen, J.G. *The Hittites and their Contemporaries in Asia Minor.* London: Thames & Hudson, 1996.

Mallory, J. P. and Victor H. Mair. *The Tarim Mummies: Ancient China and the Mystery of the Earliest Peoples from the West.* London: Thames & Hudson, 2000.

Marazov, Ivan, ed. *Ancient Gold: The Wealth of the Thracians (Treasures from the Republic of Bulgaria).* New York: Harry N. Abrams, Inc. in cooperation with The Ministry of Culture of the Republic of Bulgaria, 1997.

Marglin, Frédérique. *Wives of the God-Kings: The Rituals of the Devadasis of Puri.* New York: Oxford University Press, 1985.

Marler, Joan, ed. *From the Realm of the Ancestors: An Anthology in Honor of Marija Gimbutas.* Manchester, Conn.: Knowledge, Ideas and Trends, Inc., 1997.

Marshack, Alexander. *The Roots of Civilization.* New York: Moyer Bell Ltd., 1991.

Masson, V.M. and V.I. Sarianidi. *Central Asia: Turkmenia Before the Achaemenids.* Edited by Glyn Daniel. London: Thames & Hudson, 1972.

Meador, Betty De Shong. *INANNA Lady of the Largest Heart: Poems of the Sumerian High Priestess Enheduanna.* Austin, Tex.: University of Texas Press, 2000.

Meixner, Gabriele. *Frauenpaare in kulturgeschichtlichen Zeugnissen.* München, Germany: Frauenoffensive, 1995.

Mellaart, James. *The Chalcolithic and Early Bronze Ages in the Near East and Anatolia.* Beirut, Lebanon: Khayats, 1966.

Mellaart, James, with Udo Hirsch and Belkis Balpinar. *The Goddess from Anatolia.* Adenau, West Germany: Eskenazi, 1989.

Metropolitan Museum of Art and Los Angeles County Museum of Art. *From the Lands of the Scythians: Ancient Treasures from the Museums of the U.S.S.R. 3000 B.C.–100 B.C.* New York: Metropolitan Museum of Art, 1975.

Miroshina, T.V. "The Amazons and the Sauromatians" in *Eurasian Cultural Artifacts of the Scythian/Sarmatian Epoch*. Moscow, Russia: Royal Academy of Sciences, Institute of Archaeology, 1995.

Monaghan, Patricia. *The Book of Goddesses and Heroines* (revised and enlarged). St. Paul, Minn.: Llewellyn Publications, 1990.

Morgan, Robin. *Sisterhood Is Powerful*. New York: Random House, 1970.

Needham, Joseph. *Science and Civilization in China*, vol. II. Cambridge, England: Cambridge University Press, 1969.

Neumann, Erich. *The Great Mother: An Analysis of the Archetype*. Bollingen Series XLVII. Princeton, N.J.: Princeton University Press, 1963.

Newark, Tim. *Women Warriors: An Illustrated Military History of Female Warriors*. London: Blandford, 1989.

Nilsson, Martin. *The Minoan-Mycenaean Religion and its Survival in Greek Religion* (second rev. ed.). Lund, Sweden: Gleerup, 1950.

Nissen, Hans J. *The Early History of the Ancient Near East 9000–2000 B.C.* Chicago: Chicago University Press, 1988.

Norbu, Namkhai. *Drung, Deu and Bön: Narratives, Symbolic languages and the Bön tradition in ancient Tibet*. Dharamsala, India: Library of Tibetan Works and Archives, 1995.

Noble, Vicki. *Shakti Woman: Feeling Our Fire, Healing Our World (The New Female Shamanism)*. San Francisco: HarperSan Francisco, 1991.

———. "Sky-Walking Woman of the Night" in *Mama Bear's News & Notes*, vol. 14, no. 1, December–January 1997, Oakland, California.

———. "Medea and the Shaman Women of the Silk Road." Paper presented at conference about the Black Sea flood in Bogliasco, Italy, June 2002. Publication forthcoming.

Opsopaus, John. "Pauca Anecdota Neapolitana," from Biblioteca Arcana, a Web site, www.cs.utk.edu/~mclennan/OM/BA/JO-AN.html.

Padmakara Translation Group (translation of original text by Gyalwa Changchub and Namkhai Nyingpo). *Lady of the Lotus-Born: The Life and Enlightenment of Yeshe Tsogyal*. Boston: Shambhala, 1999.

Palaska-Papastathi, Helene. *Crete* (Tourist Guide). Athens, Greece: Adam Editions, n.d.

Pearson, Kenneth and Patricia Connor. "The Strange Case of James Mellaart or The Tale of the Missing Dorak Treasure." *Horizon* 9, no. 3 (Summer 1967).

Perera, Sylvia Brinton. *Descent to the Goddess: A Way of Initiation for Women*. Toronto, Canada: Inner City Books, 1981.

Petsopoulos, Yanni (with Belkis Balpinar). *Kilims: Masterpieces from Turkey*. New York: Rizzoli, 1991.

Rabinowitz, Jacob. *The Rotting Goddess: The Origin of the Witch in Classical Antiquity*. New York: Automedia, 1998.

Ray, Reginald. "The Origins of the Tülku Tradition in Tibet," in *Indestructible Truth: The Living Spirituality of Tibetan Buddhism*. Boston: Shambhala, 2000.

————. Secret of the *Vajra World: The Tantric Buddhism of Tibet*. Boston: Shambhala, 2001.

Redmond, Layne. *When the Drummers Were Women: A Spiritual History of Rhythm*. New York: Three Rivers Press, 1997.

Read, Donna. *Goddess Remembered,* a video presentation.

Reeder, Ellen. *Scythian Gold: Treasures From Ancient Ukraine*. New York: Harry Abrams, Inc., 1999.

Reid, Lori. *The Complete Book of Chinese Horoscopes*. Rockport, Mass.: Element Books, 1997.

Renda, Dr. Günsel, curator. *Nine Thousand Years of the Anatolian Woman*. Exhibition Catalogue. Istanbul, Turkey: Ministry of Culture General Directorate of Monuments and Museums, 1993.

Richer, Jean. *Sacred Geometry of the Ancient Greeks: Astrological Symbolism in Art, Architecture, and Language*. New York: SUNY Press, 1994.

Roscoe, Will. *Changing Ones: Third and Fourth Genders in Native North America*. New York: St. Martin's Press, 1998.

Rothery, Guy Cadogan. *The Amazons*. London: Francis Griffiths, 1910 (rev. ed. 1995).

Rudenko, Sergei I. *Frozen Tombs of Siberia: the Pazyryk Burials of Iron Age Horsemen*. Berkeley, Calif.: University of California Press, 1970.

Rutkowski, Bogdan. *The Cult Places of the Aegean*. New Haven, Conn.: Yale University Press, 1986.

Ryan, William and Walter Pitman. *Noah's Flood: The New Scientific Discoveries about the Event that Changed History*. New York: Simon & Schuster, 1999.

Salmonson, Jessica Amanda. *The Encyclopedia of Amazons: Women Warriors from Antiquity to the Modern Era*. New York: Doubleday/Anchor Books, 1991.

Samuel, Geoffrey. *Civilized Shamans: Buddhism in Tibetan Societies*. Washington, D.C.: Smithsonian Institution Press, 1993.

Schliemann, Heinrich. *Troy, Mycenae, Tiryns, Orchomenos*. Athens, Greece: National Archaeological Museum, 1990.

Seeley, Thomas. "Born to Dance: Choreography in a Beehive." *Natural History* 108, no. 5 (1999): 54–57.

Seton-Williams, Veronica and Peter Stocks. *Egypt Blue Guide*. London: A and C Black Publishers, Ltd., 1993.

Shallin, Ann-Louise. *Islands Under Influence: The Cyclades in the Late Bronze Age and the Nature of Mycenaean Presence*. Sweden: Svenskt Tryck Surte, 1993.

Shaw, Miranda. *Passionate Enlightenment: Women in Tantric Buddhism*. Princeton, N.J.: Princeton University Press, 1994.

Simmer-Brown, Judith. *Dakini's Warm Breath: The Feminine Principle in Tibetan Buddhism*. Boston: Shambhala, 2001.

Sjöö, Monica and Barbara Mor. *The Great Cosmic Mother: Rediscovering the Religion of the Earth*. San Francisco: Harper and Row, 1987.

Skafte, Diane. *When Oracles Speak: Understanding the Signs & Symbols All Around Us*. Wheaton, Ill.: Quest Books, 2000.

Snellgrove, David L. *Indo-Tibetan Buddhism: Indian Buddhists and Their Tibetan Successors*. London: Serinda Publications, 1987.

Spess, David. *Soma: The Divine Hallucinogen*. Rochester, Vt.: Park Street Press, 2000.

Streep, Peg. *Sanctuaries of the Goddess: The Sacred Landscapes and Objects*. Boston: Little, Brown and Co., 1994.

Tatton-Brown, Veronica. *Ancient Cyprus*. London: British Museum Press, 1997.

Taylour, Lord William. *The Mycenaeans*. London: Thames & Hudson, 1995.

Thadani, Giti. *Sakhiyani: Lesbian Desire in Ancient and Modern India*. London: Cassell, 1996.

Thimme, Jürgen, ed. *Art and Culture of the Cyclades in the 3rd Millennium B.C.* Chicago: Chicago University Press, 1977.

Thondup, Tulku (Rinpoche). *Hidden Teachings of Tibet: An Explanation of the Terma Tradition of Tibetan Buddhism*. Boston: Wisdom Publications, 1986, 1997.

Torday, Laslow. *Mounted Archers: The Beginnings of Central Asian History*. Durham, England: The Durham Academic Press, 1997.

Tubb, Jonathan. *Bible Lands: Eyewitness Guide*. London: Dorling Kindersley in association with the British Museum, 1991.

Tulku, Tarthang (oral translation of original text by Nam-mkha'I snying-po). *Mother of Knowledge: The Enlightenment of Ye-shes mTsho-rgyal*. Berkeley, Calif.: Dharma Publishing, 1983.

Vasilakis, Andonis. *Minoan Crete: From Myth to History*. Athens, Greece: Adams Editions, 1999.

Veen, Veronica. *The Goddess of Malta: The Lady of the Waters and the Earth*. Netherlands: Inanna-Fia Publications, 1992.

Vialou, Denis. *Prehistoric Art and Civilization*. New York: Harry N. Abrams, Inc., 1998.

Von Rudloff, Ilmo Robert. *Hekate in Ancient Greek Religion*. Victoria, B.C., Canada: Horned Owl Publishing, 1999.

Walker, Barbara. *The Woman's Encyclopedia of Myths and Secrets*. San Francisco: Harper and Row, 1983.

Warren, Peter. *The Aegean Civilizations: The Making of the Past*. New York: Peter Bedrick Books, 1989.

Weil, Andrew. *Spontaneous Healing: How to Discover and Embrace Your Body's Natural Ability to Maintain and Heal Itself*. New York: Alfred A. Knopf, 1995.

Whitfield, Susan. *Life Along the Silk Road*. Berkeley, Calif.: University of California Press, 1999.

White, David Gordon. *The Alchemical Body: Siddha Traditions in Medieval India*. Chicago: University of Chicago Press, 1996.

White, David Gordon (editor). *Tantra in Practice*. Princeton, N.J.: Princeton University Press, 2000.

Wolkstein, Diane and Samuel Noah Kramer. *INANNA: Queen of Heaven and Earth: Her Stories and Hymns from Sumer*. New York: Harper & Row, 1983.

Wood, Michael. Foreword to *The World Atlas of Archaeology*. New York: Portland House, 1988.

Yurukova, Yordanka (curator). *Glorie di Tracia: L'oro Più Antico I Tesori I Miti* [The Glories of Thrace: The Most Ancient Gold, the Treasures, the Myths]. Florence, Italy: Ermes, 1997.

Zihlman, Adrienne L. *The Human Evolution Coloring Book*. New York: Harper-Perennial, 1982.

Index